Chris Tapscott,
Tor Halvorsen, Teresita Cruz-Del Rosario (Eds.)

The Democratic Developmental State: North-South Perspectives

CROP International Poverty Studies

Edited by Thomas Pogge

Chris Tapscott,
Tor Halvorsen, Teresita Cruz-Del Rosario (Eds.)

THE DEMOCRATIC DEVELOPMENTAL STATE: NORTH-SOUTH PERSPECTIVES

ibidem-Verlag
Stuttgart

Bibliographic information published by the Deutsche Nationalbibliothek

Die Deutsche Nationalbibliothek lists this publication in the Deutsche Nationalbibliografie; detailed bibliographic data are available in the Internet at http://dnb.d-nb.de.

Bibliografische Information der Deutschen Nationalbibliothek

Die Deutsche Nationalbibliothek verzeichnet diese Publikation in der Deutschen Nationalbibliografie; detaillierte bibliografische Daten sind im Internet über http://dnb.d-nb.de abrufbar.

Cover photo: #66752523 | © okalinichenko - Fotolia.com

ISBN-13: 978-3-8382-1045-2

© *ibidem*-Verlag / *ibidem* Press

Stuttgart, Germany 2018

Printed in the United States of America

Contents

Toward a Conceptualization of the Democratic Development State in Principle and Practice

Chris Tapscott, Tor Halvorsen, and Teresita Cruz-del Rosario

Ever since the American political scientist Chalmers Johnson first coined the term "developmental state" to describe the economic successes of a number of newly industrialized East Asian countries in the aftermath of World War II, the concept has attracted considerable attention from scholars and practitioners around the globe. Of particular interest was the fact that these states, which came to be known as the East Asian Tigers, not only achieved rapid economic growth but they also managed to redistribute wealth and alleviate widespread poverty. Of further interest was the fact that they appeared to have followed a trajectory of capitalist growth, which differed significantly from that of economically advanced countries in the West. Unlike western countries that relied, at least in theory, on the self-regulatory mechanisms of the market and envisioned a restricted role for the state, the East Asian developmental states explicitly sought to influence markets in order to control and direct the orientation and pace of economic growth. However, while the economic achievements of the Tigers are indisputable, the key determinants of their success have been hotly disputed as has been the potential replicability of the model elsewhere in the developing world.

The state-led model of economic growth adopted by such states as Japan, South Korea, Taiwan, Singapore, and others has since been extensively analyzed in the literature. This has focused on what were considered to be the defining, and unique, characteristics of the East Asian developmental states, which included a capable, but autonomous bureaucracy (Evans 1995); a developmentally oriented political leadership (Fritz and Menocal 2007); a close and symbiotic relationship between certain key or "focal" agencies and key industrial capitalists; and policy interventions that promoted rapid economic growth (Beeson 2004). Key to the success of the Tigers was, indisputably, the establishment of a strong and relatively insulated state bureaucracy, manifesting what Evans (1995) has referred to as "embedded autonomy." Governed by strict meritocratic

principles, an elite group of bureaucratic decision-makers, working together with counterparts from the corporate sector, were the drivers of
state-led capitalist development. Small but powerful focal agencies, such
as the Ministry of International Trade and Industry in Japan and the Economic Development Board in Singapore, played a pivotal role in coordinating the affairs of the developmental state. In particular, they were instrumental in creating a stable and predictable business environment, in
shielding investors from risks, and in guaranteeing long-term returns on
their investments. The autonomy that these agencies enjoyed stemmed
from the fact that they were insulated from external social pressures and
enjoyed protection from the cut and thrust of political life. The public respect enjoyed by this bureaucratic elite enhanced their legitimacy and ensured that they remain embedded in, rather than isolated from, society. In
all East Asian developmental states, strong political leadership with an
unwavering commitment to the developmental vision, typified by Park
Chung Hee and Lee Kuan Yew, the presidents of South Korea and Singapore, respectively, ensured that the bureaucracy had the full support of
the executive.

The establishment of a symbiotic relationship between the state and
the industrial sector was a further distinctive feature of the developmental state. This relationship involved both regulation and support. Thus,
while industrialists were encouraged to ensure that their production
goals were in line with the developmental objectives of the state, the state
formulated policies and created an environment conducive to industrial
growth, including the sponsorship of investment in strategic sectors.

Further explicators of the success of the East Asian developmental
states included discussion on the extent to which historical, sociocultural,
and geopolitical contexts had played a role in shaping growth paths in
these states. These included the unprecedented support received from the
West as a consequence of the Cold War (which crucially included preferential access to western markets), the location of the East Asian developmental states (which favorably positioned them on key trade routes), and
the fact that as they had, in differing degrees, been ravaged by war and/or
a colonial past, their populations were more accepting of a centralizing
state. The fact that they were able to sustain such extensive state involvement for a prolonged period has been ascribed to a system of highly au-

thoritarian rule and intolerance of public dissent (trade unions, in particular, were disallowed). However, with the progression of time their political orientation is now seen to be largely incompatible with the ideals of a modern democratic state. Under these circumstances, it has been argued, why would states today wish to pursue a politico-administrative model so out of keeping with international norms and trends and so likely to provoke social and political unrest.

While Japan, South Korea, and Taiwan, and subsequently Singapore, became the poster models of the developmental state and the benchmark against which such states were measured, there has been significant variance in the factors that contributed to economic growth in the region. Despite a tendency in the literature to treat East Asian developmental states as somewhat homogenous, it is evident that their social, economic, political, and cultural contexts differed significantly. Thus China, a latecomer to the developmental club, followed a socialist route and decentralized power to a greater extent than most recognized developmental states, but nevertheless made use of the state to coordinate economic growth. China emerged as what has been termed a "socialist developmental state" during the Cold War era and during this period of relative isolation it embarked on a program of industrialization which was to lay the platform for its future economic growth. Of significance in this case has been the strategic role played by the Communist Party of China (CPC) in transforming the path of the Chinese economy as well as in reshaping its foreign relations with other developing countries. While the CPC is not, in a strict sense, a bureaucratic structure, it is the supreme organ of the Chinese state and it is responsible for the political and economic policies followed in the country. It is also the only political party and consequently enjoys relative autonomy and insulation from competitive politics, enabling it to formulate policy unfettered by political opposition. In that respect, the function of the CPC was similar to that of the "focal unit," which was key to steering developmental part in the other East Asian states. It is evident, furthermore, that there has been considerable variance in the levels of economic growth achieved among developmental states, with those making up the rear of the so-called flying geese skein, such as Malaysia and Indonesia, unable to sustain their initial momentum.

As a consequence of the particular, and arguably unique, circumstances that gave rise to the East Asian developmental state, a number of authors have asserted that the model should be considered sui generis and hence not replicable elsewhere in the world. However, irrespective of their position on the transferability of the model, there is a broad consensus that common to all these developmental states was the fact that they implemented a process of industrialization and followed what has been termed a "plan rational" approach wherein the state intervened in the market over a sustained period of time. It is this commitment to pursue a purposeful economic growth path, supported by a highly skilled and professional public service that has come to be seen as a defining characteristic of the developmental state.

Nevertheless, there has long been disagreement between those who attribute the economic growth of the Asian Tigers to a statist approach and neoliberals who, while recognizing the significance of the state's involvement, asserted that this was due to their ability to "get the prices right" and hence to maximize the impact of market forces, rather than to a heavy-handed guidance of the economy. It is this element of the developmental approach, some have argued, rather than the contextual factors unique to East Asian states in the post-Second World War, postcolonial era which gives continued relevance to the model. The neoliberal position, however, lost traction following the market crash of the 1990s and was further weakened by the global financial meltdown of 2008, which precipitated extensive and unprecedented state intervention in the economies of most major western countries and which seriously called into question the self-regulating capacity of the market. In this context, there has been broadening support for the adoption of a more state-centered approach in many emerging economies and renewed interest in the idea of a developmental state, notwithstanding the fact that the appropriateness of the model for countries located outside of East Asia remains a contested topic.

The Need for Greater Conceptual Clarity

Despite renewed attention to the concept, usage of the term "developmental state" outside of East Asia has been vague and ill-defined. While some scholars continue to assess the extent to which such states conform to a set of criteria derived from East Asia, others have argued that this is a meaningless exercise since the model, at least in its formative phases, could not be considered democratic in any contemporary sense and this, in and of itself, would prevent its adoption in all but the most authoritarian of states. In this context, the term developmental state has lost much of its explanatory power and it is frequently used to describe any state intent on economic development irrespective of the path chosen. Part of the problem with contemporary debate on the developmental state, as a consequence, relates to the fact that the term is so conceptually vague. Illustrative of this vagueness, Fritz and Menocal (2007: 533) maintain that a developmental state exists "when the state possesses the vision, leadership and capacity to bring about a transformation of society within a condensed period of time."

In a context where most emerging economies now embrace some form of democracy, the challenge has been to create a state that retains the state-led features of the original East Asian model but yet one that is underpinned by democratic principles. The quest for this hybrid model gave rise to the idea of a democratic developmental state. However, the concept of a democratic developmental state has been poorly theorized in the literature and in much of the writing it is used as descriptive device to describe a democratic state that is trying to institute greater control over the economy (however weak this might be). Alternatively, the term is used in aspirational or prescriptive fashion to describe what states should do to achieve more rapid and equitable growth yet with little indication of how this might be achieved (Edigheji 2009). In another conceptualization, the defining features of a democratic developmental state are that it "ensures that citizens participate in the development and governance processes," and it "fosters pro-poor, broad-based economic growth and humane development." This implies that the state must be capable not only of transforming its productive base, but it must also "ensure that the economic growth improves the living conditions of the majority of its people" (Kanyenze et al. 2017:20). Despite their laudable intentions, such conceptualizations are not noticeably short on detail on the steps that states might follow in pursuing this democratic ideal. However, notwithstanding the conceptual indeterminacy, a number of states in Africa (including South Africa, Botswana, Ghana, Rwanda, and Ethiopia) and elsewhere in the global South (Brazil and India) have signaled their interest in implementing what they understand as a developmental state approach. Significantly, setting aside any potential conceptual contradictions in the model, virtually all of these have committed themselves to the establishment of what has been termed a democratic developmental state.

Alternative Conceptualizations

More recently, some scholars have suggested that debates on the most appropriate modes of state intervention in emerging economies have been too narrowly focused on the characteristics of the East Asian developmental model. In so doing, it is argued, they have overlooked the achievements of other development models that have succeeded in promoting both economic growth and democracy, which might justifiably be deserving of the "developmental" label and, in particular, the term "democratic developmental state." This collection of essays seeks to broaden the debate on what the establishment of a democratic developmental state might entail and to move understandings of the concept, if, indeed, it retains any analytical value beyond political rhetoric. Conceived, in the first instance, in the context of a comparative analysis of what might be considered developmental states (or, more accurately, aspirant developmental states) in the global South and Nordic welfare states, it seeks to broaden both the case base on the study of this model of economic growth and its progression over time. Our intention is also to consider how a democratic developmental state has been conceptualized in those countries in the global South that have committed themselves to this growth path and the extent to which they have reconciled the inherent contradictions between economic growth and democratic values. Given that the controlled economy of the East Asian developmental state is now seen, contextually, as one of a kind, we are keen to explore what potential alternatives there might be to the hegemony of a neoliberal state that operates according to the rules of the World Trade Organization in support of global capitalism.

Rather than formulating an authoritative definition of a democratic developmental state, this book seeks to examine the ways in which states, in different epochs and in different parts of the world, have attempted to reconcile the inherent contradiction between the need for rapid economic growth and the democratic rights of citizens, expressed in terms of their right to influence policy that might affect their welfare, to a living wage, and to access to social services. In other words, we are interested in looking at how a developmental state that is based on democratic principles might have a more emancipatory orientation and might serve to produce a more egalitarian and less exploitative society. It is in this context that the comparative experience of the Nordic countries is of interest. Put differently, are there other ways of conceptualizing development that might be followed by countries seeking to stimulate growth and, at the same time strengthen their democracies, other than the authoritarian top-down model typified in the East Asian developmental states? Alternatively, are the experiences of states that have adopted a social welfare model so contextual and path determined that they are of little relevance to states in the global South?

The Nordic Model

The economic progression of the Nordic welfare states in the latter half of twentieth century, although perhaps not as dramatic as that of the East Asian states, was nevertheless significant and they currently rank among the most affluent and, yet egalitarian states, in the world. Of further significance is the fact that while welfare states globally are increasingly challenged by the neoliberal order, the influence of which now extends well beyond the Western world, the resilience of Nordic welfare states to the onslaught on public institutions in general, and to welfare schemes in systems in particular, has been strong although they have not entirely escaped its influence. To that extent, the impact of neoliberalism on these welfare states has been far less severe than expected and the sustainability of what has come to be referred to as the Nordic development model warrants considerably more attention.

What is of interest in this model is the manner in which it has succeeded in linking trust in public institutions with the regulation of power. In that respect, the Nordic developmental state has been based on a far more consensual approach than the top-down model adopted in East Asia. Integral to this process has been the establishment of a social compact between organized labour (which is both strong and broad in its reach), civil society, the business sector, and the state. Over time, the interaction between these constituencies has led both to a mutual understanding, although not always acceptance, of their differing vested interests and to a recognition that their common interests, and by implication the common good, will be best served through democratic processes. The increasing influence of democratic decision making has also led to growing trust between opposing forces in society and this, in turn, has also shaped state-civil society relations. Contra Marx, the state in this context is not seen primarily as an instrument of the capitalist class.

Underpinning the formation of a network of nationwide labour unions and the mobilization of civil society (particularly women's movements, citizen protection movements, and campaigns for universal child and youth support) was the development of a system of corporate negotiation between labour (which included small-scale farmers) and capital. In a process that took into consideration the strengths of the externally oriented components of capitalism, nationwide multi-sectoral negotiation was combined with local, sector-specific negotiation, in a system of economic regulation commensurate with the overall strength of the economy.

The focus of these corporate negotiations was on the rights of the workers to receive a proportion of the surplus generated by capital, and more importantly, to derive benefits from ongoing technological advancements in the workplace, in terms of both improved wages and more secure working conditions. The rationalization of production methods through technological advancements led both to greater efficiency and to greater output, but it also resulted in a sharing of the output of growth. This was a result of local-level negotiations within firms which promoted a sense of shared ownership and which ultimately led to a situation where both workers and managers assumed responsibility for promoting and steering growth. The notion of a profit-sharing system was central to the idea of the social compact which is a key feature of the Nordic model. Moreover, this is a process that has evolved over time and strong welfare arrangements have been introduced to protect individual workers from the vagaries of the economy, whether this might be the loss of a job due to technological advancement or retrenchment due to structural rationalization.

Due to the strong links developed between labour unions and labour-based parties, social democrats gained legislative power in the Nordic states and, in the process, the social compact that had been developed in the workplace was extended to all citizens as universal welfare rights (these included child support, pensions, public health systems, public schools for all, and public higher education). The welfare state, in effect,

emerged out of struggles in the workplace together with corporate negotiations at the national and state levels, which, in turn, were supported by
a variety of social movements using democratic channels to influence the
state. The coming together of these different forces in a social democratic
order created the space for the development of a welfare state and, in the
process, rights negotiated between the unions and employers became
universal rights for all citizens.

In recent years, however, these universal rights have been under attack from neoliberal ideas (which have gained political strength in the
Nordic countries) as has been the role of unions in shaping negotiations
at the corporate level. By bureaucratizing rather than democratizing politics and by embracing the international ideas of competition, the market-
ization of services and the deconstruction of public institutions, it has also
threatened the role of civil society in invigorating democracy. This process
is also evident in attempts to dismantle or diminish the role of local government. In Norway, in particular, mobilization for local government from
below took place hand in hand with the mobilization of labour unions and
civil society organizations. In that regard, the emergence of a strong state,
based on a robust system of parliamentary democracy, can be seen to have
evolved alongside popular mobilization for local-level democracy and local government, which has subsequently played a pivotal role in promoting more diversified economic growth and, more recently, for ensuring the
rights of the weak and vulnerable within the general principles of the welfare system.

Attempts to dismantle key elements of the Nordic model, however,
have met with resistance. At a theoretical level, defenders of the model
have argued convincingly that the trust that has been engendered between government (and the state) and labour, supported by the engagement of civil society and a process of democratic decision making, has led
to levels of economic growth at least as high and as sustained as that
which has occurred in so-called neoliberal economies (from Australia to
the United States). More importantly, it has been argued, in periods of crises (which have occurred more frequently in recent decades) the impacts
on the working lives and welfare of ordinary citizens have been far less
devastating than in most neoliberal countries (a fact that is supported by
the Organization for Economic Cooperation and Development (OECD)
growth statistics).

Further resistance has taken place within the unions themselves (in Norway they have grown both in number and size), as well as in the types of alliance that have been forged across the worker/white-collar divide. Despite the movement of labour across Europe, from the poorer East to the richer West, a process that has both suppressed wages and undermined the bargaining system, the growing strength of the unions is reflected in the political ideal that all who form part of working life in a country, irrespective of their origins, have the right to become social citizens with access to the welfare state. It is argued that this is the only way in which to preserve the relationship between the nation-state and citizenship, which is the very relationship that the neoliberal idea of a competitive state would effectively dissolve. Thus far, the gains of social integration appear to have overcome criticism about the growing costs of welfare support. In this way, the strength of organized labour has served to preserve the link between the corporate state and citizen-based democracy within the different Nordic communities.

A further reason for the resilience of the welfare state has been the quality of the public services which it is providing, and the fact that there is little societal impetus to replace them with the private providers advocated in neoliberal thinking and championed by international consulting firms and international bodies such as the OECD. In that regard, it must be noted, the provision of quality education, health, pensions, care for the elderly, and other services, is dependent on popular willingness to pay taxes and this, in turn, is dependent on the social compact which recognizes the need for the corporate regulation of the economy and the democratic ideal of equal access to life support and life chances. It is in defense of these values that popular resistance to the dismantling of the welfare state, established under the social democratic developmental model, is the strongest but it is also the arena where neoliberal pressure to establish a global service community is the most concerted. Thus far, the Nordic model has demonstrated its historical strength, but the question remains for how long it will be able to resist neoliberal pressures, both from within and from multilateral agencies in the global economy.

Organization of the Book

This book is divided into two parts. In the first, a number of chapters examine different understandings of the democratic developmental state in the global South as reflected in the varied policies pursued both to stimulate economic growth and to ensure that the process is informed by citizen participation. This begins with a chapter recapitulating the factors that gave rise to the East Asian developmental states, followed by chapters that discuss experiments in democratic developmentalism in Ethiopia, South Africa, Brazil, India, and Indonesia. In the second part, discussion focuses on the experiences of the Nordic countries in their construction of welfare states and the extent to which they meet what some have posited as the criteria of a democratic developmental state, and, importantly, whether they hold out any lessons for countries in the global South.

The opening chapter, by Teresita Cruz-del Rosario presents an overview of the prototypical East Asian developmental state as exemplified by Japan, Singapore, South Korea, and Taiwan. In it she discusses the factors common to the success of the East Asian Tigers. Chief among them were the historical and geopolitical factors, particularly the dynamics of the Cold War, which shaped the pro-capitalist, anti-communist sentiments that were so important in establishing national consensus in these countries and which encouraged support from their western allies. The preferential access to overseas markets granted by these allies spurred a program of industrialization, anchored in an aggressive manufacturing sector whose products found their way into the global market. Massive investments in human resource development that were closely linked to the demands of the industrial sector created a strong social consensus between the citizens' aspirations for social upliftment and the needs of society for economic and social advancement. Finally, a bureaucracy insulated from the pressures of organized interests and based on meritocratic recruitment resulted in a state with strong capacity to deliver on development objectives. These favorable conditions were ensured by an authoritarian state structure that limited all forms of political participation among a demobilized citizenry.

In the second part of her chapter Cruz-del Rosario looks at the experience of these original developmental states in transitioning to democracy. Although there are significant variances between them, she argues that most of these states might be considered hybrid regimes in that they are neither fully democratized nor authoritarian. Singapore, for example, is seen to exercise a form of "soft authoritarianism" that entails the persistence of a strong developmental tradition alongside certain democratic practices such as multiparty elections. Of interest is the fact that a number of these states have shifted their position along the authoritarian-democratic continuum over time, moving both toward and away from liberal democracy, in a process that adds complexity to the analytical authoritarian-democratic binary. She further considers the extent to which authoritarianism and democracy might have supported or hindered economic development in these hybrid states. She concludes that while authoritarianism played an important role in the formation of developmental states such as Korea and Singapore, there is no guarantee that it will always lead to economic growth as the experiences of Myanmar and the Philippines (under Ferdinand Marcos) bear testimony. Similarly, she maintains, the advent of democracy, as illustrated in the case of Indonesia and the Philippines, has not necessarily contributed to growth and in Korea it has led to widening social inequality.

The challenge of reconciling democratic principles, a respect for basic human rights and participatory forms of governance, with a state-centric and authoritarian approach to managing economic growth, is clearly illustrated in the three chapters from Africa. In the first of these, Gebremariam looks at the Ethiopian variant of democratic developmentalism. When judged against the conventional criteria of East Asian developmental states, the achievements of the Ethiopian state have been remarkable. In the decade or more since democratic developmentalism was adopted as the official policy of the ruling People's Revolutionary Democratic Front (EPRDF), the country has achieved an annual growth rate close to 11%, and this has led to significant social welfare gains for the population as a whole. The number of people living below the national poverty line decreased from 45% in 1995 to 29.6% in 2011, life expectancy increased from 55 to 62 years in the same period, and the Millennium Development Goals relating to primary education, child mortality, HIV/AIDS, and malaria control were all surpassed. However, on the democratic front progress has been far from convincing. This is because, in its quest to establish its developmental hegemony over the social and political order, the EPRDF has become increasingly authoritarian and repressive and, along with this, there has been a steady erosion of civil and political rights.

Gebremariam attributes the progressive abandonment of democratic principles in Ethiopia to the ideological roots of the EPRDF, a coalition of four political parties that formed an alliance in the late 1980s to defeat Mengistu Haile Mariam's Derg regime. On its assumption of power in 1991 the EPRDF announced that it would rule the country under a system of "revolutionary democracy." Central to this ideology, which drew its inspiration from the writings of Vladimir Lenin, was the idea that the establishment of an equitable society could only be achieved by rapid economic growth, steered by a dominant ruling party that respected the rights of the poor masses. The EPRDF's rise to power, however, occurred at a time when the Cold War had ended, and with it the bipolar world order, and the influence of the Washington Consensus was in its ascendancy. In this context, he argues, the government was compelled to adapt its ideology and moderate its political rhetoric in its attempts to solicit donor aid and financial support from international funding agencies such as the IMF and World Bank. Following this apparent volte-face a new constitution was adopted in 1995 and shortly thereafter, the first multiparty elections were held. The EPRDF and its allies won the election but in this, and in every successive election, opposition parties and independent observers have contested the fairness of the electoral process. There have been repeated complaints about vote rigging, the suppression of political opponents (through illegal arrests and imprisonment), and the closing down of independent media outlets among other measures intended to ensure the victory of the EPRDF. Thus, despite the veneer of multiparty democracy, Ethiopia has, in effect, become a one-party state.[1]

Gebremariam maintains that the state has adopted a "carrot and stick" approach in its attempts to promote democratic developmentalism, rewarding those who toe the party line (through job creation and the development of small businesses), and punishing those who dissent or who propose alternative approaches to economic development. The segue from revolutionary democracy to developmental democracy, he argues,

---

[1]   In the 2015 elections the EPRDF won 90.5% of the seats in parliament while the remaining seats were captured by its allies.

represents a continuum rather than an abandonment of the EPRDF's original revolutionary ideology, which called for the establishment of a dominant political party capable of ensuring the hegemony of its ideas and policies throughout society. The Ethiopian experience, he suggests, illustrates the inherent contradiction of trying to build a democratic developmental state through decidedly undemocratic means.

In their chapter, Penderis and Tapscott present a case study on democratic developmental local government in South Africa, where an emphasis on grassroots democracy has obscured the broader goal of state-driven economic development and which, in many respects, is the obverse of the Ethiopian model. The ruling African National Congress (ANC) party in South Africa, they maintain, has long been drawn to the idea of a developmental state as a means to pursue rapid economic growth and address the high levels of poverty and unemployment which are a legacy of Apartheid rule. However, as a political party that had recently triumphed over the oppression of the undemocratic and racist Apartheid political order, the ANC was keen to embed its economic development in a program of social transformation that placed considerable emphasis on citizen participation in planning and policy making at the local level.

A feature of the South African variant of the democratic developmental state is the fact that it has been so poorly articulated in national policy since it first entered into official discourse and there is little common understanding of what it entails. Penderis and Tapscott attribute this conceptual indeterminacy to two factors. The first relates to the fact that while there is a broad consensus in the literature on the defining elements of the East Asian developmental state, there is considerably less agreement on what constitutes a democratic developmental state other than that it should adopt the attributes of procedural democracy in its pursuit of state-driven growth. Furthermore, in the absence of an archetypal model of a democratic developmental state, it is left to the ideologues and policy makers of individual states to chart their own course in reconciling a socially and politically transformative agenda with that of rapid economic growth. In the South African case, they argue, this situation was aggravated by inconsistency in the government's economy growth path. Where ANC policy documents released in the run up to the first democratic elections stressed the importance of an interventionist state in transforming the post-Apartheid social economy, this idea was abandoned within two years with the adoption of the Growth Employment and Redistribution (GEAR) macroeconomic framework, which espoused both a diminished state and neoliberal economic policies. The failure of GEAR to achieve the growth rates necessary to create jobs and raise living standards, combined with the negative impacts of the 2008 global financial crisis, led to renewed interests in the idea of a developmental state and this now forms part of the National Development Plan, which represents the government's long-term vision for the future.

The South African developmental state, in as much as it has been defined in policy, is intended to be based on a partnership between the state and civil society, where decision making is co-determined through a process of public participation. This approach found its first expression in the 1997 White Paper on Developmental Local Government which set out the measures municipalities must follow to ensure citizen participation in planning and policy-making process at the local level. Based on a case study of a poor suburb in Cape Town, the chapter reveals that there is little or no understanding of a developmental state among municipal officials, that the participatory processes involve a very small proportion of the population, and that those who do participate have little or no influence over decision-making processes. More problematic, is the fact that the attempt to establish a developmental local government has contributed little to job creation or to improving the welfare of poor communities. This is due to the fact that municipalities have little capacity to stimulate local economic growth and this remains a responsibility of the national government. Beyond the rhetoric, Penderis and Tapscott argue, the South African democratic developmental state can be considered neither fully democratic (in the sense that it has established effective mechanisms for citizen participation) nor developmental (in the sense that an interventionist state is stimulating rapid economic growth).[2]

Braathen's chapter looks at the rise and fall of what he terms "democratic neo-developmentalism" in Brazil. In so doing, he traces the origins of development thinking in the country to the second term of the Getulio

---

2 Since the advent of democracy in 1994, the gross domestic product (GDP) growth rate in South Africa has seldom exceeded 4% per annum and the forecast for the next two to three years is for growth rates of no more than 1% per annum.

Vargas presidency (from 1951 to 1954). This was an era characterized not only by the advent of multiparty democracy, but by attempts to build a compact between the working classes and capital, known as *corporativismo*, and by strong state intervention in the economy, known in Brazilian political discourse as *desenvolvimentismo* or developmentalism. Although this initiative lapsed in the succeeding years of authoritarian rule and military dictatorship, it resurfaced during the presidency of Luis Lula da Silva. Elected in 2002, *Lula* as he was popularly known, and his *Partido dos Trabalhadores* (Workers Party) came into power promising a democratic revolution which would transform a corrupt and patrimonial social order. A key feature of what came to be known as *Lulismo* was a stated commitment to more direct forms of democracy, to state intervention in the economy, and to a program of socioeconomic redistribution through improved public infrastructure and services. The emphasis on direct democracy had been inspired by the successes of the Workers Party in its management of various municipalities prior to its victory in the national polls, and particularly in the system of participatory budgeting made famous in Porto Alegre.

On assumption of office, the Lula government set about an extensive program of citizen engagement and most prominently in a series of national conferences which were convened to discuss a range of social issues including those relating to youth and children, culture, housing, racial equality and many others. During Lula's two terms of office (from 2003 to 2010) 72 such conferences were held, involving some 5.6 million participants, and culminating in 14,000 resolutions, some of which were incorporated into national policy. These included the *Bolsa Familia* program, a federal system that transferred cash to female heads of the poorest families, and increases in the minimum wage. However, notwithstanding the objective of greater social inclusion, many of Lula's supporters in the trade unions and social movements complained that, in practice, the participatory spaces which had been created provided little opportunity to influence national policy, particularly in regard to economic policy. As a consequence, in his second term of office Lula lost considerable support from his core constituency on the left but made up for this in the support which he gained from the poor and working classes.

Lula's commitment to reducing poverty and social exclusion through major infrastructural development programs, particularly in urban renewal and housing, helped to strengthen the political influence of the working class, but, ultimately, it proved to be economically unsustainable. While the discovery of major offshore oil reserves in 2007 promised a way out of the impasse, the management of this resource marked the beginning of the end of *Lulismo*. Instead of assigning sole mining rights to the state-owned oil company, *Petrobas*, and thereby maximizing revenue returns to the state as many among his supporters had hoped, under pressure from western trading partners and in a quest to attract foreign investment in the Brazilian petrochemical industry, concessions were granted to national and international firms with exclusive rights to specific oil fields. Not only was this move seen as a betrayal of the objectives of *Lulismo*, but subsequent revelations of massive corruption in the oil sector, involving many high-ranking members of the ruling party and Lula himself, led to mass street protests and calls for a change in government. Lula's successor as leader of the Workers Party and as president, Dilma Rouseff, although herself not implicated in the scandal, further contradicted core principles of *Lulismo* when, in 2014, the country was confronted by an economic and fiscal crisis. In a move to appease the markets she introduced a series of harsh austerity measures, which she was forced to withdraw in the face of mass protests, and this, along with other misadventures, ultimately led to her impeached for financial mismanagement. The Temer government which succeeded Dilma, and which represents a coalition of parties opposed to the Workers Party, has since reverted to a set of neoliberal policies which seek to cut public spending and deregulate the economy.

The demise of democratic neo-developmentalism in Brazil is instructive for several reasons. Firstly, it is evident that the system of participatory democracy which had been a key principle of *Lulismo*, and which had succeeded so well in some municipalities under the Workers Party control, proved extremely difficult to scale up to the national level. This led to criticisms, common to invited spaces elsewhere, that they afforded limited opportunity to influence national policy substantively, and that they were subject to various forms of elite capture (the corporate sector and business associations, for example, participated in most fora). Secondly, while the state's investment in social development (driven largely through infrastructural development) succeeded in improving the welfare of the poor, it was unsustainable without significant growth in the national economy which never came close to the levels required.[3] Thirdly, although the Lula government attempted to forge alliances between the corporate sector and the unions and social movements, this was never formalized in any sort of social compact and the vested interests of big capital continued to be pursued relentlessly and regardless of their costs to the wider society.

In the second chapter on South Africa, Jeremy Seekings discusses further the consequences of the policy incoherence and inconsistency which have been a feature of the government's endeavors to establish a developmental state and in particular, he suggests, its emphasis on social development at the expense of economic growth. Commencing with its *Reconstruction and Development Plan*, which was formulated in the run up to its assumption of power, the ANC spoke of the need to "develop the capacity of the government for strategic social and economic development." A key focus of the state at this time was on replacing the racially based policies of the Apartheid regime, the establishment of an integrated state, the provision of basic social services to the majority of the population (hitherto denied access), the redressing of inequality, and attempts to de-racialize corporate ownership through a program of Black Economic Empowerment. However, although there was a massive expansion of the state's role and spending in the delivery of public health, education, municipal services, and cash transfers for the poor, issues of production, he maintains, were generally neglected and there was little investment in basic economic infrastructure.

By the turn of the millennium, it was evident that the economy had failed to grow at the rate required to address widespread poverty and inequality and, despite some welfare gains, that unemployment had worsened in the democratic era. This prompted calls from within the ruling party and its allies, the South African Communist Party (SACP) and the Congress of South African Trade Unions (COSATU), for a more interventionist developmental state than would steer the economy toward greater growth and job creation. Here the focus, in part, was on public utilities,

---

3   During the period from 1996 to 2016 the average GDP growth rate in Brazil was 0.59% per annum, reaching a height of 4% in 1996.

leveraging growth through the state's portfolio of public entities. The idea of a developmental state (characterized as a "capable and developmental state") remains part of the political rhetoric of the ANC, notwithstanding the fact, as Seekings points out, that the government's efforts in that regard have been largely unsuccessful. Over and above a lack of state capacity, the vagaries of international markets, and restrictive trade protocols, Seekings primarily attributes the failure of the government's attempts to play a more assertive role in the economy to a wrong mixes of policies. This state of affairs was exacerbated by the different ideological positions of the ANC's allies, COSATU and the SACP, which believed that, beyond the creation of a new black bourgeoisie, the government's economic policies had done little to improve the plight of the poor who made up the bulk of the population.

The state's intervention in the clothing manufacturing sector in South Africa is illustrative of the effects of poorly conceived and implemented economic growth policies. The manufacturing of clothing had historically been labour intensive, and although not offering the lowest wages in the country, it was targeted by the unions as an exploitative sector. Industrial action, and subsequent legislative intervention by the Department of Labour in support of collective bargaining, led to the raising of wages across the sector in the understanding that this would lead to both welfare gains and to higher production and improved international competiveness. Compliant companies were also promised a range of state subsidies to invest in new technology which would enhance their productive capacity. This, however, occurred at a time when the government had liberalized trade and the effects which this had on the clothing industry (which had been heavily subsidized during the Apartheid era as counter to international sanctions) were profound. The government was slow to implement its package of incentives and in a sector which remained heavily labour intensive the increase in wages made many firms either uncompetitive or unproductive. This was aggravated by the fact that the government had failed to predict the rise in Chinese clothing production, which not only captured much of South Africa's regional export market, but with easy access, also penetrated the country's domestic market. In this instance, Seekings maintains, a developmental policy intended to create jobs led to their destruction and the decimation of an industry.

While the post-Apartheid state cannot be described as a developmental one in any sense of the criteria commonly associated with the concept, Seekings argues that it does display many of the features of a welfare state and it is in this role that it has been most effective. This is evident in the introduction of a comprehensive package of social welfare grants (old age pensions, child support grants, etc.) along with a range of measures to support those deemed to be indigent (these include access to state housing and to a limited quantity of free water and electricity). These social assistance program have substantially reduced both the poverty headcount (the number of people living below a designated poverty line) and the poverty gap (the aggregate amount by which the incomes of the poor fall below the poverty line). In South Africa, and indeed across much of the southern African region, he maintains, states have proved more effective in redressing the inequalities in markets than they have at governing markets so as to reshape the economic growth path. "The welfare state," Seekings asserts, has been "the stand in for the failed developmental state."

In his chapter Törnquist looks at the attempts to establish social democracies in Indonesia and India and contrasts these with the experiences of welfare states in the Nordic community. Tracing the attempts to establish a more inclusive social order in the Indian state of Kerala from the 1950s onward, he illustrates the difficulties confronted by various social and political movements in their efforts to chart a social democratic course. Those attempting to establish broad coalitions in pursuit of this objective confronted the challenge of overcoming ethnic and other social cleavages as well as the system of clientelism and patronage, so deeply rooted in the social and political fabric of the society. Although alliances were formed over time, these were sometimes based on political horse trading between political parties and they were far from all-embracing, frequently excluding important constituents such as farmers, labourers, and the middle class. There were, nevertheless, some notable achievements, which included the introduction of participatory processes at the local level (which included women and the socially and politically ostracized Dalits) and improved access to social services. However, the drive toward social democracy in Kerala has not been sustained. This is in part due to political differences in the Left Front, which has championed this program over the past three decades, and, linked to this, the fact that it has been unable to secure a grip on political power, having lost various elections over the years. Perhaps of greater significance is the fact that the drive for greater equity has not been matched with economic growth and the uneven development to which this has given rise has led to growing inequality and greater vulnerability of the poor.

The trajectory of sociopolitical development in Indonesia was markedly different from that of India but some common trends are, nevertheless, discernible. Like India, Indonesia achieved independence in the immediate aftermath of World War II and this heralded a new era of parliamentary democracy and the promise of citizen participation under the presidency of Sukarno. This was not to be. The impacts of the Cold War and Sukarno's shift from multiparty democracy to a form of centralist government, termed "guided democracy," was followed by a coup d'etat in 1967 and three decades of military rule under Suharto. Following Suharto's resignation in 1998 Indonesia entered an era of democratic reform which has been filled with the rhetoric of citizens' rights but which has yet to result in substantive social democratic development. Törnquist attributes this to the fact that, despite its populist veneer, the political order is essentially that of an elitist liberal democracy, characterized by clientelism, rent seeking, and widespread corruption. Despite the rise of social movements and the activism of organized labour, those campaigning for a more just and democratic society have been unable to form the coalitions and alliances necessary to set and pursue an agenda for social reform.

Although, in his comparative analysis, Törnquist does not entirely discount the potential that the Nordic model holds for states in the global South, he points to the reduced possibilities that exist for the establishment of social compacts between labour, business, and the state in many emerging economies. Where the labour movement in Nordic countries was relatively homogenous, in many states in the global South it is highly diverse and fragmented. In India, where roughly 10% of the workforce is in permanent employment, the majority of workers are engaged in temporary work, in informal activities, or else they are unemployed. In this context, it is difficult to build the consensus necessary to negotiate compacts with the corporate sector and the state. They also point to the fact that social compacts in the Nordic state were formulated during periods of rapid industrialization, where the prospects for employment creation were good and unemployment levels were low. In this context the prospective gains to be derived from a social compact were clear to all. In states where the prospects for rapid job creation are limited, the likelihood of achieving such social accords is greatly reduced.

Olsen's paper on the sociocultural foundations of democratic capitalism in Norway provides further insights into the debate on the factors that gave rise to the Nordic welfare state. The origins of the welfare state in Norway, he states, can be traced back to the latter half of the nineteenth century and gained momentum in the 1920s and 1930s, when struggles, often militant, between workers and business owners had led to some concessions in the workplace. However, he maintains, the drive to establish a society based on social democratic principles only gained momentum in the immediate aftermath of World War II. Of interest to him is why, at this time, labour movements in the Nordic states (and elsewhere in the global North) abandoned the socialist goal of abolishing capitalism and opted, instead, for its transformation through democratic means. This he attributes, in part, to the growing power of the union movement and to its ability to form alliances with other social forces such as small farmers. It may also be ascribed to the declining influence of national communist parties (and radical socialists) following the onset of the Cold War.

It was during this era, he asserts, that Norwegian society embraced what has been termed "democratic capitalism." According to Rueschemeyer et al., "Democratic capitalism rests on a class compromise between labour and capital in which the interests of both sides are to varying extents accommodated" (Rueschemeyer et al. quoted in Olsen). This concept, as Olsen points, embodies an element of contradiction and by way of illustration he cites the Norwegian historian Francis Sejersted's proposition that "capitalism means that the societal power is in the hands of the capitalists...of those who have the control of the means of production," while "democracy means that the power is in the hands of the people". Nevertheless, commencing with capital and organized labour, a broad consensus was forged in Norwegian society based on the principles that the good society could only be achieved through cooperation and compromise. This process entailed an acceptance on the part of socialists of some of the principles of liberal democracy and, at the same time, the embracing of the principles of a welfare state by bourgeois capitalists. What this entailed was a major reorientation of ideas entrenched in the discourse of both capital and organized labour. While employers had to suppress their instinct to maximize profits in favor of the common good, unions had to accept the idea of a partnership with their arch enemy, big capital. Thus, in the postwar years, labour leaders played down the significance of class struggle and emphasized the importance of increased national productivity as a precondition for the establishment of a welfare state. At the same time, big business agreed to the payment of a living wage and to improved working conditions.

While Olsen sees this class compromise as an important stepping-stone toward a more equitable social order, in and of itself, he believes, it would not have been capable of establishing a platform broad enough to construct and sustain a welfare state. What was required was a broader-based coalition, embracing all social strata and bound together by a social democratic ideology. Central to this process was the universalization of rights secured in the workplace to the society as a whole. The success of the class compromise, he asserts, was not based on the ability of the state to balance the "naked power interests" of competing parties. Rather, it derived its strength from its broad-based legitimacy in society. "The hegemony of social democracy," he asserts, "was imprinted in social practices as well as in ideology (of practical political and economic thinking)."

Once the framework of a social compact had been agreed to by the unions, civil society, the state, and business, the modalities of steering the future growth of the economy had still to be negotiated. While some on the left were in favor of assigning responsibility for regulation of the economy to the state (including the power to regulate prices, investment practices, etc.), employers and those on the political right were opposed to the derogation of extensive powers to the state beyond the scrutiny of parliament. In resolving this impasse, it was agreed that all new state interventions should be negotiated on an ongoing basis—in other words, state regulation of the economy needed to be governed by political processes.

Halvorsen's chapter begins with the proposition that democratic depth is of far greater importance in defining a democratic developmental state than its capacity to promote rapid economic growth. In so saying, he affirms the position that the Nordic welfare states represent a more democratic, and hence more transformative, version of the democratic developmental state than any variants of the East Asian model. However, despite their success in establishing some form of equilibrium between the interests of organized labour, civil society, the state, and the corporate sector, he maintains that the Nordic developmental states are, themselves, now under extreme pressure to conform to what is seen as the inexorable progression of global capitalism. The influence of globalization, furthermore, is eroding many of the institutions and social practices that gave rise to the welfare state and which provided the platform for the economic success of the Nordic model. He argues that as the hegemony of global capitalism has spread it has given rise to what has come to be called the "competition state" (Münch 2012). "The goal of the competition state," he maintains, "is not the advancement of democracy, but rather that of increasing the competitiveness of its national economy within the global market." The organizing principles of such a state are no longer shaped by national constitutions or legislatures in that they respond to the needs of the global economy. States participating in the new global order subvert themselves to the prescripts of a "new constitution" (Gill and Cutler 2014) constructed by various international think tanks and regulated by the World Trade Organization, the IMF, World Bank, the OECD, and others of their kind. Under this regime, rather than receiving their orders from national parliaments, competition states are guided by the principles of the new constitution which is interpreted by various advisory councils, consulting firms, rating agencies, and other purveyors of neoliberal dogma.

Where the Nordic model of the democratic developmental state privileged solidarity, the common good of society, and collective decision making in pursuit of this objective, the competition state, he maintains, stresses the importance of innovation, the development of human capital, and the value of individual achievement. Linked to this is a reconceptualization of the notion of justice. Where, as in the welfare state, justice was to be understood as the right to access the resources provided by the good society, this has been replaced by the concept of justice as fairness (cf. Rawls 1971). In this formulation, while it is the responsibility of the state to provide an enabling environment for the social and economic advancement of all citizens, it is ultimately up to individuals to utilize their human capital to productive ends.

In order to illustrate how the new constitutionalism is subverting the welfare state, Halvorsen proposes an adaptation of Evans' "tripod model" (Evans 1995), which suggests that the success of democratic developmental states is based on their ability to maintain a balance between bureaucratic capacity, democratic engagement, and a vibrant market economy. He does so by adding Science and Science-Based Education (S&SBE) as a fourth leg in the model. S&SBE, he maintains, has emerged as a new source of power which shapes the institutions and social life of all modern societies. Control of S&SBE, furthermore, has become a site of struggle between the proponents and opponents of globalization.

In the conventional Nordic welfare state, he states, the generation of knowledge was based on an incremental model which recognized the importance of workplace learning and valued education for its contribution to the inclusiveness of the good society. In the new global dispensation, in contrast, the emphasis is on radical innovation which is seen as the driver of global economic growth. Unlike the incremental innovation economy, which set store in the value of collective knowledge, the radical innovation approach rewards the achievements of individual innovators. Taking, as an example, the tertiary education sector in Norway, he discusses how an emphasis on the establishment of a radical innovation economy has led to significant changes in the organization, funding, and orientation of research. Strongly influenced by the OECD, which has funded such initiatives, universities have become vehicles for radical innovation, oriented to the interests of global capital, and have themselves embarked on a form of academic capitalism as a source of revenue. This commodification of the tertiary education sector, he asserts, has served to undermine the solidarity which has been key to the success of the Nordic welfare state. Rather than contributing to the common good, academic program and research are now oriented to the needs of corporate capital which increasingly operates in the global arena rather than within the borders of the nation-state.

While he sees the progression of globalization as a corrosive force which is a threat to the future of welfare states, Halvorsen believes there is a push-back by democratic forces within Nordic countries. The trade unions, allied to progressive professional associations and civil society organizations, are, in various ways, resisting the logic of the radical innovation economy. This resistance has led to the establishment of hybrid institutions embodying elements of both economic orders: retaining respect for the incremental innovation regime (particularly in the workplace), but at the same time investing in the radical innovation economy. Although this contestation remains unresolved, it has, to some extent, stemmed the seemingly inexorable advance of the new constitutionalism. The solidarity re-engendered in this process, he suggests, holds the potential to establish a new global order, founded on the alliance of transnational civil society coalitions, committed to more effective oversight and regulation of the global economy.

Building on this theme, the final chapter by Halvorsen and Tapscott suggests that the debate on the democratic developmental state should be directed toward an analysis of the relationship between democracy and capitalism and the role of the state in stimulating economic growth. This would focus on the extent to which democratic systems are able to mediate the relations between politics and the economy, such that growth is pursued in accordance with democratic values. Adopting a normative proposition, they assert that states which reproduce and strengthen democracy are inherently more effective in steering economic growth and more durable (assessed in terms of their political legitimacy) than authoritarian ones. They further argue that the failure of attempts to establish democratic developmental states in countries such as South Africa, Brazil, and Indonesia, may principally be attributed to their inability to overcome the latent contradictions between democracy and capitalism. However, they maintain, it is not that democracy and capitalism are, by definition, incompatible, as the Nordic welfare states have demonstrated that this not the case. Rather, they argue, when capitalism is not directed and disciplined by democratic systems and processes, it is likely to pursue its own path to the detriment of the majority of citizens. This state of affairs has been aggravated by the globalization of capital which is now governed by the dictates of international financial institutions, such as the World Bank, IMF, and OECD, rather than by the legislatures of nation states.

Since the defining feature of a democratic developmental state is the extent to which democratic values and practices have been institutionalized in the state and in the regulation of the economy, Halvorsen and Tapscott argue, this will only be achieved through democratic mobilization. It is only through this process, they believe, that civil society will have the strength to engage with both the state and capital in shaping a new social and political order. Thus, unlike the top-down approach adopted by the East Asian developmental states, a democratic developmental state will need to be constructed from below.

Conclusion

The chapters in the first part of this book discuss the varied challenges faced by states in the global South in their attempts to reach a balance between the seeming imperatives of the market and the need to strengthen their democracies. With the exception of Ethiopia, which has emulated the authoritarian East Asian developmental model (albeit based on ideological principles diametrically opposite to those of the Tigers), the studies on South Africa, Brazil, India, and Indonesia illustrate how these countries have struggled both to build inclusive democracies and, simultaneously, to stimulate the economic growth necessary to reduce poverty and inequality. The second set of chapters describes both the factors that led to the establishment of the Nordic welfare as well as those that now threaten its continued existence. In different ways, these chapters also consider the degree to which the Nordic welfare states could be considered democratic developmental states, and the extent to which elements of the model could be replicated in the global South.

As is evident from the ensemble of chapters in the book, the essence of a democratic developmental state has been poorly articulated in theory and in policy and, as has been seen, in practice. Differentiating this second wave of aspirant developmental states from their East Asian forbears is the fact that there is considerable variance in the approaches which they have adopted. While some states have merely adopted the rhetoric of democratic developmentalism (as in the case of Ethiopia and, to a lesser extent, South Africa) others have pursued a largely populist route (as in the case of Brazil and Indonesia), seeking to mobilize the population in support of state-driven development program. This may be attributed to a number of factors, including their global distribution, prevailing national and international geopolitics, and the fact that, unlike Japan, Singapore, and Taiwan, there are no widely recognized leading geese in the skein of democratic developmental states which might serve as models for others to follow. Although Cruz-del Rosario (in this book) has pointed out that some East Asian developmental states, notably Japan, Korea, and Taiwan, have, over time, shed the authoritarianism of their early years and have become democratized, this was certainly not how they started out. Furthermore, while their transition could be seen to add fuel to the old argument that economic development is a precondition for the emergence of democracy (Moore 1966; Rueschemeyer et al. 1992) with so much contradictory evidence, this has become something of a sterile debate which lends little to our analysis of democratic developmental states. The Nordic welfare states have, in any event, demonstrated that it is possible to achieve economic growth based on sound democratic principles. Of considerably more interest is the manner in which states attempt to institutionalize democratic processes in the formulation of policies which direct economic growth.

In his chapter as indicated, Halvorsen has argued that it is the strength of democracy rather than the rate of economic growth which is the defining feature of democratic developmental states. This is because the establishment of a democratic developmental state cannot be separated from the development of democracy and, indeed, it forms part and parcel of this process. From this, it may be inferred, the notion of a democratic developmental state is more closely aligned to the developmental ideals of a social democracy than it is to the state-centric East Asian model. In other words a democratic developmental state is recognizable more by its participatory and redistributive character than by its state-driven and rapid economic growth, a point made by Seekings in his chapter in this book. According to Törnquist, social democratic development has four distinguishable features: the formation of democratic political collectives based on broad popular interests; the establishment of democratic linkages between state and society; the establishment of equitable civil, political and social rights in society and working life; and the negotiation of social growth pacts between capital and labour. As the chapters that follow relate, the achievement of these objectives remains beyond the reach of most states in the global South. As a consequence, a range of questions might be raised as to how much of the Nordic model states in the global South might feasibly be able to adopt or adapt.

Despite their different political and historical trajectories, there are a number of discernible challenges common to most aspirant democratic developmental states. The first relates to the challenge that they face in trying to forge the broad consensus necessary to support the construction of a democratic developmental state. In this endeavor their experiences have differed from those of both the East Asian and Nordic states. While the Asian Tigers stressed the importance of building a national consensus, this was a state-driven initiative, which, in the context of the Cold War, was aided by popular fears of a Communist takeover by neighboring countries. In order to preserve national sovereignty, and, in effect, their own freedom, citizens ceded the right to public participation and left to the state decisions on the economic growth path to be pursued. The Nordic states, in contrast, succeeded in establishing a social compact, which enabled the key stakeholders (trade unions, citizens, civil society organization, and the corporate sector) to reach agreement on key decisions on both the economy and the ordering of society.

Differentiating the Nordic societies from those in the South, however, was their size and homogeneity at the time in which they embarked on the journey toward a welfare state.[4] While class differences did exist in all of these states, there was considerable homogeneity in the cultural, social, and religious makeup of their societies and the ability to shape a common narrative based on a shared history inevitably facilitated the construction of a national consensus. In societies such as Brazil, India, Indonesia, and South Africa, however, which have large populations differentiated by class, race, ethnicity, and religion, the prospects of forging a broad social compact are infinitely more challenging.[5] Even among those mobilizing for universal basic rights themselves, the building of coalitions which transcend party politics, class, and ethnicity has proven difficult, and, as discussed in Braathen's chapter on Brazil, even when alliances are formed they are frequently episodic and discontinuous. Of further concern is the ability to ensure that the more powerful partners in a compact are held to account. The Lula government in Brazil, as Braathen points out, was unable, or unwilling, to restrain the corporate sector either in capturing participatory systems or in their quest to maximize profits. This, combined with the failure to stem widespread corruption in his own party, led to the collapse of the corporate compact he had aspired to construct.

---

4   The largest of the Nordic states, Sweden, has a population of less than 10 million while the combined population of all five Nordic states is less than 27 million. In contrast the state of Kerala, which makes up 2.7 of the population of India, had an estimated 36 million people in 2016.

5   It perhaps comes as no surprise that Botswana and Mauritius, the two African states now accorded the democratic developmental label, in 2016 had populations of just 2.3 million and 1.3 million, respectively.

As in the case of the East Asian developmental states, a further factor that contributed to the forging of social solidarity across social classes in the Nordic states was the existence of an external threat to national sovereignty. As Olsen points out in his paper, the Nazi occupation of Norway during World War II did much to create a common national identity, and this was reinforced during the Cold War era when the threat of communist expansion served to suppress militancy whether among socialists or trade unionists. While developmental states in the South face real threats to their economic autonomy from global capitalism, this is not perceived in the same way as a threat to national sovereignty and it has little symbolic capacity to mobilize the masses.

A further challenge raised in the chapters by Braathen and by Törnquist relates to how countries, seeking a democratic developmental path, manage to scale up citizen-based governance from the local to the national level. As the experiences of Brazil and the Indian state of Kerala have demonstrated, despite their promise, the successes of citizen involvement in participatory budgeting and in decision making in local welfare programs, are not sustainable if they are not transformed into a universal welfare system embedded in the national political economy. The failure to introduce a national welfare system in these countries, furthermore, represented a lost opportunity to build the solidarity necessary to establish a more egalitarian society. In the Nordic states welfare reforms (such as those leading to free education and health and comprehensive unemployment insurance) were embraced by the middle classes and led to their willingness to pay higher taxes. Similarly, a commitment to full employment of the workforce led to increased production and a broader tax base and, at the same time, kept industrial action to a minimum.

A further factor limiting the replicability of the Nordic welfare state relates to the fact that it emerged out of a prolonged struggle between workers and employers, which subsequently drew in the state and civil society as a whole. It was active citizenship rather than state regulation, Törnquist maintains, that was of central importance in the progression toward a democratic developmental state in Nordic countries. This was an organic process which grew out of community-based mobilization (for example among workers and local farmers) rather than through measures introduced by the state, for example, through participatory local democracy (as was the case in Kerala) or through political processes (as was evident in the participatory budgeting program in Brazil).

Herein lies a paradox for aspirant democratic developmental states. All strive to promote economic growth as rapidly as possible, and to do so through democratic means, yet the process of building active citizenship is a protracted one, as the experiences of South Africa demonstrate. The engagement of citizens in the realm of public policy-making processes, necessary as this might be in developing an inclusive democracy, also creates challenges of its own. While citizens' engagement in public decision making represents an expression of their democratic rights, it is also certain that they participate in the expectation that this will lead to improvements in their livelihoods and welfare. When this does not happen, due to slow economic growth, weak governance, and/or corruption, enthusiasm for public participation swiftly dissipates and is frequently replaced by disillusionment, anger, and protest. This is especially the case in heterogeneous societies where there is considerable class differentiation. Establishing a national consensus under these circumstances is extremely difficult and, social compacts, even when attempted as in the case of Brazil, are not easily sustained. Several conclusions may be drawn from this. The first is that states which pursue economic growth at the expense of citizen participation (as in the case of Ethiopia) cannot be considered democratic developmental states in any sense of the word. The second is that in highly unequal societies, participatory democracy without economic growth and redistribution will be incapable of establishing the national consensus necessary to build a democratic developmental state.

Yet another factor contributing to the success of the Nordic welfare states, which will not easily be replicable in the global South, was the ability of social democratic parties to retain sufficient popular support to remain in power for a sustained period of time. Thus, for example, a prolonged period in office by the Norwegian Labour Party enabled it to entrench social democratic ideals and practices in the public sector and in society as a whole.[6] Although Halvorsen's chapter indicates that the Nordic welfare systems are now under threat from the competitive state, he also suggests that they have the resilience to rebuff the onslaught of globalization. In contrast, in countries in the global South where the political environment is highly contentious and democratically elected parties are often displaced through military coups, the prospects for a sustained term in office are often restricted.[7] The experiences of Kerala and Brazil illustrate how welfare ideals and policies which have not been embedded in social values and practices can be swiftly replaced following a change in political power.

The chapters in this book suggest that despite the ambitions and rhetoric of their ruling parties, the establishment of democratic developmental states in the global South is neither path determined nor inevitable. Halvorsen, however, has suggested that states in the global South could benefit from the fact that their integration into the global economy is far less extensive than those in the North. The implications of this are that, in their attempts to create a democratic developmental state, they are less likely to be subject to the dictates of competitive capitalism which he sees as a significant threat to the future of the Nordic welfare states. The extent to which they are able to use their relative disadvantage to their advantage will, to a considerable extent, be determined by the economic growth path that they charter.

None of the countries in the global South discussed in this book could be said to have met the criteria for a social democratic state specified by Törnquist. However, despite the fact that the conditions for the creation of a democratic welfare state are not propitious, they argue that shallow democratization and uneven growth in countries in the global South have created new contradictions and, in so doing, have opened up space for the

---

6   The social democratic Labour Party in Norway ruled with an absolute majority for 17 years from 1945 to 1961 and, although not continuously, has managed to hold office periodically in the following three decades. The Swedish Social Democratic Party had a similar pattern of success, winning most votes in successive elections from the 1930 to the mid-1980s, as did the Danish Social Democrats and the Social Democratic Party of Finland.

7   This is not always the case, however, as the Congress Party in India was in power from 1947 until 1996, and ANC in South Africa has been in power since 1994. What has been lacking in these states has been a commitment to a concerted economic growth path and to a program of redistribution.

renewal of social democracy through what they term "an alternative sequencing of its basic pillars." In Nordic countries the quest for a welfare state was driven by a strong labour movement (supported by civil society organizations) which succeeded in establishing social compacts with big business and the state. In countries in the South, they suggest, the struggle for fundamental social rights, such as access to basic services and decent work, might need to precede the establishment of such compacts. It is through the struggles for such basic rights, they believe, that the alliances and solidarity necessary to establish a wider social compact might be forged.

References

Beeson, M. (2004). The rise and fall (?) of the developmental state: The vicissitudes and implications of East Asian interventionism. In: L. Low (Ed.), *Developmental states, redundancy, and reconfiguration*. New York: Nova Science Publishers.

Edigheji, O. (2009). How to construct a 21st-century developmental state in Africa. *New Agenda, 35*(3), 60–63.

Evans, P. (1995). *Embedded autonomy: States and industrial transformation.* Princeton, N.J: Princeton University Press.

Fritz, V. and Menocal, A. (2007). Developmental states in the new millennium: Concepts and challenges for a new aid agenda. Development Policy Review, 25(5), 531-552.

Gill, S. and Cutler, C. (Eds.) (2014). New constitutionalism and world order. Cambridge: Cambridge University Press.

Johnson, C. (1982). *MITI and the Japanese miracle: The growth of industrial policy, 1925–1975.* Stanford: Stanford University Press.

Kanyenze, G., Jauch, H., Kanengoni, A., Madzwamuse, M., and Muchena, D. (Eds.) (2017). *Towards democratic development states in Southern Africa.* Harare: Weaver Press.

Moore, B. (1966). *Social origins of dictatorship and democracy: Lord and peasant in the making of the modern world.* Boston: Beacon Press.

Münch, R. (2012). *Inclusion and exclusion in the liberal competition state. The cult of the individual.* Routledge. Abingdon.

Polanyi, K. (1944). *The great transformation: Social and economic origins of our times.* Boston, MA: The Beacon Press.

Ramaswamy, S. and Cason, J. (2003). *Development and democracy: New perspectives on an old debate.* Lebanon: Middleburg College Press.

Rawls, J. (1971). *A theory of justice*. Cambridge: Harvard University Press.

Rueschemeyer, D. Stephens, E., and Stephens, J. (1992). *Capitalist development and democracy*. Chicago: University of Chicago Press

Building the Democratic Developmental State: Lessons from East Asia

Teresita Cruz-del Rosario

Introduction

The notion of a democratic developmental state is at best a normative construct, given that developmental states in the East Asian experience typically flourished under more closed political systems. However, although the East Asian experience suggests that an authoritarian approach holds better prospect for the establishment of a developmental state than a democratic one, this, as shall be discussed, is by no means certain. Furthermore, where there have been moves to democratize developmental states, the often prolonged and difficult transition to democracy has frequently prompted a retreat to more authoritarian methods used in the past.

In this chapter, I elaborate on the developmental role of the state, a topic that has been the subject of long-standing debate among development scholars. An argument central to this discussion is that the state plays a critical role in either promoting or impeding development (due to weak or ineffective public policy). Linked to this is the enduring question of the *replicability* of developmental states, given their different histories and local contexts. A further point of discussion relates to the authoritarian nature of "traditional" developmental states, the prospects for democratization within them, and the extent to which economic performance and social equity may be balanced. Here I discuss what are considered to be hybrid regimes in the East Asian context, those that are neither fully democratized nor authoritarian, and the extent to which they have performed economically.[1]

---

1   These countries, also referred to as the "Asian tigers," are Japan, Taiwan, Singapore, and South Korea. Hong Kong is also classified as an East Asian development success story, yet the literature treats Hong Kong as an outlier in terms of a "nearly laissez-faire" approach to economic growth. See Page (1994).

I amplify the discussion on the original "Asian Dragons," namely, South Korea and Taiwan, both of which entered a democratic phase following their economic "take-off." The characterization of the Singapore state as one that exercises "soft authoritarianism" (Nassir and Turner 2013: 339), for example, typifies the persistence of a strong developmental tradition combined with certain democratic practices such as competitive multiparty elections. It is thus construed by scholars as an "illiberal democracy" (Mutalib 2000: 313), a categorization it shares with other Southeast Asian countries such as Cambodia, Malaysia, Vietnam, and, more recently, Thailand. Despite a range of inhibitory factors, I argue that the establishment of a democratic developmental state is possible, but that it needs to be based on a realistic assessment of a multiplicity of national, regional, and geopolitical interests. Finally, I briefly consider external actors, and the potential role of donors in redirecting aid toward the difficult but necessary task of supporting an overtly political development agenda, that of promoting democracy.

The Developmental State and Its East Asian Prototypes

The identification and implementation of appropriate economic policy has been singled out as a precondition for development success. In this regard, four countries, such as Japan, Taiwan, Singapore, and South Korea, are held up as exemplars of the way in which development policy may be directed in order to achieve desired economic and social outcomes. In a relatively short period, these countries achieved spectacular economic growth rates and have been able to sustain this growth path over the long term. Singapore, for example, achieved First World status in less than half a century, transforming from an *entrepôt* to a high-performing economy built on technological innovation and human resource development, despite its lack of natural resources, its small size, and its troubled political history. Over and above their economic performance, these early developmental states outperformed other Asian countries in terms of a number of important social indicators such as life expectancy, literacy, and maternal and infant mortality rates. While challenges remain, the record of these so-named "Asian Dragons" has been nothing short of spectacular and their performance has collectively been labeled "The Asian Miracle."

Such successful development, however, does not happen by chance. Beeson (2004: 2), among others, contends that sustained growth in the East Asian countries was "neither a fluke nor inevitable," but was rather the outcome of purposive and direct state intervention in the economy. Alongside this was a widespread social consensus on the goals and outcomes of the developmental process. In direct contrast to predatory or weak states, it has been argued, a strong-willed state is able to craft a collective vision, to fashion prescriptive policy for social transformation, to mediate conflicts and overcome internal resistance, and to make the decisions necessary to achieve a developmental vision, however difficult these might be. In the East Asian context, a state possessing these attributes came to be known as a "developmental state." While it is not within the scope of this chapter to elaborate on the different conceptualizations of the state, it may briefly be defined as "a set of processes and institutions which act as a form of domination or authority that produces particular sets of outcomes—in this case developmental ones" (Routley 2012: 4). For Wade (1990: 9), the developmental state is quite simply the "plan rational" state. The plan rational state stands in direct opposition to the "market rational" state in that it formulates and pursues social and economic goals, in a process where development is planned and managed, whereas the latter "simply establishes the rules of the economic game."

The concept of the developmental state originated from the work of Chalmers Johnson (1982) and particularly from his analysis of Japan's economic resurgence after World War II. He argued that a coherent industrial policy had been the handiwork of a relatively small group of highly trained bureaucrats, specifically within the Ministry of Trade and Industry, who had steered the formulation of a comprehensive industrial program in the aftermath of Japan's defeat in World War II. During this era, the United States, as an occupying power, undertook a massive land redistribution program in Japan, the effect of which was to create a socially egalitarian base upon which to construct an industrialization program. The same was true for Korea and Taiwan, which also underwent extensive land reform in a process that broke the stronghold of potentially obstructive landlords and other disruptive social groups and, in so doing, created a base for entrepreneurial activity. Together with a massive education drive, in which citizens received technical and vocational training which prepared them for immediate employment in an industrial sector that required modern skills, the state developed the social and administrative infrastructure necessary for the rapid expansion of economic activity (McGuinn et al. 1979).

The historical context in which the developmental state emerged in East Asian countries underscores the significance of geopolitics. The threat of communist expansion in this era was at the borders of Taiwan, Hong Kong, Korea, and Singapore. As a consequence, there was a strong impetus for these countries to craft a nationalistic vision and a broad commitment to economic transformation as a buffer against the communist threat. A side effect of this national consensus, however, was a "social contract" between state and citizen that entailed the surrender of political freedoms and civil liberties in exchange for the unfettered protection of the state and the unhampered pursuit of economic growth. The support of Western donors, particularly the United States, furthermore, benefitted these countries substantially, particularly in terms of the flow of capital, the provision of technology, and preferential trade relations. All of these countries enjoyed preferential access to American markets for their products, while Taiwan and Korea also enjoyed access to the Japanese market. The geostrategic importance which these states had assumed meant that they enjoyed an advantage otherwise denied to other developing countries.

The configuration of the original developmental states has been characterized as consisting of four key features: (i) a capable, but autonomous/insulated bureaucracy, based on the meritocratic appointment of bureaucrats (Evans 1995); (ii) a developmentally oriented political leadership (Musamba 2010; Fritz and Menocal 2007) and elite consensus over developmental goals (Wu 2007); (iii) a close and symbiotic relationship between certain key, or "focal," agencies and key industrial capitalists (Johnson 1982, 1987); and (iv) successful policy interventions that promoted growth (Wade 1990; Beeson 2004), particularly an export-led industrialization strategy premised on conducive world market conditions. All of the East Asian Dragons exhibited one or more of these features of the developmental state.

Wade's (1990) study of Taiwan, for example, demonstrates the state's capacity to effectively "govern the market." The latter entails the state's "disciplining" of the industrial sector to ensure that its focus and performance were primarily oriented to the government's development outcomes and economic growth path, and only secondarily to the maximization of profit. Where industrial (business) interests preceded the goals of overall development, the result, according to Wade, was state penetration and capture by narrow business interests (*ibid:* 158). The relationship between state and business, thus, was a key feature of the developmental process. However, it was a particular type of relationship that promoted positive development—one that required strong, state-led sponsorship of business investment in strategic sectors in order to maximize returns in an environment where financial resources were scarce. In countries like Japan, Korea, and Taiwan, this symbiotic relationship between the state and the industrial sector proved to be one of the defining features of a developmental state, which led to an era of rapid industrialization.

A further crucial feature of the developmental state was that it possessed a "depoliticized elite" sheltered from political pressures and with considerable leeway to undertake economic decisions. Johnson (*ibid.*) characterizes this as "stable rule by a political-bureaucratic elite not acceding to political demands that would undermine economic growth." He argued that a key characteristic of the East Asian economic development strategy was that it was able to maintain a built-in, long-term perspective in contrast to the short-term economic planning characteristically associated with states operating in accordance with political/electoral cycles.

Finally, there is the unquestionable role of political leadership and a commitment to the developmental vision. In all these countries, the consistent application of strong leadership was instrumental in steering, and sustaining, a long-term development path driven by their vision and executive ability. Park Chung Hee recalls the state of the economy in South Korea in 1961, and the development imperative that informed his leadership in transforming the country into an economic powerhouse.

In May 1961 when I took over power as the leader of the revolutionary group, I honestly felt as if I had been given a pilfered household or bankrupt firm to manage. Around me I could find little hope of encouragement. The outlook was bleak. But I had to rise above this pessimism to rehabilitate the household. I had to destroy, once and for all, the vicious circle of poverty and economic stagnation. Only by reforming the economic structure would we lay a foundation for decent living standards (cited in Gibney 1993: 50).

Authoritarianism and the Hybrid State

Scholars have expressed their concerns with the predominant authoritarian character of most East Asian developmental states (White 1998: 5; Fritz and Menocal 2007: 537; Vu 2007: 30, among others). In that respect, it is evident that the insulation of the focal units was relatively easy to achieve due to the state's capacity to suppress and ignore demands from interest groups. In most cases, the East Asian developmental states eliminated political opposition and suppressed many civil liberties in order to achieve bureaucratic autonomy. As a consequence of their authoritarian mode of operation, developmental states were able to project a long-term view of the economy, unimpeded by the short-term developmental interventions dictated by democratic electoral cycles. However, although authoritarianism has been seen to be a key component of the developmental state, in and of itself, it is by no means a guarantor of economic growth as the experience of other East Asian states has demonstrated. Following a period of 21 years of martial rule under the Marcos regime, for example, the Philippine economy was in tatters, a far cry from the 1960s when it was one of the strongest economies in region and, at the same time, a constitutional democracy. Myanmar, similarly, prior to the opening up of its economy in 2011 had experienced the same types of economic mismanagement under an authoritarian and isolationist regime.

Although the linkage between authoritarianism and economic growth is not a conclusive one, it is also evident that democracy too does not necessarily contribute to economic growth. Experience suggests that the pursuit of economic development under a democratic framework has been at best partial and uneven. The recent economic performance of Indonesia, the Philippines, and until recently, Thailand, would suggest that democratic states can and do promote development with positive outcomes, but they are plagued by problems of corruption, patronage, clientelism, and weak institutions of accountability.

Such states are best characterized as "hybrids," a "mixture of democracy and authoritarianism" (Fritz and Menocal 2006: 17). Table 2.1 presents a typology of regimes proposed by Diamond (2001), and later amplified by Carlson and Turner (2006), which reflects the political changes that occurred in various East and Southeast Asian countries over a five-year time span from 2001 to 2006. It is noteworthy that countries shifted their position along the authoritarian-democratic continuum over time. Diamond classified Indonesia as "ambiguous" in 2001, possibly because multiparty elections were in the offing a year before he drew up the typology (Carlson and Turner 2006: 382). Thailand, interestingly, shifted from electoral democracy in 2001 to politically closed authoritarianism in 2006 following the September coup that ousted the duly elected Prime Minister Thaksin Shinawatra. In 2011, Thailand held multiparty elections and reverted to electoral democracy, only to become a politically closed authoritarian regime once again in 2014 when the military declared martial law. This trend of alternating periods of democratic and authoritarian rule has been a feature of the Thai state as it has experienced eleven successful coups and seven attempted coups since 1932.[2] The hybrid regime typology is of interest because it enables the tracking of trends within these states, but also because it moves the debate beyond a simple authoritarian-democracy binary.

2   Fisher (2013).

Table 1: Regimes in Southeast and East Asia 2001, 2006[3]

	'01	'06
Liberal Democracy	Japan Taiwan South Korea	Japan Taiwan South Korea
Electoral Democracy	Philippines Thailand	Indonesia Philippines
Ambiguous	Indonesia	
Competitive Authortarianism	Malaysia	Malaysia
Hegemonic Electoral Authoritarianism	Singapore Cambodia	Singapore Cambodia
Politically Closed Authoritarianism	Laos China Vietnam Myanmar	Laos China Thailand Vietnam Myanmar

Source: Carlson and Turner (2006: 381).

Countries that have made the formal transition to democracy are still undergoing the arduous process of building stable institutions capable of outliving the personalities that initiated the democratic process and of withstanding attempts to undermine the gains that have been made. Aung San Suu Kyi's role in Myanmar's recent democratization process provides an illustration of the necessity of establishing and sustaining institutions capable of surviving beyond her leadership. From a developmental perspective, hybrid states suffer from a particular disadvantage: the spaces

---

3   Definitions of each regime type are provided by Carlson and Thompson (2006: 381), to wit: Liberal democracy is characterized by free, fair, and competitive elections including the related freedoms of expression, assembly, and organization. Electoral democracy is procedural democracy in which politicians "struggle for the people's vote" (Schumpeter); it does not necessarily entail free and fair elections but is usually marred by electoral violence and fraud. It is democracy in the minimalist sense. Competitive electoral authoritarianism features competitive elections with significant parliamentary opposition. Hegemonic electoral authoritarianism is a regime in which one dominant party wins nearly all if not all of the seats. The ambiguous category refers to "blurry boundaries between electoral democracy and competitive authoritarian." Finally, politically closed authoritarianism refers to regimes that have no popular competitive elections, no freedom of expression or organization, and government control of all information.

that democratic processes open up for public participation provide equal opportunity to narrow sectoral interests, which frequently run counter to the wider social goals of equity and social justice. A second disadvantage is the fragility of institutions that are designed to deliver social services, promote widespread participation in decision making, and, at the same time, provide checks and balances to enhance state accountability (*ibid*). Finally, there is the added disadvantage among hybrid regimes of continuing political instability despite the formal transition to democracy. Challenges from preexisting authoritarian structures remain not only from the military but also from some of their civilian allies, who perceive the hierarchical order as better suited to the larger political project of state formation. In Thailand, the prolonged spate of protests against the government of the democratically elected Prime Minister Yingluck Shinawatra in 2013 provides an illustration of the capacity of a minority, in the form of a vociferous and well-resourced urban elite, to successfully press for "less democracy" and a much stronger role for the monarchy in steering the affairs of the nation.[4]

Similar challenges face Myanmar. Despite the current political and economic liberalization that ushered in a period of democratic reform in 2011, the military remains a strong political force in national politics. The foremost challenge facing the country, thus, is its ability to reform a host of social institutions and, in so doing, remove the vestiges of 50 years of military rule. A country that has long depended on the extraction of its natural resources and the export of foreign labour, set within a context of fragile institutions and military dominance, faces major challenges in pursuing an industrialization program akin to that of the East Asian Dragons. Although the current liberalization of the media and the abolition of the censorship boards represent a positive step in strengthening democratic trends, the signs of illiberalism are creeping back in.[5] In this context, the prospects of establishing a developmental state, let alone a democratic one, seem questionable, and the country seems set to continue on a

---

4   "Thai Protesters Issue a Call for Less", *The International New York Times.* 13 December 2013.

5   "Myanmar 'backsliding' on path to democracy." http://www.dw.de/myanmar-backsliding-on-path-to-democracy/a-18059754. Accessed at: January 2, 2015.

growth path that aims to capitalize on the remittances of migrant workers, a risky economic path given the instability of the global labour market.

In pursuing a developmental vision, hybrid states are hamstrung by
a number of mutually interacting factors that limit their capacity to deliver
on the goals of democratic development. Among these, Fritz and Menocal
(*ibid:* 17–18) enumerate the following: the persistence of clientelistic
structures; high expectations among the citizenry that result in collective
frustration over the slow or nondelivery of public goods and services; corruption; elite domination in political affairs and especially during elections; and an all-around lack of state capacity to deliver quick results on
the promises of democracy. The example of the popular uprising in the
Philippines in 1986 and the ensuing attempts by a faction of the military
to unseat President Corazon Aquino serve to illustrate the perils of a democratic transition and the difficulties faced in pursuing a path of democratic development. While civil society organizations and social movements mobilized people for social reforms in the aftermath of the uprising, their experiences demonstrate the difficulties of pursuing policy reforms while undergoing a process of re-democratization.[6]

Singapore represents an interesting case of hybridity. Mutalib (2000:
318) describes it as an "illiberal democracy" whose defining feature is the
dominance of a single party, the People's Action Party (PAP), that manages
and regulates all aspects of social and economic life. Unlike the communist
parties of China and Vietnam, Mutalib argues that the Singapore state allows for procedural democracy through regular elections and competitive
party politics without threatening the central role of the PAP. Singapore as
a hegemonic electoral authoritarian regime, the dominant party wins almost all the seats. Political participation outside of elections is also severely restricted. Nevertheless, in the 2010 elections the dominant PAP
suffered significant losses in a development that seemed to point in the
direction of more competitive electoral authoritarianism. However, fol-

---

6   See Cruz-del Rosario (2014), especially two case studies on agrarian reform and
    commercial log ban that illustrate the pitfalls of engaging policy arenas in a con-
    text of political hybridity.

lowing the 2015 elections the PAP had regained its dominance of parliament having won 83 out of 89 seats (93%), suggesting a shift back on the continuum to a one-party model.

The Singapore state, however, holds an outstanding record of economic development having assumed an active role in shaping the development agenda and in delivering on development outcomes. This, indeed, has been its primary concern rather than the survival of the party or the regime per se. Not only have per capita incomes increased dramatically in the 50 years of its existence as a city-state, it has also outperformed most economies in Southeast Asia on both economic and noneconomic performance indicators. The argument for a "soft authoritarian" governance has been put forward assertively by former Prime Minister Goh Chok Tong, who states, "Do you think we could have done just as well if we had a government which was constantly being held in check by ten to twenty Opposition members in the last thirty years? (quoted in Mutalib: *ibid*)."

Singapore's "model of Asian authoritarianism" has drawn the attention of Chinese reformers who wish to emulate the city-state's "near perfect degree of efficiency" (Khanna 2011 as quoted in Ortman and Thompson 2014: 435) without having to introduce liberalization or a transition to multiparty democracy—in a model which is seen as having the best of all worlds. In particular, China wishes to emulate Singapore's one-party governance founded on the principles of meritocracy and pragmatism; a strong stance on corruption; and electoral authoritarianism based on a combination of election and selection. The latter involves the selection of highly qualified candidates by the ruling party before they are allowed to compete in elections. This ensures that the PAP puts forward only the most qualified candidates when competing in elections. This process achieves two goals: first, it ensures that the ruling party's selection process is *internally* competitive; and second, the party ensures its legitimacy and deflects foreign criticism by "allowing" other opposition candidates to compete and even win in elections. Other measures intended to ensure the party's dominance include community outreach activities and the promotion of public participation in nonpolitical activities (e.g., convening regular meetings with members of the public and welfare societies), and increasing the party's overall responsiveness to the citizenry. More authoritarian measures include "selective repression," which involves tar-

geting a few selected dissidents, and the monitoring, although not blocking, of Internet websites; rather than undergoing a political transition to
multiparty democracy, the Singaporean model promotes an "administrative state in which politics becomes a matter of management" through a
process of "learning authoritarian modernity" (*ibid*: 441–447).

Democratic Transitions: Lessons from South Korea and Taiwan

The experience of South Korea and Taiwan stands in sharp contrast to that
of Singapore. Today, both countries are considered liberal democracies.
However, both countries pass through a period of politically closed authoritarianism during which time the foundations of their economic success were firmly established. Syngman Rhee, an anticommunist nationalist, became South Korea's first president in 1948. He is credited with
building the developmental state through "an extremely repressive anti-
Communist political system, which effectively guaranteed long-term state
domination and a social environment conducive to capitalist development" (Vu 2007: 37). The civil war of 1950–1953 and the division of the
country into two Koreas further deepened the centralization of executive
power under Rhee. However, it was under the regime of Major General
Park Chung Hee, who came into power in 1963, that the Korean developmental state initiated a program of uninterrupted industrialization that
effectively transformed the country from Third World status to a modern
industrial economy. Annual growth rates in the 1960s averaged 9%, and
where gross domestic product per capita in 1961 was US$ 161, by 1989
this had increased to US$ 5,438. Today, South Korea is a member of the
Group of Twenty and of the Organization for Economic Cooperation and
Development, and it has graduated from being an aid recipient to an international donor, dispensing development assistance through the Korean
International Cooperation Agency.

During its prodigious growth during the 1980s, South Korea experienced political turbulence as demands for political participation escalated. Following the appointment of Chun Doo Hwan (another military
general) in September 1980,[7] state-led development continued but it was

---

7   This followed the assassination of Park Chung Hee in 1979.

far less comprehensive and all-encompassing than it had been in the previous two decades. A crucial factor in the unraveling of the developmental state, according to Kim (1993), was the expansion of the *chaebols* (family conglomerates) that had gained prominence during the period of economic takeoff and that had now succeeded in building international networks that extended their reach beyond South Korea. This meant that businesses that were once under the discipline of the Korean developmental state now felt capable of challenging and obstructing its directives. Ironically, the state now faced a challenge from the very sector that it had protected and nurtured during the phase of economic modernization. By 1981, big business was clamoring for less state intervention and this stance is reflected in the annual report of the Federation of Korean Industries which read:

> We must quickly establish a civilian-led economic management and control system which will enable us to utilize the rules of the market economy most efficiently ... . We must actively seek and adopt the opinions and expertise coming from various corners of our society, and in particular from the *business elites* ... Thus we will be able to improve the total efficiency of our economic and social activities. (The Federation of Korean Industries 1981: 79–80, quoted in Kim *ibid*: 238)

A further impetus to democratize came from the labour movement that had grown during the era of heavy industrialization in the 1970s and 1980s. In the largest companies, employing over 1,000 employees, union membership grew from 48.3% of the workforce in 1973 to 58.7% in 1979 (Choi 1989: 73, quoted in Kim *ibid*: 236), despite repressive state policies aimed at restricting unionization. The role of militant student movements and church groups, often in alliance with labour unions, played a further role in shaping and expanding the democratization movement in the 1980s. Newly established civil society organizations, notably the Coalition of Movement for People and Democracy and the National Congress for Democracy and Reunification, also combined forces to support opposition candidates in the 1985 legislative elections. Following this mass pressure, in June 1987, President Roh Tae Woo announced the Declaration for Democracy, ending an era of almost four decades of authoritarian rule in South Korea. Multiparty elections took place in December 1987 and since then they have become a regular feature of South Korean democracy. However, some observers have suggested that the dissolution of authoritarianism contributed to the eventual dismantling of the developmental state.[8]

In Taiwan, the authoritarian Kuomintang (KMT) party also pursued a path of rapid economic development to buttress its legitimacy and its survival as a regime. The KMT was, after all, a foreign regime that had transplanted itself on foreign soil. Security threats from the Chinese mainland called for consensus among the ruling elite on the development trajectory to follow. Further to this, a development strategy was needed to manage ethnic tensions between the émigré KMT and the indigenous Taiwanese population and to placate the latter through greater economic inclusion. Unlike South Korea, Taiwan's industrialization push was founded not on heavy industry but on "a network of flexible, small and medium factories" (Chu 1998: 190). The state at no stage privileged large enterprises and, as a consequence, Taiwan does not have any powerful interest groups resembling the Korean *chaebols.* The absence of big businesses had implications for the formation of labour unions that did not develop autonomously as had done in Korea, but rather were co-opted and integrated into the KMT party structure. As a result, a labour movement in Taiwan never flourished and trade unions never provided a backbone of support to the pro-democracy movement as had been the case in South Korea. Instead, it was civil society organizations, intellectuals, middle-class activists, local politicians, and the Democratic Progressive Party that led the effort. In the early stages of democratization, issues were framed not around progressive politics (such as human rights or environmental rights), but rather around the equitable distribution of political power among ethnic groups. Activists for democracy were predominantly Taiwanese, and their pro-democracy struggles were focused on issues of national identity and claims to self-determination (Wong 2003: 246). In later years, as Taiwan's democracy deepened, competitive politics would incorporate progressive issues related to social welfare, and these were

---

8   For an extensive discussion of South Korea's democratic transition from the perspective of actors and agents that include President Ronald Reagan, the US Ambassador in Seoul, President Chun Doo Hwan, civil society organizations and social movement actors, and the opposition leaders Kim Dae Jung and Kim Young Sam, see Adesnik and Kim (2008).

articulated in political parties' electoral platforms. Alongside these issues, however, was the perennial question of Taiwan's relationship to mainland China and alternating positions on independence or unification—a question that continues to invigorate Taiwanese politics to this day.

The developmental paths of both South Korea and Taiwan are particularly interesting despite differences in their societal dynamics. Their current status as liberal democracies, furthermore, is worthy of study, given their histories and the starting points of their economic growth. Both countries are relatively small and neither has a rich natural resource base. In the 1950s their populations were predominantly employed in the agricultural sector because both had undergone major land reform programs: Taiwan between 1949 and 1953, and Korea in 1949 (under the tutelage of the United States). As a consequence of this, having successfully redistributed land to small farmers and broken up wealth concentration in the landowning classes, neither country encountered resistance from landed interests at the onset of the development decade in the 1960s (Ranis 1995: 512). One of the positive results of land redistribution was the emergence of rural entrepreneurs whose livelihoods were derived from a mix of farm and off-farm sources. As a result, rural incomes increased through a critical mass of small- and medium-size rural-based enterprises which in turn spurred growth, productivity, employment, and equity elsewhere in the economy. Between 1960 and 1980, nonagricultural production rose in both countries, reflecting a fundamental change in the Taiwanese and Korean economies, whereby labour had drawn out of agriculture and into the industrial sector. This was particularly the case in Taiwan where virtually the entire workforce had been absorbed into the industrial sector and agricultural output was negligible. Significantly, increased participation of the labour force in the wider economy led not only to increased incomes but also to a relatively equitable distribution of wealth.

Despite their successful transition to liberal democracy, a new generation of problems has emerged in South Korea and Taiwan. For one, pork barrel politics, characteristic of many competitive electoral systems, undermine the political party system. In Taiwan, what has been termed "Black-gold" politics, or political corruption, has been a feature of this trend (Rigger 2000: 113). Policy coherence, once a hallmark of developmental states, has also proven to be more difficult to achieve, along with bureaucratic insulation and autonomy. Wu (2007: 982) considers the democratization of the 1980s and 1990s to have been a "political shock" that "primarily dampened Taiwan's developmentalism and tarnished its track record of growth." The globally televised parliamentary fist fights between the ruling party and opposition legislators aside, Taiwan's rambunctious democracy also exhibited worrying signs of factionalism, indecision, and gridlock. In South Korea, democracy is thought to be "faltering" as regional divisions and personality-based politics, rather than institutionalized party politics, have come to dominate elections (Im 2004). A presidency based on a single five-year term together with four-year terms for parliamentarians is also thought to have weakened the state's power and effectiveness. It is argued that short electoral cycles produce political leaders who pursue short-term policies rather than, as in the past, those who consider the long-term national interest. In this context, populist policies are an easy option for politicians whose immediate goal is electoral victory rather than long-term collective welfare. More worrying is the rising inequality in South Korea. The Asian Financial Crisis of 1997–1998 had a profound economic and social impact on the country. In 1998, South Korea's growth rate had dropped to −6.9% and the unemployment rate which had been 2.6% in 1997 increased to 7.9% by the end of 1998. A package of rescue reforms underwritten by the International Monetary Fund converted what had been a limited developmental state of the 1980s into a neoliberal regime in the 1990s and thereafter. This neoliberal transformation of the Korean economy, argues Koo (2007), is the "major source(s) of increasing income inequality." Wealth inequality is even sharper than income inequality. According to Koo (ibid), the top 10% of the population owned 46% of the country's total wealth, while the bottom 50% owned just 9.5% of national wealth. Poverty is likewise on the increase. In 2001, 4% of the population lived below the poverty line but by 2003 the figure had risen to 15%. Taiwan's poverty profile stands in sharp contrast to that of South Korea and is encouraging for liberal democracies. During the period from 2001 to 2007, less than 1% of the population lived below the poverty line, suggesting that despite the dire prognoses following the advent of democracy and the decline of the developmental state, Taiwan continues to deliver positive developmental outcomes.

Building a Democratic Developmental State

The historical experiences of East Asia demonstrate that developmental states flourished under more closed political systems. Although Japan, Taiwan, and South Korea have since become full-fledged liberal democracies, this has not come about without a range of attendant problems: economic stagnation (in the case of Japan), political patronage, corruption, and a whole host of social problems that plague many open political systems. Although it would appear that authoritarianism has played an important role in the formation of developmental states, as the case of Singapore illustrates, there is no guarantee that it will always do so. The experiences of Myanmar, the Philippines, and Thailand refute the argument that authoritarianism is a necessary condition for the emergence of a developmental state. It remains to be seen whether Thailand, which has shifted from a democratic order to a more authoritarian one, and Myanmar, which transitioned from military rule to democracy, can deliver on their respective developmental promises. Still more recently, despite being officially classified as a liberal democracy, Philippines appears to be sliding perilously close to authoritarianism since President Rodrigo Duterte assumed office in June 2016.

Despite the pitfalls of transitions, White (1998: 64) argues, "external agents—whether international institutions, national donors, or foreign non-governmental organizations (NGOs)"—can make a positive contribution to the creation of a democratic developmental state, provided these agencies have the skill and understanding to provide support to what is a highly sensitive process. The building of a democratic developmental state, White asserts, requires purposeful "institutional design" which will expand the "consultative arena" such that political access is extended to a wider range of social groups beyond regular election cycles. Concretely, this entails the inclusion of different social groups in policy-making discussions (*ibid*: 66). Depending on the context, countries will need to decide whether a presidential or parliamentary system is best suited to an inclusive democratic developmental state. In a similar vein, Siegle (2004) proposes expansion of Evan's concept of embedded autonomy to include civil society and community organizations in the state-business coalition. This tripartite coalition for democratic development, he argues, ensures authentic democracy rather than one that just "goes through the motions" and, more importantly, it serves to prevent traditional bipartisan coalitions from lapsing into state capture by business interests. Siegle also insists on a free and independent media, with broad access to the public, both to ensure accountability and to promote a broad public discourse on the goals and directions of development. The combination of these ingredients, White and Siegle argue, could contribute to the formation of a democratic developmental state.

References

Beeson, Mark. (2004). The rise and fall (?) of the developmental state: The vicissitudes and implications of East Asian Interventionism. In: L. Low (Ed.), *Developmental states, redundancy, and reconfiguration.* New York: Nova Science Publishers.

Carlson, Matthew and Turner, Mark. (2006). Popular perceptions of political regimes in East and Southeast Asia. Democratization, 16(2). http://www.tandfonline.com.ezlibproxy1.ntu.edu.sg/doi/pdf/10.1080/13510340902732615. Accessed at: December 14, 2014.

Chu, Yin-Wah. (1998). Labor and democratization in South Korea and Taiwan. Journal of Contemporary Asia, 28(2), 185-202.

Cruz-del Rosario, Teresita. (2014). The state and the advocate: Development policy in Asia. UK: Routledge.

Evans, Peter. (1995). Embedded autonomy: States and industrial transformation. Princeton, N.J: Princeton University Press.

Fisher, Max. (2013). Thailand has had more coups than any other country. This is why. The Washington Post. Washington, DC, December 3, http://www.washingtonpost.com/blogs/worldviews/wp/2013/12/03/thailand-has-had-more-coups-than-any-other-country-this-is-why/. Accessed at: January 3, 2015.

Fischer, Stanley and Rotemberg, Julio J. (Eds.) (1994). NBER Macroeconomic annual 1994. Cambridge, MA: MIT Press. http://www.nber.org/chapters/c11004.pdf. Accessed at: August 9, 2014.

Fritz, Verena and Menocal, Alina Rocha. (2007). Developmental states in the new millennium: Concepts and challenges for a new aid agenda. Development Policy Review, 25(5), 531-552

Gibney, Frank. (1993). Korea's quiet revolution: From Garrison state to democracy. New York: Walker and Co.

Im, Hyug Baeg. (2004). Faltering democratic consolidation in South Korea: Democracy at the end of the "Three Kims" Era. Democratization, 11(5). http://dx.doi.org/10.1080/13510340412331304642. Accessed at: December 14, 2014.

Johnson, Chalmers. (1982). MITI and the Japanese miracle. Stanford: Stanford University Press.

Kim, Eun Mee. (1993). Contradictions and limits of a developmental state: With illustrations from the South Korean case. Social Problems, 4(2). http://www.jstor.org.ezlibproxy1.ntu.edu.sg/stable/3096924. Accessed at: January 4, 2015.

Koo, Hagen. (2007). The changing faces of inequality of South Korea in the age of globalization. Korean Studies, 31. http://eds.b.ebscohost.com.ezlibproxy1. ntu.edu.sg/ehost/pdfviewer/pdfviewer?sid=26d1e1b4-4109-4936-bed8-d 40f84ae6e97%40sessionmgr198&vid=3&hid=111. Accessed at: January 4, 2015.

McGuinn, Noel, Snodgrass, Donald, Bong Kim, Yong, Kim, Shin Bok, Kim, and Quee Yong. (1979). Education and development in Korea. Harvard East Asian Monographs 90. Harvard University Asia Center.

Mutalib, Hussein. (2000). Illiberal democracy and the future of opposition in Singapore. Third World Quarterly, 21(2). http://www.jstor.org.ezlibproxy1.ntu.edu.s g/stable/3993422. Accessed at: December 28, 2015.

Nassir and Turner. (2013). Governing as gardening: reflections on soft authoritarianism in Singapore. Citizenship Studies, 17(3-4), 339-353

Ortman, Stephen and Thompson, Mark R. (2014). China's obsession with Singapore: Learning authoritarian modernity. The Pacific Review, 27(3). http://www.ta ndfonline.com.ezlibproxy1.ntu.edu.sg/doi/pdf/10.1080/09512748.2014.90 9522. Accessed at: December 14, 2014.

Page, John. (1994). The East Asian miracle: Four lessons for development policy. In: Stanley Fischer and Julio J. Rotemberg (Eds.), NBER Macroeconomic annual 1994 (p. 219). Cambridge, MA: MIT Press. http://www.nber.org/chap ters/c11004.pdf. Accessed at: August 9, 2014.

Ranis, Gustav. (September 1995). Another look at the East Asian miracle. The World Bank Economic Review, 9(3), 341-371.

Routley, Laura. (2012). Developmental states: A review of the literature. ESID Working Paper No. 03. Manchester, UK: Effective States and Inclusive Development Research Centre, School of Environment and Development, The University of Manchester.

Seigle, Joseph 2004 "Developing Democracy: Democratizers' Surprisingly Bright Development Record." Harvard International Review (Massachusetts, USA) Vol. 26(2), 20-25

Vu, Thuong. (2007). State formation and the origins of developmental states in South Korea and Indonesia. Studies in Comparative International Development, 41(4). http://download.springer.com.ezlibproxy1.ntu.edu.sg/static/pdf/87 /art%253A10.1007%252FBF02800470.pdf?auth66=1420449019_3665ae db240376a9a7212016ba2be5ac&ext=.pdf. Accessed at: January 4, 2015.

Wade, Robert. (1990) Governing the Market: Economic Theory and the Role of Government in East Asian Industrialization. Princeton, New Jersey: Princeton University Press.

White, Gordon. (1998). Building a democratic developmental state: Social democracy in the developing world. Democratization, 5(3). http://www.tandfonline.com/loi/fdem20. Accessed at: December 7, 2014.

Wong, Joseph. (2003). Deepening democracy in Taiwan. Pacific Affairs, 76(2). http://eds.b.ebscohost.com.ezlibproxy1.ntu.edu.sg/ehost/pdfviewer/pdfviewer?sid=aa3c0838-0258-4d5c-812f-2a793cfb3d88%40sessionmgr111&vid=3&hid=111. Accessed at: January 1, 2015.

Wu, Yu-shan. (2007). Taiwan's Developmental State: After the Political and Economic Turmoil. Paper delivered at the Conference on A Decade after the Financial Crisis. Thammasat University, Bangkok, Thailand. 23-24 February 2007.

The Carrot and Stick of Ethiopian "Democratic Developmentalism": Ideological, Legal, and Policy Frameworks

Eyob Balcha Gebremariam

Introduction

Over the course of the past decade the ruling Ethiopian's People's Revolutionary Democratic Front (EPRDF) government has declared its commitment to establish a "stable and democratic developmental state" and this goal has been reflected in the policy objectives of two successive Growth and Transformation Plans spanning from 2010 to 2020. There has been some contestation in the literature over the essential features of democratic developmental states, as, for example, discussed in the case of Mauritius, Botswana, South Africa, and Brazil (Leftwich 1996; Sandbrook 2005; Edigheji 2010; Evans and Heller 2013), and the debate has largely revolved around the extent to which they have resolved the inherent contradiction that exists between democracy and development (Leftwich 1998; White 1998). Reflecting this dichotomy, discussion about the Ethiopian variant[1] of the democratic developmental state typically falls into two categories: that which lauds the economic growth and welfare gains and that which is critical of the government's authoritarianism and disregard for fundamental human rights.

The country has been praised for its success in reducing poverty (UNDP 2014), for achieving six of the eight millennium development goals (except those on maternal mortality and gender equality), for sustained economic growth since 2004 (World Bank 2016), and also for running Africa's largest social protection program (Lavers 2016). The country's annual economic growth rate averaged 10.9% from 2004 to 2014 and this contributed to an increase in the GDP from US$ 8.5 billion in 2003 to more than US$ 61.5 billion in 2015. As a consequence of this growth, the poverty headcount ratio (based on the national poverty line) decreased from

---

1   This chapter focuses primarily on the Ethiopian political-economy up until the May 2015 elections. Political developments that have taken place subsequent to the elections require further investigation although the broad trends outlined here still persist.

45.5% in 1995 to 29.6% in 2011, and life expectancy at birth improved from 55 years in 2003 to 62 in 2013 (UNDP 2014).

In contrast to these economic and welfare gains, many political analysts argue that, notwithstanding the fact that multiparty elections are regularly held, the ruling regime has become increasingly more authoritarian and oppressive, and there has been a progressive erosion of civil and political rights (Bach 2011; Lefort 2010; Tronvoll 2010; Vaughan 2012; de Waal 2013). Illustrative of this, the human and political rights of citizens have been grossly violated by legislation which labels, and criminalizes, all dissent as terrorism and which has led to the incarceration of opposition party leaders, journalists, bloggers, and activists (Arriola and Lyons 2016; Mengesha 2016). This repression forms part of a concerted drive to ensure the dominance of the ruling party's ideology and to eliminate political opposition which might stand in the way of its quest to build a democratic developmental state. This authoritarian and repressive trait, it is argued, can be attributed to the fact that the ideology of democratic developmentalism, currently espoused by the EPRDF, represents an untransformed version of its earlier ideology of revolutionary democracy. This was based on the notion of democratic centralism and was both undemocratic and intolerant of political opposition. There is, nevertheless, a clear overlap between the political objectives and strategies of revolutionary democratic ideology and the current discourse of "democratic developmentalism/developmental democracy."[2] Thus, despite a formal commitment to multiparty democracy, the EPRDF has consistently sought to establish itself as the dominant political force in what is effectively a one-party state.

The consolidation of democracy is an essential requirement if transformative development is to be institutionalized without threatening powerful interests in society. This chapter, however, examines the way in which the EPRDF is bypassing both the process of democratic transition and that of democratic consolidation in its efforts to build its version of a "democratic developmental state." In that respect the government can be seen to have adopted a carrot and stick approach in its efforts to construct

---

2   The author is aware of arguments that analytically dissect the two notions of *developmental democracy* and *democratic developmentalism*, but for the purposes of this chapter they are used interchangeably.

such a state, coercing and rewarding those who comply with its dictates, and punishing those who dissent and advocate alternative approaches to economic development. A central argument of the chapter, thus, is that there is an inherent contradiction in the authoritarian way in which the EPRDF government has set about constructing a democratic developmental state and it reflects on the paradox that such a state is being established in a decidedly undemocratic way.

Democratic Developmentalism—Prospect or Façade?

The debate on democratic developmentalism, as intimated, primarily revolves around the relationship between democracy and development. According to Leftwich (1998: 55–57) there is an inherent paradox between the dominant notion of democracy and what he considers to be one of the central features of development. He argues that democracy, particularly liberal democracy, once institutionalized, perpetuates a system which is oriented to the political and economic interests of the elite and the consensus which is built between them, along with the negotiations and settlements which they reach, largely excluding the majority of the population from the process of political decision making (*Ibid*: 56). Development on the other hand, Leftwich argues, may be understood as "a radical and commonly turbulent process..." (p. 56), which significantly affects "the use and distribution of resources...." If effectively carried out, development inevitably alters the socioeconomic and political structures of the society and facilitates the creation of new political interests and priorities that challenge the existing ones (*ibid*).

For Leftwich, overcoming the "structural contradiction" between democracy and development represents the most significant challenge in realizing democratic developmentalism. This is because there is an inherent contradiction between the consensual processes of democratic decision making and the transformative and sometimes radical decisions required to eradicate poverty and inequality. Leftwich maintains that democratic consolidation has three fundamental features, namely legitimacy, the institutionalization of rules and procedures, and the exercise of policy restraint by winning parties (Leftwich 2000: 127–150). In this analysis, he assigns equal importance to the role of formal and informal institutions in the process of democratic consolidation. When informal institutions ensure democratic consolidation, he asserts, "the winner is not winning everything"; "the loser is not losing everything" and the winner is committed to "policy restraint" (Leftwich 1998: 67–60, 2005: 696–697). Leftwich's analysis, as shall be seen, is of particular relevance in examining political processes in Ethiopia.

Following a protracted period of authoritarian rule[3] in Ethiopia, a new constitution was adopted in 1995 ushering in an era of democracy (FDRE: Proclamation 1/1995). However, despite the introduction of a system of multiparty democracy, the establishment of a range of democratic institutions, and the holding of elections at regular five-year intervals, a number of authors have argued that a substantive transition to democracy has yet to be achieved, let alone for it to be consolidated (Kefale 2011; Gudina 2011; Aalen and Tronvoll 2009). It is argued that not only has there been no devolution of power since the advent of democracy in 1995 (Kefale 2011: 682), but in the intervening four elections since then, there has been a progressive shift to the establishment of "a de facto one-party state with undiminished rule of the EPRDF as a vanguard party" (Gudina 2011: 664). Aalen and Tronvoll (2011: 199–202) further argue that the 2005 elections, in particular, were a watershed moment in Ethiopian politics for two key reasons. In the first instance, they took place during a period of unprecedented liberalization in the political sphere which enabled the opposition to win a number of seats in both the federal and regional parliaments. In the second, the post-election crisis and violence which followed the elections enabled the ruling party to strengthen its grip on power through various legal and political means. As a consequence, it has been argued, rather than consolidating democracy, the 2005 elections led to a consolidation of the authoritarianism of the EPRDF regime (*ibid*).

In an analysis of the role which dominant parties have historically played in the formation of democratic developmental states, Leftwich

---

3   From 1974 until its defeat in 1991, Ethiopia was ruled by the Coordinating Committee of the Armed Forces, Police and Territorial Army Commonly, commonly known as the Derg, and its successor the Peoples' Democratic Republic of Ethiopia, both of which were led by Mengistu Haile Mariam. The Derg, which adopted Marxist-Leninist rhetoric, executed and imprisoned thousands of Ethiopians without trial.

points to the experiences of Botswana and Singapore in addition to that of Japan. He argues that both the People's Action Party in Singapore and the Botswana Democratic Party in Botswana managed to establish themselves as dominant developmental parties in the early years of their independence from Britain (Leftwich 1998: 64–66). He maintains that the historical context of the time, both national and international, played a significant role in establishing these ruling parties as the custodians of a remarkable period of economic growth and development. In both countries, Leftwich argues, "the combination of a relatively undeveloped economy, few organized interests and a weakly differentiated social structure, relative socio-cultural homogeneity, and no longstanding military apparatus which had to be controlled or conciliated..." facilitated the relatively smooth progression toward the establishment of dominant party regimes (*ibid*:65). The significant success achieved by these parties, he asserts, may, in no small measure, be ascribed to their ability to resolve the structural contradictions that exist between democracy and development and, in so doing, to establish a political system that favors developmental transformation without placing at risk the political and economic interests of the elite (*ibid*: 66).

In Ethiopia a gradual shift in the discourse of the ruling party is discernible, from that of championing multiparty democracy to one of becoming a dominant "vanguard party," with all the associated revolutionary connotations of that status (EPRDF 2010; Gudina 2011). The attainment of legitimate dominant party status, however, has proven to be extremely challenging in the Ethiopian political domain. Due to the huge diversity of the society, and despite the absence of a formal democratic system, Ethiopian political life has historically accommodated competing political groups and interests. This was especially the case in the postrevolutionary era, from the mid-1970s onward, where ethnic politics, class struggles, and international geopolitics were a feature of the political domain (Abbink 2011; Gudina 2003; Asrat 2008). In this context, it is evident that despite having established itself as the most powerful player in the political arena, the ruling party has been unable to build the broad legitimacy that has characterized democratic developmental states elsewhere in the world. As a consequence, the transition from authoritarianism to democratic plurality remains incomplete and this continues to undermine attempts to consolidate and deepen democracy in Ethiopia.

White, having a different take, locates the democratic dimensions of a developmental state within the broader notion of "political development." In this conceptualization, political development is a long-term process of building "efficient and accountable public institutions and the spread of real as opposed to titular democratic citizenship through an increasingly pervasive process of social empowerment" (White 1998: 21). In this understanding, he underscores the need for states to move beyond procedural democracy to more substantive forms of citizen participation. Substantive democracy includes the opportunities that citizens have to influence the processes of socioeconomic and political decision making that affect their lives (Kaldor and Vejvoda 1997: 62). In a similar vein, Robinson and White (1998: 5) argue that the democratic features of a developmental state should include the possibility of mass mobilization, popular pressure, and the representation of disadvantaged/marginalized social groups such that their concerns are recognized in the political processes.

In his detailed analysis of the features of a democratic developmental state, White asserts that democratization is best understood as a continuous process rather than as a "sudden rupture" of social and political life. This process of democratization coupled with the need to progressively improve the socioeconomic well-being of a country's citizens inevitably gives rise to the challenge of "managing the tension between the political and economic logic of development" (White 1998: 29). In a position similar to that of Leftwich, White also stresses the inherent contradiction between democracy and development but suggests that a solution to the impasse may be reached through a different institutional design and a different mode of state-society relations.

White sets out a framework of the structural and institutional parameters necessary to integrate effective socioeconomic development with a capable and inclusive political apparatus. In so doing, he stresses the essential, and albeit complex, relationship, between three phenomena, namely the institutional design of the state, the character of political society, and the character and role of civil society (ibid: 32–42). In considering the contextual factors that influence the processes and institutional features of state building, he maintains that democratic developmental states require an institutionalized system which is capable of entertaining the diverse views, interests, and political ambitions of both individuals and organized groups. The institutional design of such a system should correspond to the unique socio-historical features of a society without limiting the effectiveness of the state, while, at the same time, promoting its governance systems and responsive decision making (*ibid*: 33). Such a design could include the features of a presidential or parliamentary system, a centralized or federal government, and a decentralized or devolved administration. Here, it is important to note that institutional design is not an end in itself, but rather a contributory factor in a state's capacity to effectively combine the political and institutional arrangements necessary to establish democratic developmentalism.

In its institutional design the Ethiopian state is a federal one governed by a parliamentary democracy. Among the central features of the federal state is the fact that it is based on ethnolinguistic groups, called "nations and nationalities," and that it combines a "decentralised and non-centralized mode of governance" (Tsegaye 2014: 5). Historically, the Ethiopian state had been characterized by a strong central government, dominated by the elites of certain ethnolinguistic groups. One of the stated primary goals of the state in the democratic era, as a consequence, was to address the "uneven relationship among the various constituent nations" of the country and to transform the country into a "multi-foundational, multi-vocal, multi-confessional, secular, socially just federal republic" (*ibid*: 6). The fulfillment of this goal, indeed, provided the rationale for the creation of a decentralized state where the federal government has no supreme authority other than that which has been delegated to it by the regional states. Political power, furthermore, is divided between the federal and state governments, with areas of concurrent responsibility between them and others which are exclusive to the regional states, which exercise a measure of self-rule prescribed by their own constitutions (*ibid*: 8). Policy formulation, the day-to-day administration of the state, and intergovernmental power sharing are legally enshrined in the constitution which sets out the responsibilities of the three arms of the government, namely the executive, the legislature, and the judiciary. The constitution also prescribes a multiparty democracy where political office is contested through national elections held every five years.

As a consequence of its consolidation of power, the EPRDF government has been able to significantly improve intergovernmental coordination and, with it, to align the legislative frameworks of the federal and state governments. In so doing, it has been able to ensure coherence in the implementation of national policies and, in particular, those intended to improve socioeconomic services at the regional level. Through its centralized political structure, the ruling party has also been able to exercise direct influence over the administrations of the four big regional states, and it has the support of affiliates in the remaining regional states. Policy coherence and the politically driven execution of national programs have contributed immensely to the efficiency of the state in fulfilling its socioeconomic development objectives.

The second feature of a democratic developmental state identified by White, the character of political society, refers to the manner in which political power is exercised by the state in its interaction with its citizens. This aspect of a democratic developmental state is of central importance in that it relates both to the state's authority and capacity to pursue development and its willingness to respond to the diverse interests of its citizens (White 1998: 36). This includes its ability to negotiate with powerful political players, the extent to which it includes or excludes citizens, and the manner in which it facilitates the redistribution of resources. In his assessment of the feasibility of striking a balance between the contending priorities of democracy and development, White suggests that this would be most likely achieved in a one-party-dominant system. He argues that a political system dominated by one party would be best positioned to pursue both developmental and democratic goals effectively. However, he also stressed that such political systems (as the ones that exist in Botswana, Japan, and Singapore) have been tested through regular elections and by the competing interests of organized civil society groups. The effectiveness of such a system, he states, is in "maintaining the coherence, authority, and capacity for long term decision making" (*ibid*: 38).

The third contingent factor in the building of a democratic developmental state, according to White, is the character and role of civil society. Here, he refers specifically to the role played by citizens in influencing the course of both developmental and democratic processes through organized and collective engagement. In this realm, civil society can play a role in either defending the status quo or by inducing change in a political system. In a society with a highly differentiated socioeconomic structure and one which is also divided along ethnic and religious lines, he maintains, civil society plays a limited role in the consolidation of democracy. On the other hand, there is also a possibility that a civil society might be captured by certain interest groups that have the resources and capacity to organize themselves more effectively than the society at large (White 1998: 40). In both instances, the political inclusiveness and the meaningful engagement of citizens, along with the redistributive and welfare elements of democratic developmentalism, might be at risk (*ibid*). In an ideal context, he asserts, the existence of a vibrant and organized civil society assists in formalizing the institutional design of the state and in establishing political procedures that facilitate citizen participation in decision making through consultation. The risks of elite capture aside, consultation is seen to be of central importance in ensuring the inclusiveness of the developmental and political processes (*ibid*).

Common to the arguments of both Leftwich and White is the central role that political negotiations and processes play in establishing systems that determine how power is accumulated, distributed, and maintained. Such processes move the establishment of a democratic developmental state beyond the merely technical and administrative aspects of state formation (such as a focus on industrial policy and on an effective and efficient bureaucracy), to concerns about the political processes necessary to sustain a developmental approach. "(I)deational and political capacities," Edigheji argues, are essential factors in in ensuring that the technical and administrative aspects of a developmental state are successful (Edigheji 2010: 8). This is a view shared by Mkandawire who also emphasizes the significant role that ideological orientation and structural capacity play in defining the developmental role of the state (2001: 290). Taking into consideration the central role of politics and political practice in the construction of a democratic developmental state, the discussion which follows looks at the ideology which underpins the political outlook of the ruling EPRDF.

The EPRDF's Revolutionary Democracy Ideology

In June 1993, two years after it had seized power, the EPRDF published a policy document, entitled *Our Revolutionary Democracy Objectives and Next Steps*, which declared that its future policies would be guided by the ideology of revolutionary democracy (EPRDF 1993: 2). Historically, the concept of revolutionary democracy ideology was pioneered by V.I. Lenin who saw it both as the means through which a proletarian dictatorship would be established and as the antithesis of bourgeoisie (parliamentary) democracy (Berhe 2008: 234; Bach 2011: 641). Revolutionary democracy, in this context, called for a "vanguard party" that was committed to the principles of "democratic centralism." Democratic centralism thus had its roots in the Marxist-Leninist principle that all had the "complete freedom to discuss and criticize" any idea within the party before a decision was reached. However, once a decision had been reached, all were obliged to "implement the decision of the [party] no matter what their view" (Angle 2005: 525). Based on these Marxist-Leninist principles, the EPRDF proceed to reshape the Ethiopian state by combining the ideology of revolutionary democracy with the establishment of a hierarchical social structure which encouraged secrecy, obedience, and total submission to the party.

In its early years in power, the EPRDF portrayed the ideology of revolutionary democracy to be central to its goal of building a socialist state. In order to do so, it was stated, the party needed to liberate the oppressed masses from the shackles of Western imperialism and from the dominance of the local "oppressive class" (EPRDF 1993: 1). Two broad economic objectives were also identified and these related to the need to establish a "complementary and regionally balanced economy" and rapid economic growth. Revolutionary democracy bestowed a key role on the state to "co-ordinate, shape and guide" economic forces with the necessary fiscal and monitory policies (*ibid*: 43–44), the ultimate outcome of which would be "self-reliance and prevalence of economic justice" (*ibid*: 14–19).

The ideologues of revolutionary democracy dismissed "liberal democracy" for its emphasis on electoral representation which provided little room for meaningful participation by the masses. In its stead, the EPRDF advocated a form of "popular democracy" which would be based on the collective and organized participation of the people. In this model the party favored persuasion, rather than a majority vote, as the means to achieve consensus among its supporters (Vaughan and Tronvoll 2003: 116; Lefort 2010: 442). Significantly, it was intended that "popular democracy" would be advanced under the auspices of the EPRDF as the vanguard party. Notwithstanding the fact that the concept of democratic centralism was something of an oxymoron, put into practice through the mechanism of "popular democracy," it had an immediate restraining effect on both civil and political rights.

Despite the EPRDF's stated commitment to entertaining a plurality of political views, from the outset it was evident that competing political views would only be accommodated within the party itself. Thus, according to its 1993 strategy document:

> Ethiopia has *one and only one opportunity* to continue its existence as a state—that is the realization of our revolutionary democracy objectives. Without our revolutionary democracy objectives; not only the improvement of peoples' living standard is in jeopardy but also the very existence of Ethiopia as a state. (EPRDF 1993: 22) [Emphasis added]

Key to the party's success in achieving political dominance and in establishing the hegemony of its ideology was stated to be its victory in the first, and all subsequent, elections:

> (O)ur revolutionary democracy forces need to have sustained support that ensures legitimate superiority by winning all regular elections through continuous popular support to govern the country. *Losing even a single election can create serious danger. Hence the road to a hegemonic dominance must be paved by winning the first election.* (EPRDF 1993: 49) [Emphasis added]

The EPRDF pursued its mission to entrench the hegemony of the ideology of revolutionary democracy on three fronts: the partisan process of state building, the establishment of affiliate political parties, and the control of socioeconomic institutions. In so doing, the EPRDF capitalized on calls by Western donors to dismantle the centralized socialist bureaucracy of the Dergue to restructure the form of the state in its favor. It did so by diffusing potential opposition by bureaucrats from the previous regime and by restructuring both the federal and regional governments in line with the thinking of revolutionary democracy (*ibid*: 56). This assault on officials opposed to the new ideology (now labeled enemies) in what has been described as a "war on the *birokrasi*" (Young 1996: 541; Henze 1998: 49; Vaughan 2011: 627); it is also illustrative of the extent to which EPRDF consciously set about embedding its political ideals in the post-1991 Ethiopian state structure.

The EPRDF further extended its civilian control over political rights by organizing different ethnic groups into their own political parties. In line with the ethnically based federal structure delineated in the new constitution, "Peoples' Democratic Organizations (PDOs)" were established and served as the EPRDF's "satellite representatives" in regions where it had no direct representation (Henze 1998: 44; Gudina 2011: 667; Vaughan 2011: 627). In this endeavor the EPRDF recruited farmers, the proletariat, as well as educated but economically poor members of society, such as teachers, to establish the PDOs and to make them the "forces of revolutionary democracy" (EPRDF 1993: 51–55). In addition, other social institutions, such as community-based organizations, and religious and educational institutions have also been targeted as vehicles through which revolutionary democracy might be advanced. Thus, according to the EPRDF's strategy document, the party must aim "to make them [the religious and educational institutions] apparatuses of revolutionary democracy or at least to diminish their potential of becoming an obstacle" (*ibid*: 63). Although the engagement of the youth was not a feature of the early stages of political mobilization, it has since become a focal area of the EPRDF's hegemonic project.

There has not, however, always been consensus within the EPRDF about the ideological orientation of revolutionary democracy and the essence of the concept has been contested in struggles which have led to schisms within the party. According to Gebru Asrat, a veteran of the TPLF who left the party in 2001, there had long been ideological ambiguity in the discourses and practices of revolutionary democracy within the EPRDF. He refers to internal power struggles which took place in the EPRDF council in 2001 to illustrate the conceptual confusion that existed among senior party cadres as to whether revolutionary democracy should be considered a transitional Marxist ideology or an instrument of capitalism. According to Gebru, Meles Zenawi, then chairperson of the EPRDF and president of the country, managed to circumvent this ideological impasse by "wearing different hats," at different times, presenting himself as a revolutionary democrat, as a Marxist, or as an advocate of capitalism and supporter of the IMF and World Bank (Asrat 2014b: 313).

Thus, while EPRDF cadres were still being taught that imperialism was the enemy of revolutionary democracy, the government had already concluded an agreement with the IMF and the World Bank to implement a program of structural adjustment. In this move, a central tenet of the ideology, which assigns responsibility for control of the economy to the state, had clearly been compromised by liberal policies which promoted deregulation and privatization. Gebru maintains that the EPRDF wished to avoid confrontation with the IMF and World Bank in its early days in power, particularly due to the collapse of the Soviet Union which had provided support during the struggle against the Derg regime. In an attempt to get around this contradiction and to ensure that the government could play a central role in the management of the economy, "economic development organizations" were established in each of the coalition parties which make up the EPRDF. These organizations were set up as charitable foundations, to avoid criticism by the IMF or World Bank, but their intention was to play a role in steering the economy (Asrat 2014b: 156–158). However, these party-affiliated "development organizations" failed to introduce any vibrancy into the economy by promoting strategic and large-scale industrial development. Instead, they focused predominantly on retail trade, the production of nondurable consumer goods, and various import and export activities. Those involved in these development activities were politically supported and gained an unfair advantage over business people without any political affiliations. More importantly, Begru argues, these organizations became the breeding ground for rampant corruption (*ibid*).

A further ideological inconsistency within revolutionary democracy which triggered fierce debate was the contradiction between the political objective of establishing a multiparty democratic system and that of ensuring the hegemony of a revolutionary democratic state. The answer to this contradiction was to work for the complete adoption of revolutionary democracy thinking by the wider public such that it would become the dominant societal ideology regardless of whether or not the EPRDF was in power. In retrospect, Gebru states, "our entire move was not founded on a clear ideology and strategy, rather we were adaptable and followed flexible policies and directions that would help us remain in power" (*ibid*: 158).

Gebru's analysis supports that of Bach who asserts that the ideology was "neither revolutionary nor democratic" (Bach 2011: 653). Bach maintains that the revolutionary democracy has passed through different phases and has evolved from being an "ideological strategy" to becoming "a codified discursive strategy" (Bach 2011: 649). The discursive strategy of the ideology, in particular he asserts, is used as a powerful "political weapon" (*ibid*: 655) to attack competent political critics within the party, in the national political sphere, and even perceived opponents in international arena.

In national politics, where revolutionary democracy is portrayed as the antithesis of liberalism, at least in principle, opposition parties which advocate neoliberal policies are labeled as "anti-development," "anti-democracy," and "anti-peace," and hence as enemies of the people. In this way, revolutionary democracy has been used to undermine the legitimacy of opposition parties as occurred in the highly contested 2005 elections as well as in those held in 2010 (Bach 2011: 655). Finally, at the international level, the ideals of revolutionary democracy are used to counter the accusations of human rights groups and organizations advocating for freedom of speech and freedom of the press. Official government responses to reports produced by the US State Department, Human Rights Watch, and Amnesty International among others accuse these organizations of promoting a neoliberal agenda which is intended to delegitimize the developmental program underway and the demonstrable welfare benefits which it is bringing to the Ethiopian people (EPRDF 2010: 3–15; Bach 2011: 655). The section which follows considers the shift in EPRDF policy from revolutionary democracy to developmental democracy and discusses the continuity and discontinuity in the discourse and strategies than underpin them.

From Revolutionary Democracy to "Democratic" Developmentalism

During the course of the past decade, the EPRDF has managed a relatively "smooth transition" from the once dominant discourse of revolutionary democracy to that of democratic developmentalism. Reflective of this, one of the central objectives of the Growth and Transformation Plan (GTP) (2010–2015), was to "establish suitable conditions for sustainable nation building through the creation of a stable democratic and developmental state" (MOFED 2010: 22). This objective is reiterated in the Second Growth and Transformation Plan (GTP II) which stresses the importance of "establishing (a) developmental political economy by strengthening the democratic developmental state" (MOFED 2015: 78).

The EPRDF has articulated the mission of a democratic developmental state in Ethiopia as encompassing two key goals: the restructuring of a rent-seeking political economy and selective state intervention in the economy, both to address market failures and to eliminate bottlenecks to development (EPRDF 2010: 45). In order to fulfill this mission, according to EPRDF, the Ethiopian developmental state must display three basic features: development must be treated as an existential question, it must maintain political and economic autonomy from the economic elite, and it must ensure the hegemony of developmental thinking (*ibid*). The EPRDF has argued that its ideology of revolutionary democracy distinguishes it as a party which supports the rights of the rural masses to dismantle an exploitative system that has denied them both their economic and political freedom (EPRDF 2010: 56). In that regard, although South Korea and Taiwan are cited as models of best practice in constructing developmental states, the EPRDF has asserted that, unlike these East Asian countries, it will not alienate rural farmers. Instead, the developmental state which it aims to create is one that will prioritize the rights and the benefits of the rural masses which it considers its primary constituents (*ibid*: 55–57). However, the party argues, due to changing national and geopolitical contexts, it has been necessary to transform the orientation of the EPRDF from that of revolutionary democracy to developmental democracy.

As previously discussed, the notion of revolutionary democracy had been used both as a political strategy and as a means to renew the party by resolving the power struggles that had emerged in the central committee of the TPLF (Bach 2011: 650). Following this, the dominant faction in TPLF accused those they had ousted of a rent-seeking mentality and rent-collecting practices. In a similar fashion, the EPRDF has characterized the political economy of Ethiopia as one that is dominated by rent-seeking elites and zero-sum politics. Based on this critique, it is stated that a democratic developmental state will eliminate the conditions which give rise to rent-seeking practices and will establish a stable and democratic political order. This will be achieved by transforming revolutionary democracy into developmental democracy. According to the EPRDF:

> (T)he only way that our organization's revolutionary democracy direction and behaviour can survive is in a developmental democracy line. It can be said that combining the common features of developmental states with the unique elements of our organization's revolutionary democracy is a developmental democracy line which is the only way that revolutionary democracy can happen at the present time both at national and international context. In other words, it can be said that developmental democracy can be seen as the only timely manifestation of revolutionary democracy. Revolutionary democracy reveals the historical emergence, revolutionary and democratic behaviour of our organization; hence it is our correct name. Likewise, developmental democracy is also our correct name, because it describes the present day essence of revolutionary democracy as well as the true face of its emergence and realization. (*ibid*: 57)

This statement, bold in its intent, is a declaration by the leadership of the EPRDF that developmental democracy is, in effect, a new form of revolutionary democracy. Furthermore, the political processes seen as necessary to ensure the hegemony of developmentalism are exactly the same as those previously required to safeguard the dominance of revolutionary democracy. Following this logic:

> There is one and only one way that can ensure the continuity of the developmentalist direction. It only by ascertaining a hegemonic position that developmentalism can penetrate into the public and become the dominant thinking and cultural orientation. In order to do so, we have learnt that a massive public relation and indoctrination task is required. (*ibid*: 69)

The proposed process of building "ideational and political capacities" in a developmental state is also the same as the one that was introduced by the EPRDF to entrench the ideology of revolutionary democracy throughout the public service as well as in state-civil society relations. In establishing the hegemony of developmentalism it is evident that the EPRDF is using the same political strategies and mobilization techniques deployed in its earlier years in power. From this it becomes clear that, rhetoric aside, rather than positing a new democratic vision, the construction of a democratic developmental state in Ethiopia represents a continuation of the revolutionary, and implicitly undemocratic, policies of the past.

In establishing the hegemony of developmentalist thinking the government is explicit in its intent to target, among others, universities, research institutions, civil society organizations, and religious institutions, all of which are seen as battlegrounds in its struggle against neoliberalism, imperialism, and what it perceives as reactionary, and foreign-supported, thinking. Thus the EPRDF asserts that "it is essential to involve all societal initiatives in the state building struggle in an organized and effective manner so that the hegemony of developmental and democratic thinking is ensured both in the practical and ideational struggle" (*ibid*: 70). In addition to underscoring the fact that religious institutions are constitutionally prohibited from engaging in politics, the EPRDF argues that:

> (I)t is very important that the religious beliefs are crafted in a developmental and democratic sense. For instance, the culture of democracy can be enriched if all religious institutions preach equality of religions and plurality. They can also preach about the virtues of hard work, the negative aspects of corruption, theft and being idle...therefore high regard should be given in making sure that religious institutions are disseminating democratic and developmental messages to their believers without interfering into politics and without compromising their believes. (*ibid*: 71)

There is a remarkable similarity between the state-society relations that the advocates of revolutionary democracy had intended to create in Ethiopia in the early post-Derg years and the kind of sociopolitical order envisaged in democratic developmentalism. In the early years of its ascendency it was stated that revolutionary democracy would provide a platform where all ideas could be heard and debated in public. Its egalitarian veneer aside, this call for an open expression of views was a strategy to surface and then to nullify or defeat the ideals of so-called imperialists, the bourgeoisie, and those deemed irresolute. In a similar fashion, the EPRDF has asserted that the democratic developmental state will also provide a platform that will entertain competing ideas and perspectives. It is only when subjected to public debate and scrutiny, it is stated, that contentious ideas will be exposed and ultimately rejected by the wider public:

> A wrong and backward thinking is defeated not because it is covered or despised rather only if it is opened, exposed and [then] removed from the minds of the people. It will be very difficult to publicly expose the backwardness and dangerousness of an idea and to remove it from peoples' mind if it is covered. Entertaining wrong ideas in an impartial debating platform contributes more for the prevalence of the right ideas than to the promotion of wrong ideas. Wrong ideas will have better chance of remaining invisible and expanding if they are not openly debated and defeated in free debating platform. (*ibid*: 72)

Having declared that freedom of speech and the open expression of ideas are essential to the dominance of developmental democracy, the EPRDF has also made explicit its position on multiparty politics and a dominant party discourse. In that respect, it has stated that the hegemony of developmental democracy will only be achieved if it transcends the life span of the EPRDF, either as a government or a political party. In light of this, its primary focus has been to ensure that the ideology of democratic developmentalism is entrenched within the public sector and that it is inculcated throughout society. However, although the EPRDF has never openly endorsed the notion of a "dominant party," it is implicitly preparing itself for a prolonged period in power by suppressing it opponents and scaling up its developmental achievements, both of which have contributed to its successive electoral victories (*ibid*: 73–75).

The Balance Sheet of Revolutionary Democracy and Developmental Democracy

Current trends suggest that the EPRDF has decided that its legitimacy will be derived from the delivery of socioeconomic services, rather than from its successes in national elections, which have become mere ceremonial moments to renew their mandate to remain in power. Ambitious development plans play a significant role in pursuit of this objective. Thus, despite some success with the first Growth and Transformation Plan (GTP-I), the GTP-II was launched with the ambitious goal of transforming Ethiopia into a lower middle-income country by 2025 (NPC 2015: 16). Continuing with the target set in the first development plan, the stated of objective of GTP II is to maintain economic growth at "an average real GDP growth rate of 11%," and to achieve "rapid, broad-based, sustained and equitable economic growth" which will be the basis for "stable democratic developmental state" (*ibid*: 3–4).

In pursuit of these goals the government has initiated a series of new programs and mega projects intended to transform the economy and enhance the social welfare of citizens. At various levels, these programs have had both a direct and indirect impact on the social and economic rights of citizens. This has included massive investment in the establishment of micro and small-scale Enterprises (MSEs), particularly in the urban areas, which have benefited from extensive financial, technical, administrative, and political support. The creation of MSEs is primarily intended to create employment opportunities for new graduates and for unemployed urban youth. In July 2011, the government also introduced a compulsory pension scheme for all private-sector employees, a welfare benefit which in the past had been restricted to those working in the public sector. The legislation introducing the new scheme states that widening the scale of social security available to citizens contributes to "social justice, industrial peace, poverty reduction and development" (Proclamation No. 715/2011). In the same year, the government issued a proclamation introducing a social insurance scheme (Proclamation No. 690/2010) and another to pilot a Community Based Health Insurance program in selected rural areas and small towns across the country (Yilmaet al. 2014). The mega projects embarked upon have primarily been of an infrastructural nature and have included the construction of hydroelectric dams, railway lines, education and health centers, a light rail transit network in the capital Addis Ababa, and the establishment of industrial zones for foreign and domestic investors and government-owned enterprises.

There is clear evidence that the socioeconomic development policies introduced have positively impacted the livelihoods of the population and that they hold the possibility of further gains in the future. Thus, for example, during the period of the first GTP state support to MSEs resulted in the creation of 4 million jobs (NPC 2015:9), the national coverage of electricity services increased from 41% to 54%, and the percentage of the rural population with access to a telephone service (within a radius of 5 km) increased from 62.1% to 96% (NPC 2015:10–11).

In the area of manufacturing and industry, the government is committed to providing a package of incentives (including, land, financing, an enabling policy framework, and tax relief), as a means to stimulate economic growth. The returns on this investment are to be seen in the fact that during the four years of GTP I the annual growth rate of the industrial sector increased from 10.8% to 20% (NPC 2015:4).[4] Although significantly lower than rates in some other sectors of the economy, the agricultural sector still recorded an annual average growth rate of 6.6% during the period from 2009/2010 to 2013/2014. More importantly, given the large proportion of the population who are subsistence farmers, the production of major food crops (cereals, pulses, and oil seeds), increased by 52% during the same period (NPC 2015:8).

However, a closer examination of the Ethiopian government's programs reveals that the discourse of democratic developmentalism is deeply embedded in both the political machinery of the ruling party and throughout the administrative structures and policies of the state. In this system, developmental and political processes are deeply intertwined in a mutually reinforcing process which reinforces the legitimacy of the government and the policies which it is implementing. This is evident in its efforts to expand its support among small-scale and subsistence farmers, who make up nearly 80% of the total population and who have historically constituted its political power base (EPRDF 1993: 5; Ohino 2009: 6). In building its support base it has also elicited the support of certain social groups in the urban centers, irrespective of their size, as these are also considered to be part of the broad-based coalition which underpins the "embedded autonomy" of the state. These social groups include business elites, and women, youth, and civil servants who have, in various ways, been incorporated into the government's political and developmental program.

---

4   Although the bulk of this growth took place in the construction sector (which increased from 10.9% to 29.9%), the manufacturing sector recorded a credible increase from 11.6% to 13% (NPC 2015:4).

The methods used in this process of incorporation include the establishment of multiple rural neighborhood administrations comprising between 10 and 90 households. These are ostensibly intended "to make service delivery at local level more efficient and to mobilize people for development work," but they also serve to increase the ruling party's presence in the rural areas and, with this, increased surveillance and increased pressure to comply with the dictates of government (Aalen and Tronvoll 2009: 198). As an incentive to those who are willing to comply, as indicated, thousands of MSEs have been established for women and youth at every level of the governing hierarchy (Aalen and Tronvoll 2009: 198–203; Lefort 2010: 445–451; Vaughan 2012: 631).

Over and above the mobilization of the urban and rural population under such structures, the ruling party has embarked on an aggressive campaign to expand its membership. As part of this strategy, a pyramid recruitment program (commonly known as One-for-Five) was introduced in government departments with the objective of expanding the EPRDF's membership base. As a consequence of this campaign, the EPRDF's party membership increased exponentially from around 700,000 at the time of 2011 elections to 6.5 million in 2013 (EPRDF 2013). Through this process of political mobilization and control, and the concomitant punishment of dissent, the institutional and structural distinction between the ruling party and the state has been effectively eliminated and the undisputed dominance of the EPRDF has been assured (Aalen and Tronvoll 2009: 197–198; Vaughan 2012: 623).

Under these circumstances, it is perhaps not surprising that the human rights record of the Ethiopian government is at its worst since the advent of democracy.[5] This is evident in the state closure of newspapers and magazines that are thought to be critical of the government, and the intimidation, harassment, and imprisonment of journalists (and lately also bloggers) who have written critically about state policies and practices. It is also to be seen in the use of anti-terrorism legislation against perceived political dissidents (including the leadership of opposition par-

---

5   Among the legal instruments used by the government to consolidate its authoritarian dominance of society are the Charities and Civil Societies Law (2009), the Anti-Terrorism Law (2008), and the Press Law (2008).

ties, religious leaders, and journalists), which has become part of the eve-ryday of Ethiopian politics (Human Rights Watch 2012). In recent years, the government has deployed all of its media outlets (television, radio, and print) to attack and delegitimize its political opponents, labeling individ-uals and groups "terrorists" even while judicial processes against them are still underway.[6] In almost all of these cases, the constitutionally guar-anteed rights of citizens to freedom of "thought, opinion and expression" (Article 29) and "to be presumed innocent" until proven guilty (Article 20 (3), have clearly been violated. This is aggravated by the fact that all those accused by the government are typically portrayed as being "anti-devel-opment," "anti-peace," and "anti-democratic" and, hence, as being a threat to the common good.

Conclusions

The carrot and stick of "democratic developmentalism" in Ethiopia can clearly be seen in the mix of successful socioeconomic policies and strat-egies and in the authoritarian and undemocratic nature of the politi-colegal system. From this, three interrelated conclusions can be drawn. First, taking into consideration the conceptual arguments advanced by Leftwich and White, it is unlikely that a "democratic" developmental state can be established in Ethiopia based on a democratically consolidated po-litical platform. This is because the ideology which has driven the ruling party since the transition to democracy in the early 1990s is in inherent conflict with the ideal of consolidated plural democracy. It is thus unreal-istic to expect political pluralism to emerge from a system controlled by a ruling party committed to the principles of "democratic centralism."

Second, the discourse of "democratic developmentalism" currently espoused by the ruling party represents a simple evolution of its ideology of revolutionary democracy. Stemming from this, the need to build the ide-ational and political capacity necessary to realize development has been a long-standing feature of the policies and practices of the EPRDF govern-ment. At the same time, while it is undeniable that the government has

---

6   For example, a number of documentaries have been released which target Muslim religious leaders, opposition party leaders, and journalists, accusing them of terrorism based on secretly recorded, and heavily edited, clips of interrogation sessions, or on the subjective views of selected panellists.

achieved significant economic growth through its developmentally driven political processes and politically crafted development initiatives, it is also certain that these achievements would not have been realized without the imposition of highly authoritarian policies.

Third, the continuity of the EPRDF's political ideology in the new narrative of democratic developmentalism has provided the government an unprecedented opportunity to present the drive for economic growth as a justification for the political repression of its opponents, the criminalization of dissent, and the suppression of alternative viewpoints. Furthermore, by portraying contending viewpoints as "anti-development and anti-democratic" the hegemony of revolutionary democratic developmentalist thinking is perpetuated.

References

Aalen, L. and Tronvoll, K. (2009). The end of democracy? Curtailing political and civil rights in Ethiopia. *Review of African Political Economy, 36*(120), 193–207.

Abbink, J. (2011). Ethnic-based federalism and ethnicity in Ethiopia: Reassessing the experiment after 20 years. *Journal of Eastern African Studies, 5*(4), 596–618.

Angle, S. C. (2005). Decent democratic centralism. *Political Theory, 33*(4), 518–546.

Arriola, L. R. and Lyons, T. (2016). The 100% election. *Journal of Democracy, 27*(1), 76–88.

Asrat, G. (2014a). *Sovereignty and democracy in Ethiopia* (Autobiography in Amharic).

Asrat, G. (2014b). *Sovereignty and democracy in Ethiopia.* (Signature Book Printing Press).

Bach, J.-N. (2011). Abyotawi democracy: Neither revolutionary nor democratic, a critical review of EPRDF's conception of revolutionary democracy in post-1991 Ethiopia. *Journal of Eastern African Studies, 5*(4), 641–663.

Berhe, A. (2008). The political history of Tigray People's Revolutionary Front (1975–1991): Revolt, Ideology and Mobilization in Ethiopia. Vrije Universiteit. Amsterdam.PhD Dissertation.

de Waal, A. (2013). The theory and practice of Meles Zenawi. *African Affairs, 112*(446), 148–155.

Edigheji, O. (2010). Constructing a democratic developmental state in South Africa; potentials and challenges. In: O. Edigheji (Ed.), *Constructing a democratic developmental state in South Africa; Potentials and challenges.* Cape Town, South Africa: HSRC Press.

EPRDF. (1993). Our revolutionary democracy objectives and next steps (Party document in Amharic).

EPRDF. (2010). The path of the renaissance and the renewal of Ethiopia (Party document in Amharic).

EPRDF. (2013). *EPRDF in brief.* Addis Ababa, Ethiopia: Ethiopian People's Revolutionary Democratic Front.

Evans, P. and Heller, P. (2013). Human development, state transformation and the politics of the developmental state. In Leibfried, S. Nullmeier, F. Huber, E. Lange, M. Levy, J. and Stephens, J. *The Oxford handbook of transformations of the state.* Oxford: Oxford University Press.

Federal Democratic Republic of Ethiopia.(1995). Federal Negarit Gazetta, 1st year, No. 1.

Federal Democratic Republic of Ethiopia.(2010a). Federal Negarit Gazetta, 16th year, No. 50.

Federal Democratic Republic of Ethiopia.(2010b). Federal Negarit Gazetta 17th year, No. 4.

Federal Democratic Republic of Ethiopia.(2011). Federal Negarit Gazetta 17th year, No. 79.

Gudina, M. (2003). *Ethiopia: Competing ethnic nationalisms and the quest for democracy, 1960-2000.* Addis Ababa. Shaker Publishers.

Gudina, M. (2011). Elections and democratization in Ethiopia, 1991-2010. *Journal of Eastern African Studies, 5,* 664-680.

Henze, P. B. (1998). A political success story. *Journal of Democracy, 9*(4), 40-54.

Human Rights Watch.(2012). *World Report.* Accessed at : https://www.hrw.org/world-report/2012

International, C. S. A. a. I. (2012). *Ethiopia demographic and health survey 2011.* Addis Ababa, Ethiopia and Calverton, Maryland, USA.

Kaldor, M. and Vejvoda, I. (1997). Democratization in central and east European countries. *International Affairs (Royal Institute of International Affairs 1944), 73* (1). 159-82.

Kefale, A. (2011). The (un)making of opposition coalitions and the challenge of democratization in Ethiopia, 1991-2011. *Journal of Eastern African Studies, 5*(4), 681-701.

Lefort, R. (2010). Powers-mengist-and peasants in rural Ethiopia: The post-2005 interlude. *Journal of Modern African Studies, 48,* 435-460.

Leftwich, A. (Ed.). (1996). *Democracy and development: Theory and practice.* Cambridge. Polity Press.

Leftwich, A. (2000). *States of development: On the primacy of politics in development.* Cambridge: Polity.

Leftwich, A. (2005). Politics in command: Development studies and the rediscovery of social science. *New Political Economy, 10*(4), 573–607.

Mengesha, S. Y. (2016). Silencing dissent. *Journal of Democracy, 27*(1), 89–94.

Ministry of Finance and Economic Development. (2010). *Growth and transformation plan 2010/11 -2014/15*. Addis Ababa: Ministry of Finance and Economic Development.

Ministry of Finance and Economic Development. (2015). *Growth and transformation plan 2015/16 -2019/20*. Addis Ababa, Ministry of Finance and Economic Development.

Mkandwire, T. (2001) Thinking about developmental states in Africa. *Cambridge Journal of Economics, 25*, 289–313.

National Planning Commission. (2015). *The Second Growth and Transformation Plan 2015/16 -2019/20*. Addis Ababa: National Planning Commission.

Robinson, M. and White, G. (1998). *The democratic developmental state: Political and institutional design*. New York. Oxford University Press.

Sandbrook, R. (2005). Origins of the democratic developmental state: Interrogating Mauritius. *Canadian Journal of African Studies/La Revue canadienne des études africaines, 39*(3), 549–581.

Tronvoll, K. (2011). The Ethiopian 2010 federal and regional elections: Re-establishing the one-party state. *African Affairs, 110*(438), 121–136.

UNDP. (2014). *National Human Development Report 2014*. Addis Ababa: UNDP.

Vaughan, S. (2011). Revolutionary democratic state-building: Party, state and people in the EPRDF's Ethiopia. *Journal of Eastern African Studies, 5*(4), 619–640.

Vaughan, S. and Tronvoll, K. (2003). *The culture of power in contemporary Ethiopian political life*. Stockholm: Sida.

White, G. (1998). Constructing a democratic developmental state. In: M. Robinson and G. White (Eds.), *The democratic developmental state: Politics and institutional design*. Oxford: Oxford University Press.

World Bank. (2016). *Ethiopia – Systematic country diagnostic: Priorities for ending extreme poverty and promoting shared prosperity*. Washington, D.C.: World Bank Group.

Yilma, Z., Mebratie, A., Sparrow, R., Abebaw, D., Dekker, M., Alemu, G., and Bedi, A. S. (2014). Coping with shocks in rural Ethiopia. *Journal of Development Studies, 50*(7), 1009–1024.

Young, J. (1996). Ethnicity and power in Ethiopia. *Review of African Political Economy, 23*(70), 531–542.

The Establishment of a Democratic Developmental Local State in South Africa: Between Rhetoric and Reality

Sharon Penderis and Chris Tapscott

In various formulations, the idea of a developmental state has appeared in official discourse in South Africa since the ending of Apartheid and the advent of democratic government in 1994, albeit that its adoption as state policy has been slow and inconsistent (ANC 2007b; Manuel 2013; Evans 2010; Fine 2008). As has been the case in many other emerging economies, South Africa was drawn to the idea of a developmental state in the hope of replicating the economic successes of the East Asian Tigers. However, in the context of a newly democratized state which had just recently overcome more than three centuries of colonial and Apartheid rule, there was a reluctance to replicate the authoritarian features of the East Asian developmental states which permitted little dissent, imposed restrictive labor legislation, and, in their early years at least, generally thought little of exploiting the working class who were poorly paid and often labored under very poor conditions (Burkett and Harl-Landsberg 2003). Instead, South Africa was committed to global trends which have increasingly linked economic development to the need to strengthen basic rights and entitlements. This trend has also been extended to the idea of a developmental state where emphasis has now been placed on the need to embrace democratic principles and practices (Leftwich 2002; White 2006) which include notions of good governance (Fritz and Menocal 2007) and the promotion of citizen participation (Welch and Nuru 2006).

While there is a broad consensus in the literature, country variances aside, on the defining features of the East Asian developmental states, there is considerably less agreement on the essence of what has now come to be called a democratic developmental state. Edigheji (2005:22) defines a democratic developmental state as one which has the "institutional attributes of the classical developmental state, that is, being autonomous and coherent, but (which) also takes on board the attributes of procedural democracy. In addition, the democratic developmental state is one that forges broad-based alliances with society and ensures popular participation in the governance and transformation processes." To that extent, there is some consensus in the literature that a democratic developmental state should have a transformative agenda which extends beyond economic growth to a focus on broader social and political goals (Maphunye 2009; Gumede 2009). In support of this perspective, White (2006:60) asserts that "the process of development involves more than just economic growth but includes life-and-death issues such as poverty, personal security, distributive equity, social justice and environmental sustainability." Such a state must also embody the principles of democracy, which Leftwich (2002) refers to as a developmental orientation and democratic political system. Thus, a key determinant of a democratic developmental state, Edigheji (2005) maintains, is its competence in promoting development and growth and, at the same time, its capacity to engender consensus and popular participation. The ability to provide mechanisms for effective citizen participation, in particular, has been seen as a key characteristic of the democratic developmental state. The extent to which citizens accept the legitimacy of the state, moreover, is believed to be contingent on the effectiveness of these participatory processes as well on the extent to which the gains of economic growth are redistributed (Leftwich 2002; Welch and Nuru 2006).

A further component of a democratic developmental state is seen to be its capacity to decentralize administrative and political responsibilities to lower echelons of government. Although decentralization had been fashionable in development circles for some decades (Conyers 1984), interest in the concept gained momentum in the 1980s and 1990s (Turner 1999) and programs aimed at devolving power away from central government have since been extensively supported by international donor organizations, by various United Nations agencies and international funding organizations such as the World Bank and the IMF (Blair 1998). Decentralized governance, indeed, has frequently been portrayed as not only desirable but also as inescapable (Blondel 1990). This is because the process is associated with good governance, greater efficiency, and the deepening of democracy through participatory processes which give voice to the poor (Klugman 1994).

What is noteworthy in much of the writing on democratic developmental states, however, is its aspirational nature and the fact that it is seldom grounded on empirical evidence. Furthermore, perhaps because of its conceptual vagueness or perhaps because the term democracy has positive associations in both the national and international realms, there is a significant degree of self-labeling, where states ascribe to themselves the status of a democratic developmental state irrespective of whether they permit freedom of speech, freedom of association, the right to peaceful protest, etc. Conversely, as shall be seen, South Africa has aspirations of becoming a democratic developmental state, and while it continues to hold true to the tenets of democracy there is little to suggest that it is succeeding in its endeavors to promote economic growth through an interventionist state.

Aspirations Toward a Democratic Developmental State in South Africa

An interest in the establishment of a developmental state in South Africa was evident in the policy thinking of the ruling African National Congress (ANC) both in the lead-up to the first democratic elections in 1994 and on its assumption of office thereafter. Thus, the 1994 White Paper on Reconstruction and Development, although not explicitly referring to a developmental state, nevertheless asserted the need for an interventionist state which would play a leading role in steering the economy and in reconstructing South African society:

> Reconstruction and development will be achieved through the leading and enabling role of the State, a thriving private sector and active involvement by all sectors of civil society. The role of the Government and the public sector within the broader economy has to be redefined so that reconstruction and development are facilitated. In a wide range of areas the GNU will take the lead in reforming and addressing structural conditions. In doing so its guidelines will remain the basic people-driven principles of the RDP. (RSA 1994, Sections 3.1.2 and 3.1.3)

While interest in advancing a strongly interventionist developmental state waned following the adoption in 1996 of the neoliberal Growth Employment and Redistribution (GEAR) macroeconomic framework which espoused a diminished state, the idea never entirely lost currency and in the course of the past decade it has resurfaced both in ANC policy documents (ANC 2005, 2007b) as well in official discourse (PSC 2008; The Presidency 2009, 2010; Poon 2009). The concept received new impetus following the global financial meltdown in 2008, which exposed the weaknesses of unregulated markets, and as it became increasingly apparent that GEAR had failed to deliver the economic growth it had promised. For the ruling ANC government a developmental state is now portrayed as the most viable vehicle to overcome the legacy of Apartheid, to address poverty and social inequality, to improve service delivery, and to promote people-centered development (Manuel 2009; ANC 2009; Edigheji 2010). Significantly, official South African understanding of a developmental state (in as much as it has been formally articulated) is one that is both developmental and democratic (Olayode 2005; Van Dijk and Croucamp 2007). Thus the ANC's 2007 "Draft Strategy and Tactics Document" stresses that a South African developmental state should, in addition to advancing sustainable economic development, "mobilise the people as a whole, especially the poor, to act as their own liberators through participatory and representative democracy" (ANC 2007b: para. 59). The 2012 National Development Plan (NDP), which sets out the government's long-term strategy to address poverty, inequality, and economic transformation, is also directly linked to the vision of a developmental state. The NDP refers both to the role of "citizens being active in development" and to the need for "a capable and developmental state able to intervene to correct our historical inequities" (National Planning Commission 2011:1).

Unlike the top-down and authoritarian East Asian model, the government envisages a South African developmental state which is infused with democratic content, where state/society synergies are created by a mobilized civil society working side by side with a committed and development-oriented government in a process of informing policy from below. In its emphasis on a bottom-up approach to policy formulation, the South African model differs markedly from the conventional idea of a developmental state. Reflective of this approach, the first policy document to propose a developmental approach was the White Paper on Developmental Local Government which was launched by the Ministry of Provincial Affairs and Constitutional Development in 1998 (RSA 1998b). According to the White Paper, the four characteristics of developmental local government are:

> (E)xercising municipal powers and functions in a manner which maximises their impact on social development and economic growth; playing an integrating and coordinating role to ensure alignment between public (including all spheres of government) and private investment within the municipal area; democratising development; and building social capital through providing community leadership and vision, and seeking to empower marginalised and excluded groups within the community. (RSA 1998b:8)

Although this focus on the local state is reflective of an unusual understanding of the nature of a developmental state, it was justified in terms of a conventional belief that municipalities, as the tier of government closest to the people, are best positioned to be the key drivers in overcoming economic exclusion and uneven development (Pieterse 2007). A central tenet of this bottom-up approach was the need for local authorities to institutionalize participatory processes at grassroots level and devise effective structures and processes to facilitate citizen participation in local affairs. In support of this objective, a comprehensive legislative framework was set in place for directing municipalities to implement a system of participatory governance (Moodley 2006). This included the Municipal Structures Act (RSA 1998a) and the Municipal Systems Act (RSA 2000) which prescribed the participatory processes that municipalities needed to follow in their engagement with local communities. Noticeably, as shall be discussed, little thought was given to how greater citizen participation might lead to economic growth or how different levels of government might combine to achieve this goal.

Among a number of measures introduced to promote citizen participation at the local level, and implicitly democratic developmentalism, is the Integrated Development Planning (IDP) process (Achmat 2002). In terms of the Municipal Systems Act of 2000, an IDP must be drawn up following municipal elections and the assumption of office of a new local government council (RSA 2000). In that respect, it is intended to be a means through which all development initiatives are planned at the local level, the views of ordinary citizens are heard and their needs prioritized in policy (Harrison 2002, 2006). The act further obliges municipalities to establish appropriate structures to ensure that effective citizen participation takes place (FCR 2002; Goldman 2005). The IDP was thus identified as the key mechanism by which local government would contribute to the creation of a national developmental state. It has been described as the "cornerstone of developmental government in South Africa" and the mechanism through which sectorial plans, strategic priorities, budgets, and resources will be aligned and coordinated (GGLN 2008:53).

From the above it is evident that, formalistically at least, there is in place both the legislative and policy framework necessary to promote developmental local government and that this has the potential to contribute to the broader program of establishing a developmental state in South Africa. However, aside from the somewhat anomalous approach of establishing a developmental state from the bottom-up, there is mounting evidence that the notion of developmental local government is failing in its attempts to promote effective citizen participation, to improve the welfare of the poor or, indeed, to advance the establishment of democratic developmental state at the national level. A review of the literature reveals that local authorities are unable to actualize their developmental mandate and that a substantial proportion of South Africans continue to live in poorly resourced localities, with limited opportunities for meaningful participation in development initiatives and with equally limited prospects of economic advancement (Chagunda 2007; Fakir 2007; Van Dijk and Croucamp 2007; Tapscott 2008; Thompson et al. 2011a, 2011b, 2011c; Van Donk 2012; Andani and Naidu 2013). In that respect, mounting service delivery protests across the country are reflective of citizen frustration and anger both at unfulfilled expectations and the failure of institutionalized participatory structures (Atkinson 2007; Kimemia 2011; Plessing 2011; Sowetan 2012). These protests can be viewed as the final resort of citizens attempting to make their voices heard through popular and non-institutionalized means.

In the context of the above, this chapter examines the manner in which a system of developmental local government is being implemented in the City of Cape Town. Taking as a case study the suburb of Delft[1], a poor area on the margins of the municipality, it focuses on three key aspects of the developmental approach, namely the extent to which there is a coherent national vision of a democratic developmental state which has been adopted by the local state, the extent to which democracy is being consolidated through citizen participation, and the extent to which this model is leading to economic growth and improved welfare at the local level.

Delftis, a high-density urban community located approximately 25 kilometers from Cape Town's central business district on what is known as the Cape Flats, is an impoverished region which has its origins in the segregationist policies of the Apartheid era. As a result of discriminatory legislation and policy, African, Indian, and mixed-raced Colored people from diverse backgrounds and traditions were uprooted from more central areas of Cape Town and forcibly resettled in segregated racially based residential areas on the Cape Flats in a process which radically altered the social and physical fabric of the city (Cook 1991; Western 1981). Low levels of physical and social well-being characterize most communities in an area which is characterized by widespread poverty, unemployment, poor social services (a lack of educational opportunities in particular), health problems, high infant mortality rates, poor nutrition, drug addiction, and crime (Penderis 2003). Despite 20 years of democratic governance, many of these socioeconomic conditions remain prevalent in Delft.

The Coherency of the Developmental State Vision

Constitutionally, South Africa is a unitary state with a three-tiered hierarchy of national, provincial, and local governments. However, since the adoption of a democratic constitution in 1996, the government has strug-

---

[1]   Data presented in this chapter are derived from quantitative and qualitative research conducted in Delft between January 2011 and October 2013.The qualitative research included observation, key informant interviews, and focus group discussions with municipal and provincial officials, local political office bearers, ward committee members, and other residents of the area. The quantitative data generated were derived from a stratified random sample of 470 households in Delft using a survey instrument which included both closed and open-ended questions.

gled to ensure effective intergovernmental relations, and weak coordination between the three tiers has adversely affected policy coherence and
the implementation of national strategies at the local level. This problem
is particularly apparent in the attempt to build a developmental state. Interviews with provincial and local government officials in metropolitan
Cape Town revealed that, for the most part, they had a very limited understanding of the concept of a developmental state. This lack of a "common
developmental grammar," which Johnson (1999 asserts is a prerequisite
for a successful developmental state, has been an inhibiting factor in attempts to construct a developmental local state. Reflective of this, the City
of Cape Town's IDP for 2012–2017 makes only one reference to a developmental state and its interpretation of the essence of such a state is noteworthy both for its conceptual vagueness and its minimalist interpretation of what the municipality's role should be in the process. Referring to
the NDP's objective of building a capable and developmental state, the IDP
states that:

> This objective relates to the state playing a developmental and trans-
> formative role. It entails that staff at all levels should have the compe-
> tence, experience and authority to perform their jobs, and that the re-
> lationship between the spheres of government should improve and be
> managed more proactively. To comply, the City will use property and
> land to leverage social issues and implement a human resources, talent
> management and skills development programme. The City will also
> contribute to the creation of a capable and developmental state through
> ongoing collaboration with the National Department of Transport,
> Province and the Passenger Rail Agency of South Africa (PRASA)/Me-
> trorail on the rail services improvement and upgrade programme, and
> will partner with Province in providing and maintaining education and
> school sites. (City of Cape Town 2016:33)

In light of the above, it is perhaps not surprising that the majority of officials interviewed had either "not heard of the term" or else stated that it
was not used in their departments or in any official documentation. According to one senior municipal official: "I must be honest, but I have not
heard of a developmental state in the work I do in this department or at
any meetings with other departments. Even when I attend mayoral meet-

ings this term is not used" (Male Official, Cape Town: 20/05/2013). Reference to the developmental state is similarly lacking in the Western Cape Provincial government's 2012/2013 assessment of the IDP process in the municipalities under its purview (WCGDLG 2016) which makes no mention of the concept at all.[2]

Formalistically, integrated development planning is supposed to be fully aligned with the NPD and other national and provincial planning strategies. According to the director of the city's IDP Office "planning the IDP is a total, iterative process and it is carefully aligned to the NDP. Although some documents take a longer term view, all development in a municipal area must be aligned. Sometimes the long view is different to problems that we face today" (Van der Merwe, 02/05/2013). However, an examination of the way in which the city's IDP objectives are aligned with those of the NDP, as in the above excerpt from the 2012–2017 plan, reveals the process of planning is far from integrated. This is because interpretation of the goals and objectives of the NDP are left to the discretion of the city which determines which aspects of the national plan it wishes to pursue in its IDP and in which way. In this context, the alignment of IDP is little more than an exercise in legislative compliance with little consideration given to how this might be put into practice.

Interviews with officials from different tiers of government revealed that there is very limited collaboration between them and that there are only nominal efforts to align national programs with development priorities identified by residents at the local level. According to a municipal councilor in Delft:

> In terms of the development state vision, there is a disconnect between national, provincial and local government. They start with a blank canvas, but the disconnect is between the needs of the people and higher decision making bodies. What the people's real needs are is not understood and the diversity in wards is not understood. Emotional forces and the political landscape play a major role. If one goes into the community we can see what the real needs of people are. We cannot predetermine this. We must really listen to the people, not the other way around. We are not doing this at grassroots level. If we do not deal with

---

2   No mention of a developmental state either is made in the provincial Department of Local Government's Annual Report for 2015–2016.

this, things will just get worse. We talk about freedom, but look at our informal settlements—still the same people are living there. (Van Wyk, 24/09/2013)

Citizen Participation in Developmental Local Government

A key feature of the IDP process, and a central dimension of developmental local government, as indicated, is its role in eliciting public participation in the formulation of policy. In recent years the city has made much of its success in canvassing the views of its residents in its integrated planning process. The Mayoral Forward to 2012–2017 IDP proclaims that the plan represents not only a blueprint of the city's vision but that "It is a plan that belongs to all the people of our city, who have all been given the opportunity to have their say in how we move Cape Town forward"(City of Cape Town 2016). However, when asked to comment on their knowledge of the integrated planning process and the extent to which they had provided input for the formulation of the current plan, 98.9% of respondents in Delft reported that they had never heard of the IDP while 99.5% stated that they had never been asked to provide input for its formulation. This level of response correspond to statistics for the municipality as a whole[3] which reveal that the overwhelming majority of residents are effectively excluded from a processes which is intended to be the centerpiece of participatory local governance. Thus, although public participation is prescribed by statute in the design of the IDP, this is not the case in practice and the process is ultimately a top-down exercise where ordinary citizens have little say in influencing decisions which will impact on their welfare.

In addition to the IDP process, the city has established several other structures to promote citizen participation. These mechanisms include subcouncils[4] and ward committees which constitute the institutionalized "participatory spaces" mandated by legislation to further facilitate community engagement in the formulation of the IDP and in other decision-

---

[3]   Of those interviewed in the city's 2011 Customer Satisfaction Survey 91% had never heard of the IDP (City of Cape Town 2011:57).

[4]   Sub-councils are generally only established in metropolitan municipalities (of which there are 8). All other municipalities only have ward committees.

making processes. Because it is a metropolitan government with a sizeable population (in excess of 4 million) dispersed over a large area (2,461 km²), the Cape Town City council has devolved some of its responsibilities to 24 subcouncils. These subcouncils comprise between ten and twelve ward councilors, who each represent a ward, together with an equivalent number of councilors appointed through a system of proportional representation.[5] The duties assigned to a sub-council include responsibility for monitoring service delivery, expenditure of funding allocated to the wards, encouraging public participation in decision-making processes, and for making recommendations to the council with respect to the development needs and priorities of the constituency they serve (City of Cape Town 2011).

Ward committees are intended to be the interface between the municipality and the communities which they represent and, as such, they serve as the primary vehicle for ongoing citizen participation in municipal affairs. The city has elected to make use of a system of sector representation in the wards rather than an area-based one. Under this arrangement, the ward committee is made up of the representatives of various identified sectors such as faith-based organizations, sports associations, or business organizations. Each of the sectors elects or nominates an individual to represent them on the ward committee in a measure intended to ensure that a wide range of interests is accommodated. Ward committees are chaired by ward councilors elected during local government elections and, hence, mandated to represent their constituency at sub-council meetings.

Despite the existence of an elaborate participatory system, substantively, it is evident that, ordinary citizens have little opportunity to influence decisions which might affect their welfare. Thus, although members of the public are invited to sub-council meetings, they are not permitted to participate in their deliberations. Instead, they must channel their concerns through a laborious process which entails a written submission to the relevant sector, which is then forwarded to the ward committee, and is thereafter presented to the ward councilor who then decides whether to raise the matter at a sub-council meeting or to engage directly with the

5   Local government councillors in South Africa are elected in a 50:50 split between proportional and ward constituency-based systems.

relevant municipal department. Concerns raised by citizens through their ward committee members travel through a similarly circuitous route through the ward committee, and by way of the ward councilor to the sub-council, and then on to the council where decisions of substance are ultimately taken. Furthermore, due to predefined budgets, requests from ward committees which will incur significant costs (such as the construction of a crèche or a new park), are seldom, if ever, dealt with in the same financial year and they are also unlikely to receive attention if they have not already been prioritized in the IDP.

The ineffectiveness of the ward committee system was a recurring theme raised by municipal officials and local office bearers in Delft. This related to the process through which ward committee members were selected, their lack of legitimacy, the limited power which ward committees have to influence decision making, and the fact that committee members generally do not serve as the interface between their communities and the sub-council. Linked to this was the concern that the control of ward committees and the sectors which they represent was often captured by local elites. "In my ward," according to one councilor, "all the same people are members of the different sector organizations. All they do is change their names around and then they serve together on the ward committee" (Female Councilor, Bonteheuwel: 19/06/2013). As a consequence of these concerns some councilors viewed the ward committee system as both an ineffective and largely superfluous structure:

> It is my belief that there is not really a role for the ward committee. I know as a ward councillor what the problems are in the ward. Perhaps when there is a diverse ward, then there is a role for a ward committee but, where you have a single community there is not really a role for a ward committee if the ward councillor is doing a proper job. (Female Councilor, Delft: 20/09/2012)

Ward committee members, too, were frustrated with the ward committee system and the fact that they had so little opportunity to inform the sub-council of the needs of their ward or to influence its decision making. Concerns were also expressed about the level of commitment shown by some ward councilors and the fact that they seldom engaged with the ward committee members. Commenting on this fact a ward councilor conceded that:

> The ward committee does not have much power—and its impact is very dependent on the ward councillor who might not represent all in the ward. Although there are some ward councillors who work very hard and really try to make a difference, others do just the absolute minimum. (Female Councilor, Bonteheuwel: 20/09/2012)

It is also evident that there are very unequal power relations between the councilors and ward committees. This was evident in the limited trust which ward councilors displayed in their ward committees and in the paternalistic and patronizing manner in which they interacted with them. It was also evident that they often exerted a strong and undue influence in determining which proposals emanated from a ward committee. From this it is evident that the councilors do little to promote effective citizen engagement in local decision making, and although this may, in part, be attributed to their limited understanding of the objectives of public participation, it can also be ascribed to weaknesses in the design of the participatory systems in place. These include the system of sector representation on ward committees (which effectively excludes individuals who are not affiliated to a sector), to the ascriptive manner in which ward committee members are appointed (typically by nomination rather than election), to the laborious channels through which the requests of ward committee must be processed, and, ultimately, to the fact that citizens' participation so seldom yields any tangible results.

Developmental Local Government and the Means to Improved Welfare

A key element of all developmental states has been their ability to promote sustained economic growth and, thereby, to improve the living standards of their citizens. The advocates of a democratic developmental state also aspire to this goal, albeit through more inclusive and democratic processes than those adopted in East Asia. However, the South African state's achievements in this regard have fallen well below its own expectations. At the national level the government has estimated that the economy will need to grow by at least 6% per annum (The Presidency 2008:4) in order to reduce high unemployment levels (around 25%) and address extensive backlogs in the delivery of basic services. However, although economic growth rates in excess of 4% have periodically been achieved in the past two decades these have never come close to the target set (Trading Economics 2016) and the growth forecast for the next two to three years suggests rates of no more than 1% per annum. While the slowdown in the national economy may be attributed to a variety of factors including the depressed global demand for commodities and diminished investor confidence in emerging markets and currencies, it is also evident that the government's indecision over the choice of a growth path (coupled with growing state corruption) has contributed to this uncertainty. This relates to the shift from the initial notion of an interventionist state proposed in the Reconstruction and Development in 1994, to the neoliberal vision of GEAR in 1996, and back to the hybrid notion of a capable and developmental state in the NDP in 2012.

The South African notion of developmental local government was also intended to improve the socioeconomic standing of communities through improved service delivery and the reduction of poverty. In this endeavor too, the results have been disappointing. While the local state is charged with responsibility for the delivery of basic services (such as water, electricity, sanitation, and, to a limited extent, housing) it has minimal capacity to influence the path of economic development either within its own boundaries or nationally. Although municipalities are expected to stimulate local economic development, this is largely an enabling function related to zoning of land for industrial development and the creation of an environment attractive to potential investors. Major infrastructural developments, fiscal policy, and the regulation of terms of trade remain the responsibility of the central state. Furthermore, however limited a municipality's capacity to stimulate economic growth might be, at the subcouncil level such as pertains in Delft, its influence is largely meaningless. Although they are supposed to motivate for the needs of their communities in the city council, the actual discretionary funding available to local councilors amounts to no more than US$ 65,000 annually and this is typically assigned to minor public works. What this means in practice is that the elaborate system of citizen participation which has been established at the local level holds little prospect for addressing the most pressing problems facing the poor, namely unemployment and poverty.

Conclusion

For much of the past two decades, the South African government has declared its intention to establish a developmental and democratic state. However, since it first entered official discourse the concept of a developmental state has never been clearly articulated in policy or in legislation, and its key principles remain opaque. Furthermore, in portraying itself as a developmental state South Africa differs from other states which have assumed this label only after they achieved a significant degree of economic success. In that respect, a number of scholars have pointed out that the litmus test for any state seeking to adopt a developmental approach is not the intensity of its rhetoric but rather its visible development outcomes which will be the determining factor.

While the government has been eager to build a developmental state which embraces a democratic ethos, this has been at odds with the idea of a strong central government which is able to steer a consistent economic development path with or without the direct participation of the masses. This weakness, as discussed, is illustrated in its efforts to establish a system of developmental local government which is premised on extensive citizen participation in strategic planning processes and in policy formulation at the local level. The case study of Delft serves to highlight a number of the shortcomings evident in the South African developmental state model. The first relates to the fact government has yet to formulate a clear vision of a democratic developmental state and to instill this in all three levels of government, and nor has this been communicated to the public at large. This is aggravated by endemic weakness in the system of intergovernmental relations which means that national developmental goals are either not effectively transmitted to the local level or are not transmitted at all.

A further shortcoming relates to the fact that while public participation is portrayed as a cornerstone of developmental local government, the evidence from Delft reveals that the mechanisms in place to advance citizen engagement are both cumbersome and ineffective in eliciting the input of local residents. For most residents, participation in these structures was both disempowering and unproductive and, more pointedly, their participation did little or nothing to improve their own welfare. From this it may be inferred that while the idea of a democratic developmental state is a feasible one, the latent tensions between the need for a central state to steer a concerted course of economic action and the need to elicit citizen participation in this process cannot be underestimated. Without the resolution of these tensions the mere labeling of a state as "developmental and democratic," as has been the case in South Africa, is unlikely to ensure socioeconomic development beyond political rhetoric.

References

Achmat, F. (2002). *Public participation in the Western Cape, South Africa.* Paper presented at the International Workshop on Participatory Planning Approaches for Local Governance, Bandung, Indonesia: 20–27 January.

ANC (African National Congress). (1994). *Reconstruction and development programme: A policy framework.* Johannesburg: Umanyano Publication.

ANC (African National Congress). (2005). Statement of the National Executive Committee of the African National Congress. Retrieved on January 2012 from http://www.anc.org.za/ancdocs/history/jan8-05.html

ANC (African National Congress). (2007b). Building a national democratic society: Strategy and Tactics Document. Johannesburg: Umanyano Publications.

ANC (African National Congress).(2009). *Election Manifesto.* Retrieved on 5 January 2011 from http://www.anc.org.za/elections/2009/manifesto/policy_frame work.html

Andani, A. and Naidu, R. (2013). From subject to citizen: Building active citizenship through community dialogues and radio stations. In: GGLN (Good Governance Learning Network) (Ed.), *Active citizenship matters: Perspectives from civil society on local governance in South Africa* (pp. 79–89). Cape Town: GGLN and Isandla Institute.

Atkinson, D.(2007). Taking to the streets: Has developmental local government failed in South Africa? In: S. Buhlungu, J. Daniel, R. Southall and J. Lutchman (Eds.), State of the nation: South Africa (pp.53–77). Cape Town: Human Social Science Research Council.

Blair, H. (1998). *Spreading power to the periphery: An assessment of democratic local governance.* Washington, DC: USAID.

Blondel, J. (1990). *Comparative government: An introduction.* New York, NY: Philip Allan.

Burkett, P. and Harl-Landsberg, M. (2003). A critique of 'catch up' theories of development. *Journal of Contemporary Asia, 33*(2), 147–171.

City of Cape Town.(2011). *Community satisfaction survey, project Robben*. TNS Research Services.

Chagunda, C. (2007). *South Africa as a development state*. Briefing Paper 178. Paper presented at the South African Catholic Bishop Conference: August.

City of Cape Town.(2011). *Council overview*. Cape Town: City of Cape Town.

City of Cape Town. (2016). *Five-Year Integrated Development Plan 2012–2017: 2016/17 Review and Amendments*. Accessed at: http://www.capetown.gov.za/Fam ily%20and%20home/meet-the-city/our-vision-for-the-city/cape-towns-int egrated-development-plan

Conyers, D. (1984). Decentralization and development: A review of the literature. Public Administration and Development, 4(2), 187–197.

Cook, G. P. (1991). Cape Town. In: A. Lemon (Ed.), *Homes Apart: South Africa's segregated cities* (pp.26–42). Cape Town: David Phillip.

Edigheji, O. (2005). *A democratic developmental state in Africa? A concept paper.* Centre for Policy Studies. Pretoria: University of Pretoria.

Edigheji, O. (Ed.). (2010). *Constructing a democratic developmental state in South Africa: Potentials and challenges*. Cape Town: HSRC Press.

Evans, P. (2010). Constructing the 21st century development state: Potentials and pitfalls. In: O. Edigheji (Ed.), *Constructing a democratic developmental state in South Africa: Potentials and challenges* (pp. 37–58). Cape Town: HSRC Press.

Fakir, E. (2007). *Public service delivery in a democratic developmental state*. Policy Issues and, Volume 20, No. 3. Johannesburg: Centre for Policy Studies.

FCR (Foundation for Contemporary Research). (2002). *Integrated development planning and community participation handbook*. Cape Town: Foundation for Contemporary Research.

Fine, B. (2008). *Can South Africa be a developmental state?* Paper presented at the Human Sciences Research Council/Development Bank International Policy Dialogue conference: The potentials for and challenges of constructing a developmental state in South Africa, Magaliesburg: 4–6 June.

Fritz, V. and Menocal, A. (2007). (Re)building developmental states: From theory to practice. London: Overseas Development Institute.

Good Governance Learning Network (GGLN). (2008). *Local democracy in action: A civil society perspective on Local Governance in South Africa*. Cape Town: GGLN.

Goldman, I. (2005). *Community based planning and the IDP. A guide for decision-makers.* Produced by the African Institute for Community–Driven Development (AICDD) and Development Works. Pretoria: Government Printer.

Gumede, W. (2009). Delivering the democratic developmental state in South Africa. Development Planning Division. Working Paper Series No. 9. Midrand: Development Bank of Southern Africa.

Harrison, P. (2002). *Towards integrated inter-governmental planning in South Africa: the IDP as a building block.* Cape Town: HSRC Press.

Harrison, P. (2006). Integrated development plans and third way politics. In U. Pillay, R. Tomlinson, & J. du Toit (Eds.), Democracy and delivery: urban policy in South Africa (pp. 186–207). Cape Town: HSRC Press.

Kimemia, P. (2011). Community dissatisfaction: A direct result of non-responsiveness by government. Cape Town: Human Science Research Council Press.

Klugman, J. (1994). Decentralization: A survey of literature from a human development perspective. Occasional Paper 13. UNDP. New York: Human Development Report Office.

Leftwich, A. (2002). Forms of the democratic developmental state: Democratic practices and development capacity. In: M. Robinson, and G. White (Eds.), *The democratic developmental state: Political and institutional design* (pp. 52–83). New York, NY: Oxford University Press.

Manuel, T. (2009). Budget Speech delivered on 11 February 2009. Issued by the National Treasury. Retrieved on 16 June 2013 from http://www.info.gov.za/spee ches/2009/09021114561001.htm

Manuel, T. (2013). An Overview of the National Development Plan in South Africa: Implications for Higher Education. Seminar presented at the University of the Western Cape, Bellville, on 27 August, 2013.

Maphunye, K.J. (2009). Public Administration for a democratic developmental state in Africa: Prospects and possibilities. Research Report 114. Johannesburg: Centre for Policy Studies.

Moodley, S. (2007). Public participation and deepening democracy: experiences from Durban, South Africa. *Critical Dialogue, 3–8.* Centre for Public Participation.

National Planning Commission. (2011). *National development plan: Vision 2030.* Pretoria: The Presidency.

Olayode, K. (2005). *Reinventing the African state: Issues and challenges for building a developmental state.* Draft paper for the 11th General Assembly of the Council for the Development of Social Science Research in Africa.

Penderis, S. (2003). *The organisation of space on the Cape Flats: People, place and community participation.* Bellville: University of the Western Cape.

Pieterse, E. (2007). South *African local governance: ambitions, experiences and challenges: Trilateral Dialogue on the Role of Local Government within a developmental state.* Paper presented at the Planning Workshop with experts from Brazil, India and South Africa. Bonn, Germany: 26 February – 3 March.

Plessing, J. (2011). Makana Municipality: SAHA lodges complaint with the Public Protector. Retrieved on 12 August 2012 from www.saha.org.za

Poon, D. (2009). South Africa's developmental state makeover. Trade and Industrial Policy Strategies (TIPS) Working Paper Series.

Public Service Commission (PSC). (2008). Report on the assessment of public participation practices in the public service. Pretoria: Public Service Commission.

RSA (Republic of South Africa). (1994). *Reconstruction and development programme.* Pretoria: Government Printer.

RSA (Republic of South Africa). (1998a). *Municipal structures act (Act 117 of 1998).* Pretoria: Government Printer.

RSA (Republic of South Africa). (1998b). White Paper on Local Government (Notice 423 of 1998). Pretoria: Government Printer.

RSA (Republic of South Africa). (2000). Municipal systems act (Act 32 of 2000). Pretoria: Government Printer.

Tapscott, C. (2008). The challenges of deepening democracy in post-Apartheid South Africa. In: F. Saito (Ed.), *Foundations for local governance: Decentralization in comparative perspective* (pp. 213–232). Heidelberg: Physica-Verlag.

The Presidency.(2008). *Annual Report. Accelerated and Shared Growth Initiative for South Africa.* Republic of South Africa. Accessed at: https://www.goo gle.co.za/#q=asgisa+growth+targets

The Presidency. (2009). *State of the Nation Address.* Retrieved on 10 October 2013 from http://www.thepresidency.gov.za

The Presidency. (2010). *New growth path.* Pretoria: Government of the Republic of South Africa.

Trading Economics. (2016). South Africa GDP Growth Rate, 1993–2016. Accessed at: http://www.tradingeconomics.com/south-africa/gdp-growth

The Sowetan. (2012). Protesting Delft Residents block road with tyres. Retrieved on 21 October 2013 from http://www.sowetanlive.co.za/news/2012/05/08/protesting-delft-residents-block-road-with-tyres

Thompson, L., Nleya, N., and Africa, C. (2011a). *Government and service delivery score-card in Delft Cape Town: A score card report.* Bellville: African Centre for Citizenship and Democracy, University of the Western Cape.

Thompson, L., Nleya, N., and Africa, C. (2011b). *Government and service delivery scorecard in Kahelitsha Cape Town: A score card report.* Bellville: African Centre for Citizenship and Democracy, University of the Western Cape.

Thompson, L., Nleya, N., and Africa, C. (2011c). *Government and service delivery scorecard in Langa Cape Town: A score card report.* Bellville: African Centre for Citizenship and Democracy, University of the Western Cape.

Turner, M. (1999). *Central–local relations in Asia–Pacific: Convergence or Divergence?* New York: Macmillan and St Martin's.

Van Dijk, H., and Croucamp, P. (2007). The social origins of the developmental state: Reflections on South Africa and its local sphere of government. *Journal of Public Administration*, *42*(7), 664–675.

Van Donk, M. (2012). Tackling the 'governance deficit' to reinvigorate participatory local governance. In: GGLN (Good Governance Learning Network) (Ed.), *Active Citizenship matters: Perspectives from civil society on local governance in South Africa* (pp. 12–27). Cape Town: GGLN and Isandla Institute.

Welch, G., and Nuru, Z. (2006). *Governance for the future: Democracy and development in the least developed countries.* Geneva: UNDP.

Western Cape Government. (2016). Annual Report 2015–16. Department of Local Government. Accessed at: https://www.westerncape.gov.za/dept/local-government/documents/annual_reports/2015

White, G. (2006). Towards a democratic developmental state. *IDS Bulletin, 37*(4), 60–70.

Western, J. (1981). Outcast Cape Town. Minneapolis: University of Minnesota Press.

The "Developmental" and "Welfare" State in South Africa

Jeremy Seekings

Introduction

Enthusiasm for the idea of a "developmental state" in South Africa first emerged in the early 1990s, in the lead-up to the first democratic elections in 1994 and since then it has ebbed and flowed in the intervening two decades. The incoming African National Congress (ANC) government, with Nelson Mandela as president, inherited an economy characterized by very high inequality, with deep poverty—unmatched in other comparable middle-income economies—coexisting with conspicuous affluence. The ANC leadership repeatedly committed itself to transforming the economic growth path through a mix of "reconstruction" and "development," redressing the racial and class discrimination of the Apartheid era and making future growth inclusive of the poor. A "developmental state" was integral to this vision. The ANC government also inherited a welfare state that had hitherto provided high-quality public education and health care as well as cash transfers to white citizens. Although the new government sought to address racial discrimination in the delivery of public services by reallocating resources to poorer, black citizens, ANC leaders repeatedly distanced themselves from the idea of a "welfare state,", emphasizing that they would ensure (inclusive) "development" not "handouts."

The ANC's ambivalence about the welfare state coincided with rising enthusiasm over "social protection" in the rest of the world, partly on the grounds that cash transfers to the poor are conducive to development, and partly on the grounds that poor citizens had a right to a share of national (and global) resources. A wide range of international organizations (including both the World Bank and the International Labour Organization, ILO) and donor agencies embraced social protection as both a mechanism for reducing poverty quickly and a developmental or even "transformative" tool, encouraging the economic, social, and political conditions favoring inclusive development (Von Gliszczynski and Leisering 2015).

South Africa is a global outlier in at least two respects. Firstly, its unemployment rate (close to 40%, if we include the "discouraged" unemployed who want work but have given up looking for it) is matched outside of the region only by economies emerging from civil war (such as Iraq). Secondly, one in three South Africans receives a monthly grant from the government under one or other social assistance program. These facts testify to the country's simultaneous developmental failure and reliance on welfare. In South Africa, and indeed across much of the Southern African region, the state has proven more effective at redressing the inequalities generated in markets than it has at governing markets so as to reshape the economic growth path. Even Botswana, which achieved very rapid economic growth from the 1970s, relies heavily on social assistance programs to mitigate poverty.

The South African experience forces us to reexamine the appropriateness of foreign models, including the "Nordic model." Under mostly social democratic governments, the postwar Nordic countries combined steady economic growth, driven by private companies but steered by the state, with a massive and redistributive welfare state. This was a very different combination to the subsequent developmental states of East and Southeast Asia, which attached overwhelming priority to state-steered growth, including public education, while neglecting welfare programs for the poor (at least until the very end of the twentieth century). One or other version of the East/Southeast Asian model has proven very attractive to some African countries, including Kenya and Ethiopia (Fourie 2014, 2015). Some South African policy-makers were similarly enamored with the Asian model(s), but the South African state in practice followed policies more similar to the Nordic model of hybrid developmental welfare states. The outcomes, however, were disappointing with respect to inclusive growth and development.

In this chapter, I argue that the standard explanations for the "failure" or, at best, partial success of the democratic developmental state in South Africa are insufficient. Neither external constraints nor politics within the ANC nor state (in)capacity explains the disappointing developmental record. I argue instead that the design of developmental state policies was inappropriate. The Nordic mix of developmentalism and welfare was appropriate, but the underlying assumption that the developmental imperative was to raise productivity across all sectors was inappropriate in the conditions of massive labor surplus that existed in South Africa.

The Promise of Development in Democratic South Africa

In its 1994 *Reconstruction and Development Programme* (RDP), the ANC government in waiting promised that a democratic state would act to steer the mixed economy down a new economic growth path. The RDP asserted that "The central goal for reconstruction and development is to create a strong, dynamic and balanced economy which will eliminate the poverty, low wages and extreme inequality in wages and wealth generated by the Apartheid system, ... develop the human resource capacity of all South Africans so the economy achieves high skills and wages, ... and create productive employment opportunities at a living wage for all South Africans" (ANC 1994: 79). This would entail transforming the state itself since the Apartheid state had become:

> ... secretive and militarized, and less and less accountable even to the constituency it claimed to represent. The legal and institutional framework we are inheriting is fragmented and inappropriate for reconstruction and development. It lacks capacity to deliver services, it is inefficient and out of touch with the needs of ordinary people. It lacks coordination and clear planning. (*ibid*: 119)

The ANC promised instead a state that was not only democratized but was also modernized and efficient:

> We must develop the capacity of government for strategic intervention in social and economic development. We must increase the capacity of the public sector to deliver improved and extended public services to all the people of South Africa. (*ibid*: 120)

The ANC proposed that the democratic state would shape development in three ways. First, it promised "an infrastructural programme that would provide access to modern and effective services like electricity, water, telecommunications, transport, health, education and training for all our people" (*ibid*: 6). This would not only meet basic needs denied by the Apartheid state, but would also lead to improved productivity and output. Secondly, the state would embark on a program of land reform. This would meet basic needs and reverse the injustices of Apartheid, and serve as the "central and driving force of a programme of rural development" that would generate "large-scale employment" and raise rural incomes (*ibid*: 20). Thirdly, the government would intervene in a mixed economy through industrial, trade and other policies, with the promise of growth of 5% p.a. and massive job creation (the RDP even specified "300,000 to 500,000 non-agricultural jobs per annum ... within five years") (*ibid*: 87).

The industrial policy agenda was developed through the union-linked Industrial Strategy Project (ISP) in the early 1990s. The ISP recommended that the poor performance of South Africa's manufacturing industries be rectified through higher productivity and moving "up the value chain" (Joffe et al. 1995). The ISP's recommendations meshed with unions' demands for higher wages, resulting in the use of labor market and industrial policies to raise productivity through higher ("decent") wages, skills development, and the upgrading of industrial processes (which in practice mostly meant mechanization).

In practice, the bold vision was implemented unevenly. Under the Mandela (1994–1999) and first Mbeki (1999–2004) governments, state energies were directed primarily at redressing the worst aspects of the legacy of Apartheid. The focus, thus, was on building an integrated state out of the fragments of the late Apartheid era, dealing with an acute fiscal crisis, removing racial discrimination in public policy (including labor market policies, social policies and municipal services) and then on beginning the deracialization of corporate ownership through "Black Economic Empowerment" (BEE) (Hirsch 2005). This entailed a massive expansion of the state's role in service provision, especially for the poor, with heavy expenditure on public education, health care, municipal services, and cash transfers for the poor (Seekings and Nattrass 2015). The state embraced the discourse of development—including the short-lived appointment of a minister responsible for "reconstruction and development" and the framing of welfare and local government policy along "developmental" lines[1]—but issues of production were generally neglected. The ANC's trade union allies were frustrated by its reluctance to implement their recommendations for industrial policy. It was later revealed that the state failed even to invest in basic economic infrastructure. These failures may have reflected the strained relationship between Mbeki and white business leaders who continued to control the economy.

Calls for a developmental state intensified in the 2000s as it became clear that unemployment and poverty had worsened after 1994. In his 2005 "State of the Nation" address, the first after his re-election the previous year, Mbeki promised a developmental state that would, especially, invest heavily in public utilities (including electricity). This emphasis on a developmental state was repeated in other Mbeki speeches and was endorsed by the ANC at its National General Council in 2005, its national policy conference in mid-2007, and at its National Conference in Polokwane at the end of 2007. The 2006 Accelerated and Shared Growth Initiative South Africa envisaged the developmental state accelerating and reshaping growth so that unemployment and poverty would halve by 2014 (South Africa 2006b). By 2007, the call for a developmental state had been taken up by the coalition behind Jacob Zuma's successful removal of Mbeki as ANC leader and president, and the developmental state proposal was unsurprisingly central to the ANC's election campaign in 2009. Following the election, the now-president Zuma appointed a Minister of Economic Development (the former trade unionist, Ebrahim Patel) and a National Planning Commission (chaired by the former Minister of Finance, Trevor Manuel).

It soon became very clear just how ineffective South Africa's supposed developmental state had been. In an article published in 2010, Fine pointed to the telling failure of the state to ensure sufficient capacity in the generation of electricity, with the result that both private and corporate consumers experienced power cuts: "The simplest task of a developmental state—to keep the electricity on—has not been achieved" (Fine 2010: 178; see further Styan 2015). Economic growth was slow in relation

---

[1]   The first mention of the "developmental state" in South African government documents may have been in the 1998 local government policy document. I am grateful to Chris Tapscott for pointing this out.

to the global economy, and growth per capita was very slow. The state had also clearly failed to steer the economy down a more inclusive growth path. Between 1994 and 2012, the unemployment rate rose by at least 5 percentage points, the employment rate fell by at least 5 percentage points, and the actual number of unemployed South Africans doubled. In global terms, South Africa was an outlier with respect to employment and unemployment (Nattrass and Seekings 2015).

In 2012, the National Planning Commission completed its National Development Plan (NDP) (South Africa 2012). The NDP acknowledged a failure to fully remake South Africa into a country that provided *all* of its citizens with meaningful economic opportunities. The schooling system failed to equip young people with skills, too few people worked, and poverty (as well as inequality) persisted. The NDP acknowledged that state institutions performed unevenly and often poorly (*ibid*: 54). What was needed was "an economy that is more inclusive, more dynamic and in which the fruits of growth are shared equitably" (*ibid*: 38). "Progress over the next two decades means doing things differently" (*ibid*: 26), with reformed public policies and institutions achieving "a change in the structure of the economy and the pace at which it grows" (*ibid*: 39).

The recommendation of the NDP, as in almost every government strategic document since 1994, was that a "capable and developmental state" would be key to doing things differently (*ibid*: 26, 54). As we shall see below, the NDP combined a realistic reassessment of some of the constraints on inclusive economic growth with continuing indecision and caution in its proposals for tackling these constraints. The point to be made now is a simpler one: After eighteen years in government, the ANC's major policy document suggested that the economy had not only grown too slowly but more importantly had followed the wrong growth path, such that the benefits of modest growth had not been shared adequately with the poor. As Fine recognized, the state had failed to perform even the most basic tasks of any developmental state: keeping the lights on. It had failed completely to generate significant job creation. The economy was littered with sectors in decline, in terms of employment if not of both output and employment.

The Failure of the Developmental State

The democratic state's failure to steer the economy down the desired economic growth path has often been explained in terms of the external constraints of international agreements in a globalized world, the political character of the ANC, and the incapacity of the South African state. All three arguments are well-founded, but incomplete.

Post-Apartheid economic planners concurred that the economy needed to become more competitive and export-oriented, escaping from the restrictions of Apartheid-era protectionism. The South African state's ability to deploy more selective policies to promote exports was, however, constrained. Kaplan (2007) explains how the changing global policy context made it impossible for South Africa to replicate all of the "development state" industrial policies so successfully employed by the initial East Asian "tigers". Korea and Taiwan were able to provide targeted support for key industries while avoiding the dangers of inefficiency by linking subsidies and related support to good export performance. South Africa implemented a similar industrial policy for the motor industry, making subsidies conditional on export performance. Such subsidies ceased to be legal, however, under the 2000 international Agreement on Subsidies and Countervailing Measures. South Africa's motor industry policy was revised in order to avoid challenges through the World Trade Organization. Subsidies henceforth could only be linked to production (not export performance), which raises the cost and blunts the efficacy of the intervention (*ibid*: 96–97).

Kaplan—who was integral to the ISP and between 2000 and 2003 served as Chief Economist in the Department of Trade and Industry (DTI)—also details the institutional obstacles to effective industrial policy in South Africa. Kaplan identifies two "key institutional requirements for an effective industrial policy": "the professionalism and capacities of the government" and an effective strategic collaboration between government and business. Both, Kaplan argues convincingly, were very limited in South Africa.

Effective industrial policy requires effective policy management and coordination, and clear communication with industry. Industrial policy in South Africa was never consolidated under a single state department, however, but was rather shared between the DTI, public enterprises, the treasury, and even defense. Much of it remained "hidden," including direct support and subsidies for armaments production, subsidized infrastructure and energy, support for the development and production of nuclear energy plants (notably the development of a pebble bed modular reactor), and a proposed windfall tax on SASOL (a commercial venture producing oil from coal) (Kaplan 2007: 98–99). This lack of policy coordination resulted in industrial policy preceding in a piecemeal way, and with no attention being paid to maximizing the potential advantages of agglomeration or to facilitating planned up-stream and down-stream development of industry. It also opened up the danger of particular projects being seen in isolation (as pet projects) rather than in an overall development planning context in which opportunity costs could be spelled out. This is particularly evident with regard to the attempts to develop a pebble bed nuclear reactor for which over a billion rand was allocated by the Treasury in 2006 (*ibid*: 109). Stand-alone approaches to specific sectors were also more vulnerable to corruption and mismanagement, as investigations into a highly publicized arms deal have demonstrated (Feinstein 2007; Holden and van Vuuren 2011).

The quality of the bureaucracy also constrained implementation. The government's "transformation" agenda meant that it appointed new, often inexperienced officials.

> Currently most of those responsible for government industrial policies are new recruits to their positions. They have a limited understanding of their sectors. So-called sector specialists have very limited, if any, direct work experience in the sector to which they have been appointed. Indeed, very few personnel have experience of working anywhere in the private sector. In South Africa, there is no "revolving door" as between business and government that, for example, has characterised the Japanese MITI. (Kaplan 2007: 101)

Subsequent to Kaplan's article, it began to seem that there was a door between government and business, with senior government officials as well as ministers taking up well-paid positions in business. Some officials from regulatory agencies took up posts in the businesses they had themselves licensed. But this door did not revolve: There was little evidence of people with experience in the private sector taking up positions in the state. The bureaucracy enjoyed considerable autonomy from business, but was not "embedded" (as discussed by Evans 1995).

State incapacity in departments dealing with economic management was in part due to the generic weaknesses of the post-Apartheid bureaucracy. These have been analyzed most thoroughly with respect to public health and education. Von Holdt and Murphy (2007) documented management failures in public hospitals in Gauteng in the early 2000s. In their analysis, these failures were at least in part due to overload, with public hospitals not having the resources required to perform adequately. Management practices, however, exacerbated the problems. Decision making was overly centralized, with hospital managers lacking operational discretion. Managers were preoccupied with the administration of rules and regulations and neglected actually managing either people or operations. Insofar as managers solved problems, it was found, they focused on immediate crises. Von Holdt (2010) subsequently identified five factors that underlay mismanagement in sectors such as health. First, affirmative action policies, intended to address racial imbalances inherited from the Apartheid era, combined with a shortage of skills contributed to very high turnover in management, with as many as one in three public-sector managers moving jobs each year (Naidoo 2008). A culture of "moving onwards and upwards" prevailed. Not only did managers focus on their future opportunities rather than doing their job, but their actual performance in their current job rarely affected their future prospects. Secondly, there was a widespread ambivalence toward skill, especially given the racialized distribution of "skill" under Apartheid. Race also informed the importance of "face": Deference was often more important than competence. Fourthly, there was a general breakdown of discipline. Union shop stewards exercised a veto over many management decisions, while professionals used public facilities for private practice. Finally, budgetary rituals further detracted from actual service delivery. Similar problems characterized the administration of the public school system (see, for example, Fleisch 2002).

Problems of capacity were most pronounced at the level of the local state, which was responsible for the delivery of basic services—including water, electricity, and sewerage—and the improvement of housing and related infrastructure. Nevertheless, overall, there was marked progress in service delivery, entailing considerable redistribution from rich to poor

(Seekings and Nattrass 2015: Chapter 7). Despite a dramatic increase in transfers from central to local government in the 2000s, however, many municipalities failed to ensure adequate quality, squandered resources through incompetence or corruption, and were completely unable to play the developmental roles imagined in national policy. Widespread problems included "stalemates between councils and officials; rivalries between mayors and municipal managers; tensions between senior and junior staff; a loss of moral and an ethic of service delivery amongst staff members; convoluted procedures and red tape; and the appointment of staff with inadequate formal qualifications, expertise and experience." Rapid transformation had undermined municipal capacity: "Valuable skills had been lost, institutional memory had been dissipated, senior posts had become sinecures for the party faithful and junior posts had been filled by inadequately trained people" (Atkinson 2007: 61). In the face of rising wages and salaries, "savings" were often affected by freezing posts. In summation, according to Atkinson: "The combination of inexperienced, poorly qualified staff, with similarly inexperienced councilors, in a context of substantial financial flows in and out of municipalities, creates fertile ground for irregularities, malpractice and ineffective expenditure" (*ibid*: 63; see also Makgetla 2007).

The post-Apartheid state certainly had uneven capacity, and lacked meaningful capacity in many areas. But the state did have evident capacity to do many things. It raised taxes and paid pensions and grants very efficiently. It employed teachers and nurses, even if it was unable to manage them well. It also disciplined companies in a range of ways, including through Black Economic Empowerment (BEE) legislation. The state also sought to regulate the labor market. Although compliance was poor in "unorganized" sectors (i.e. sectors without trade unions, such as domestic work), "organized" sectors (including almost all industry) was effectively and tightly regulated. As we shall see below, the evidence suggests that the state did not *lack* the capacity to implement industrial policy. It just did not design (and then implement) policy very sensibly.

A third explanation for the apparent failure of the developmental state in South Africa focuses on politics within the governing ANC. In the mid-2000s, the coalition supporting Jacob Zuma's challenge to the incumbent Thabo Mbeki began to point to the so-called "1996 class project." The Congress of South African Trade Unions (COSATU) and South African

Communist Party (SACP), which partner the ruling party in a tripartite alliance, denounced the attempt by ANC leaders to steer the "National Democratic Revolution" away from a "radical" orientation. "The current ANC NEC is simply not representative of the ANC constituency," said COSATU general secretary Zwelinzima Vavi in 2007; "It is made up of the middle- and upper-classes and is dominated by people with business interests" (quoted in *Mail and Guardian*, March 9, 2007). The ANC, it was argued, was dominated by a new black bourgeoisie that sought to use control of the state to expand their personal stakes in the capitalist economy, but was ultimately dependent on that capitalist economy.

As critics of the "1996 class project" themselves argued, however, the vision of a "developmental state" was part of a "center-left" project. In this view, the "parasitic and compradorist" black bourgeoisie sought to use the state as a means of accumulation. It is not clear why this class or faction would have been opposed to interventions that would have accelerated the growth rate or made the growth path more inclusive, as long as the economy remained a mixed one, with a substantial capitalist sector. Moreover, in 2007 the critics of the "1996 class project" succeeded in securing the presidency of the ANC for their candidate, Zuma, and eighteen months later he became president. His new Minister of Trade and Industry, SACP member Rob Davies, introduced a new Industrial Policy Action Programme (IPAP), described by the SACP as "a critical component of changing our present semi-colonial capitalist growth path." Davies and his cabinet colleague Patel (the new Minister of Economic Development) embraced the concept of the developmental state.

The post-Apartheid state was certainly constrained by international agreements, by poor coordination and uneven capacity, and by the political power of the emerging black bourgeoisie and middle classes. It is not clear, however, that these precluded the possibility of a developmental state. Indeed, the state did intervene extensively in many aspects of the economy. Indeed, substantial parts of the economy were run by public enterprises. Overall, the critics of the "1996 class project" were right in observing that even the "center-left" leadership of the ANC—many of whom were involved in business—envisaged a developmental state of some sort. This points to an alternative explanation of the failure of the "developmental state" to achieve inclusive or shared growth: They were pushing for the wrong mix of policies.

The Flawed Design of the Developmental State

An alternative interpretation of the failure of the developmental state in South Africa, in terms of its failure to achieve inclusive development or growth, focuses on the design of the project. It was the adoption of an ill-conceived policy mix that resulted in the economy traveling—or more precisely continuing to travel—down an inappropriate economic growth path that ensured that the benefits of growth were not widely shared, and probably even stunted growth itself.

ANC governments might have failed to implement the grand ISP vision, but they did implement policies that transformed various economic sectors. The case of the clothing manufacturing sector is especially revealing, because this was the last major labor-intensive industrial sector in South Africa. If South African industry was to contribute to job creation and thereby render the growth path more inclusive, then sectors such as clothing needed to expand. Rather than expanding, however, the clothing sector experienced massive job destruction, as producers were squeezed between intensified international competition (primarily due to the extraordinary expansion of Chinese production) and rising domestic costs. The high cost of textiles contributed to the high costs of South African clothing manufacturers, but the major factor was a policy commitment by the South African state to a higher productivity, higher wage strategy in the sector. Subsidies under IPAP encouraged the shift to a more capital- and skill-intensive sector, which inevitably meant continued job destruction. In the case of the clothing sector, a mix of public policies associated with the developmental state project, rather than job creation, exacerbated job destruction.

South Africa's industrial strategy was profoundly shaped by a misdiagnosis of the challenges facing the clothing industry. Under Apartheid, many clothing producers had located industrial sites in the ethnically defined enclaves known as Bantustans, where they were heavily subsidized and were exempted from any wage regulation. Low wages were understandably associated with Apartheid-style exploitation. In the 1990s, the Southern African Clothing and Textile Workers Union (SACTWU), and its influential deputy general-secretary Ebrahim Patel in particular, developed a strategy that entailed raising wages, especially at the bottom end, and forcing employers to mechanize, raise productivity and move up the value chain (as proposed by the tripartite Swart Commission). This strategy meshed with the ideas coming out of the ISP, as well as with the concept of "decent work" that was later developed in the ILO (in which Patel was active). The ISP itself had cautioned that its strategy was not a recipe for *net* job creation (Joffeet al. 1995: 17), but no one imagined that there would be massive job *destruction*. At that time South African firms were producing for export as well as for the domestic market, and it seems to have been believed that higher productivity and wages would in fact enhance South Africa's international competitiveness.

The strategy revolved around two interventions. The first entailed using the collective bargaining machinery to raise minimum wages. The 1995 Labour Relations Act of—which Patel helped to draft—provided for unions to negotiate with employers' associations over minimum wages and employment conditions. A "collective agreement" bound the parties to it. Crucially, the bargaining council could then request that the Minister of Labour extend this agreement to all workers in the area covered by the bargaining council, including those employed by firms that were *not* party to the collective agreement. This meant that SACTWU could reach an agreement with the higher wage metropolitan employers, based in Cape Town, and then the Minister of Labour would use the extension mechanism to impose the agreement on the lower wage firms that had opposed the agreement. In the clothing sector, SACTWU and the Cape Town-based employers agreed to raise the minimum wages in lower wage areas such as Newcastle in northern KwaZulu-Natal province. Bargaining council inspectors pursued non-compliant firms through the courts and shut many of them down (Nattrass and Seekings 2014). The second intervention entailed providing subsidies to compliant firms (i.e., firms that were compliant with minimum wages) to improve productivity. The goal was to occupy global niches that were more skill- and capital-intensive than low-wage producers in places like Bangladesh but were less skill- and capital-intensive than the much higher wage producers in Europe. The ANC government liberalized trade, providing a stick to the clothing industry, but did not immediately implement the proposed carrots of subsidies for investment in new technology.

The strategy did not anticipate the rise of production in China (and elsewhere) in the 2000s. Chinese exports exploded, not only capturing

South Africa's export markets, but also penetrating deeply into the domestic South African market. Consumers benefited from sharply declining clothes prices, but employment plummeted. The Minister of Trade and Industry rejected the recommendation, in a report commissioned by his own chief economist, that a new wage model be introduced that allowed workers' wages to be linked to their individual productivity. Instead, the DTI continued to emphasize sector-wide skills development and industrial upgrading. Under the IPAPs from 2007, this entailed massive capital subsidies to compliant clothing manufacturers (as the Swart Commission and SACTWU had earlier proposed). Between 2001 and 2014, Seardel, the largest South African producer, received about R643 million (roughly US$100 million over time) in production subsidies for its textile and clothing divisions. During this time, Seardel was effectively taken over by the trade union, through its investment arm. The huge investment of public funding proved futile. By 2014 Seardel had almost closed down most of its textile and clothing plants (see Nattrass and Seekings 2016). Ironically, at the same time bargaining council inspectors and court sheriffs were trying to shut down unsubsidized firms in places like Newcastle, because they were not paying the increased minimum wages. Many of the jobs in the industry that were "lost" were actively destroyed.

The "high-productivity, high-wage" strategy was premised on the assumption that there was no alternative. This assumption was echoed in the 2012 NDP, but not without some ambiguity. Living standards would be raised in part through productivity growth, but in part also through increased employment. "In the medium term", the NDP suggested, South Africa had to bolster competitiveness and investment in high value-added industries (as well as increase its mineral exports). The NDP stated that South Africa's "high cost structure" made it uncompetitive in low-skill manufacturing markets, and so most job creation would occur in small- and medium-sized businesses, mostly producing for the local market. In the longer term, however, "South Africa has to do more to enhance competitiveness in areas of comparative advantage that can draw more people into work," and such areas included mid-skill manufacturing, agriculture and agro-processing, as well as nonindustrial export sectors such as tourism. The NDP acknowledged that the question of "whether South Africa can mobilise unemployed people into production for export markets" was "contentious": "Some argue that the economy is not competitive in labour-intensive manufacturing because the cost structure is too high, the exchange rate is too volatile, infrastructure is inadequate and the skills base is too limited. Yet South Africa could compete in a range of categories should these concerns be addressed—and in large part, they can be addressed." The NDP suggested that labor market reforms were necessary: "In moving towards decent work for all, the short-term priority must be to raise employment and incentivise the entry of young people into the labour market ... Difficult choices will have to be made. To promote large-scale job creation, the functioning of the labour market will have to improve." (South Africa 2012: 25, 31, 32, 39, 41).

While the idea that the developmental state should promote *only* higher productivity and higher wages in industry, even if this meant job losses, predominated within the ANC, it was not unchallenged. Repeatedly between 2010 and 2014, ANC and government leaders clashed over the possibility of creating low-wage jobs, including through wage subsidies, and over the regulation of labor brokers. What was at issue was not simply whether the state should be "developmental," but what kind of policies were appropriate in the South African context for a developmental state.

The Unexpected Successes of the Welfare State

The NDP also recognized that improving living standards depended also on "a social wage and good-quality public services" (*ibid*: 26). The NDP sometimes referred to the "social wage" as including cash transfers (through social assistance and public employment programs) as well as free (or subsidized) public services (i.e. education, health care, and municipal services), but sometimes seemed to limit the scope of the "social wage" to the latter. The ANC government was happy to praise public services (even when the quality was low), was keen on public employment (or workfare), but displayed deep ambivalence over social assistance. The ANC government expressed repeated misgivings about social assistance, on both clearly ideological grounds ("handouts" created "dependency") and supposedly fiscal ones (were these programs "sustainable" in the long term?). But the strong evidence that the expansion of social assistance was the primary cause of the decline of the income poverty rate in the 2000s and the fact that they benefited a huge number of voters made it difficult for the ANC government to resist praising and claiming credit for these programs.

Like their Apartheid-era predecessors, ANC governments since 1994 insisted that South Africa did not and should not have a "welfare state." The ANC's policy was to promote development, not expand welfare. President Mandela himself spoke, in his first State of the Nation address, of his government's commitment "to confront the scourge of unemployment, not by way of handouts but by the creation of work opportunities." The Department of Welfare reported that spiraling costs meant that the government "can no longer afford the social security function" (South Africa 1995: 7). The government was obsessed with fraud, and promised to apply the means test more strictly. The Department of Welfare said that it accepted the need for social grants, but, "to ensure that those receiving welfare do not become permanently dependent on state aid, social grants for certain target groups will be closely linked to job creation and other anti-poverty programmes. Successful development programmes will empower people to earn a living, move off the social security system and achieve economic independence" (South Africa 1996a: 19–20). In 1996, the government proposed abolishing altogether the "unaffordable" State Maintenance Grant for poor mothers with children. Persuaded to appoint a committee (chaired by Professor Francie Lund) to consider alternatives to abolition, the department described its role as looking "at ways of linking social grants with developmental programmes, so that single parent families can move towards becoming self-supporting," and that it would also look at ways of making absent parents contribute to the costs of raising their children (*ibid*: 22). A 1997 White Paper committed the government to the goal of "developmental social welfare" and "re-orienting [its] services towards developmental approaches." This meant helping people to meet their own needs, through "the development of human capacity and self-reliance," rather than relying on the state (South Africa 1997). The Minister of Welfare, Geraldine Fraser-Moleketsi, revealingly told parliament in 1998 that "welfare has become associated with charity and hand-outs, with food parcels and pensions, something in which it was alleged bleeding hearts got involved." She called for a shift in thinking about "welfare," "from paternalism to self-reliance" and investment in development. The Department's flagship program involved training unemployed women with young children so as to reduce their "dependence on social security" (Hansard, May 27, 1998, col 3193-5, 3201). The following year, her successor as Minister, Zola Skweyiya, also emphasized "the promotion of self-reliance to reduce dependency on … social grants" (South Africa 1999: 6). Following this, the Department of Welfare was renamed the Department of Social Development.

Despite this, the number of social grants expanded rapidly in the 2000s. The major reason for the expansion was that the government accepted the Lund Committee's recommendation that, rather than abolish all provision for poor children, the State Maintenance Grant should be replaced with a parsimonious but wide-reaching Child Support Grant. The means-tested Child Support Grant was initially provided for poor children to the age of seven, but the government repeatedly raised the age threshold, eventually to the age of eighteen. The age threshold for men to receive the old-age pension was also reduced to sixty years (the same as for women). At the time of the 1994 elections, about 2.4 million people received social pensions or grants, costing less than 2% of gross domestic product (GDP). By the time of the 2014 elections, about 16 million grants and pensions were paid every month, at a cost of about 3.5% of GDP.

The expansion was not boundless, however. When a new committee of inquiry—chaired by Viviene Taylor—tentatively recommended a basic income grant, the government recoiled. The then government spokesperson Joel Netshitenzhe said that able-bodied adults should not receive "handouts" but should rather be helped to "enjoy the opportunity, the dignity and the rewards of work." The government could not support the basic income grant, he maintained, because it had a rather different "philosophy" (*Sunday Times*, July 28, 2002; see Matisonn and Seekings 2003; Meth 2004; Seekings and Matisonn 2012). The Department of Social Development continued to refer to the need for a "paradigm shift" from a welfarist approach to "developmental welfare" (South Africa 2006a). The ANC, in its 2007 policy discussion document on "social transformation," emphasized the "dignity of work" and the importance of public employment programs as an alternative to social assistance. Arguing (rather unclearly) against a basic income grant, the ANC suggested that discussion should take place "in the context of our challenges as a *developmental state* rather than against the ideological backdrop of a *welfare state*" (ANC 2007: 3, emphasis added; see also Barchiesi 2011).

The expansion of social grants in the face of ambivalence within the ANC and government was driven in part by litigation, citing the social and economic rights included in the constitution. More importantly, it reflected the shrewd leadership of Zola Skweyiya, who served as Minister of Social Development from 1999 to 2009. Skweyiya mobilized research that showed not only that the expansion of grants was behind the (modest) decline in income poverty rates, but also that many of the objections to grants—for example, that they encouraged teenage pregnancy or discouraged labor market participation—were unfounded. Indeed, Skweyiya mobilized research that argued that grants were developmental, in that they facilitated education, job search, and entrepreneurship.

While the state as a whole displayed very uneven capacity to deliver, the administration of grants and pensions proved a success story. This had not been true initially, when the administration of pensions and grants was the responsibility of provincial governments. In 2002, the press reported that 120 people were bringing high court claims each week against the Eastern Cape provincial government for non-payment of grants. A judge blasted the provincial government: "Many persons in this province are suffering real hardship through the ineffectiveness of the public service at provincial level" (*Mail and Guardian*, September 6, 2002). It allegedly took as long as two years to process applications. When Members of Parliament conducted a study tour to the Eastern Cape in 2003, they found dirty offices, shambolic filing systems, long queues, and officials who were absent or delinquent, treating the public with contempt. More than 10,000 state officials were also implicated in fraudulent claims. In the face of repeated embarrassments, especially in the Eastern Cape, a centralized South African Social Security Agency (SASSA) was established in 2004. SASSA described its "mission" in terms of cost effectiveness, efficiency, and the use of modern technology, so as to "pay the right social grant to the right person at the right time and place." The actual payment was outsourced through competitive tendering procedures to private contractors. While the award of the national contract to Net1 CPS was later found in court to have been unprocedural, the actual payment of grants and pensions seems to have improved greatly.

In terms of ensuring that any of the benefits of economic growth reached the poor, the welfare state was a modest success, in contrast to the general failure of the developmental state. Social assistance reduced

substantially both the poverty headcount (i.e., the number of people below a designated poverty line) and the poverty gap (i.e., the aggregate
amount by which the incomes of poor households fall below the poverty
line) (Armstrong and Burger 2009; Leibbrandt et al. 2010; Devereux et al.
2011; Heinrich et al. 2012; World Bank 2014). Because they were well targeted on the poor and were financed out of general taxation, social assistance programs were highly redistributive (Van der Berg 2005; World
Bank 2014). The rising coverage of the social assistance program meant
that, by 2006, social grants constituted the primary source of income for
one-half of all households in the poorest two income quintiles (Leibbrandt
et al. 2010: 61). The old-age pension, child support grant, and disability
grant increased the income share of the two poorest income quintiles in
2006 from 3.3% of total pre-transfer income to 7.6% of income including
grants (Van der Berg and Siebrits 2010: 20). By 2011, cash transfers reduced ultrapoverty massively, from a rate of 34.4% to less than 12% (using a poverty line of US$1.25/day, at purchasing power parity)—although
the reduction was less dramatic using higher poverty lines. In reducing
poverty, tax-financed cash transfers also reduced inequality. The Gini co-
efficient for income inequality was reduced by social assistance from 0.67
to 0.58 in 1995, and from 0.69 to 0.52 in 2006 (Van der Berg 2009: 24; see
also World Bank 2014).

Conclusion

The social assistance system was the unanticipated hero of poverty reduction in post-Apartheid South Africa. Reluctantly, the ANC government embraced cash transfers, pending job creation on a scale large enough to reduce unemployment and poverty. The welfare state was the stand-in for
the failed developmental state. Yet, even in 2012, the ANC government had
no clear sense of how it would navigate around the political, social, and
economic obstacles to inclusive economic growth, given that this would
require the large-scale creation of jobs for less skilled workers, which
would require low-wage jobs. One possible solution was some kind of a
wage subsidy, but neither the design nor the short-term performance of
the government's 2013 wage subsidy scheme (under the Employment Tax
Incentive Act) were encouraging. COSATU proposals to double the mini-

mum wage in most sectors, through the introduction of a national mini-mum at a high level, posed a further obstacle to job creation. Of the various scenarios considered in the NDP, the one that looks most likely is the one in which jobs are *not* created. In this scenario, the NDP envisaged that the state would need to run a massive public employment program, effectively providing a national employment guarantee. Whether through grants or workfare, the welfare state is likely to continue to be called on to mitigate poverty.

In this regard, the South African state is not out-of-line with shifting international opinion. The idea of "just giving money to the poor" has come to constitute a new paradigm of development, embraced in different ways by the World Bank, ILO, and donors such as Department for International Development (see also Barrientos and Santibáñez 2009; Von Gliszczynski and Leisering 2015). The South African model of unconditional but categorical grants—that is, grants targeted on deserving categories of poor people, but not tied to specific behaviors—had spread to most of South Africa's neighbors. Namibia has old-age pensions and disability grants, as well as a limited child grant programs. Old-age pensions were introduced in Botswana in 1996, in Lesotho in 2004, and Swaziland in 2005. Botswana has an extensive set of cash transfer programs, including public employment programs, while Lesotho has introduced a child grant. Zimbabwe, Zambia, and Malawi are in varying stages of introducing cash transfer programs. Cash transfer programs are being piloted, and in some cases expanded, in East Africa also: Zanzibar introduced pensions in 2016, Uganda is slowly rolling them out district by district, and Kenya is considering a national old-age pension program. The costs of such programs are generally modest in comparison to the total flows of aid into countries, or to GDP. In a region in which development planning has generally been underwhelming, such programs offer an important mechanism for addressing the worst of poverty.

These emerging welfare states, built around social assistance programs, are crucial to combating poverty, and the experience of Nordic countries (as well as Britain and Britain's overseas dominions) in the early twentieth century is instructive here. But critics of welfare state-building—including critics with the ANC and South African state—are correct to point out that the welfare state is not and cannot be a substitute for inclusive economic growth. The Nordic model revolved around a social pact (to which unions agreed) that delivered wage compression and generous welfare provision. The purpose of the welfare state was not only to mitigate poverty but also to promote opportunity, including through retraining the unemployed to facilitate economic restructuring.[2] In South Africa, developmental policies prioritized productivity over employment, and social grants provided an extensive but nonetheless inadequate safety net. The lesson of the Nordic model is not that the South African state should replicate the precise design of the Nordic cases, but rather that it should promote inclusive development and poverty reduction in a coordinated way through policies that are appropriate to local conditions. Postwar Europe generally succeeded in ensuring full employment. South and Southern Africa, in contrast, have a massive and chronic labor surplus. A developmental state pursuing inclusive development in Southern African conditions must promote labor-intensive sectors, even if they pay low wages, as well as promoting productivity growth.

References

ANC. (1994). *The reconstruction and development programme.* Johannesburg: African National Congress.

—-. (2007). Social Transformation, African National Congress Policy Discussion Document, available online at www.anc.org.

Armstrong, Paula, and Burger, Cobus. (2009). *Poverty, inequality and the role of social grants: An analysis using decomposition techniques.* Stellenbosch Economic Working Paper 15/09. Stellenbosch: University of Stellenbosch.

Atkinson, Doreen. (2007). Taking to the streets: Has developmental local government failed in South Africa?. In: Sakhela Buhlungu, John Daniel, Roger Southall and Jessica Lutchman (eds.), *State of the nation 2007* (pp. 53–77). Pretoria: HSRC Press.

Barchiesi, Franco. (2011). *Precarious liberation: Workers, the state, and contested social citizenship in post-Apartheid South Africa.* Albany: State University of New York Press.

Barrientos, Armando, and Santibáñez, Claudio. (2009). New forms of social assistance and the evolution of social protection in Latin America. *Journal of Latin American Studies, 41,* 1–26.

---

2   I am grateful to Olle Törnquist for this point.

Devereux, Stephen, Adato, Michelle, Sabates-Wheeler, Rachel, McConnell, Jesse and Becker, Elisabeth. (2011). *Child Support Grant Evaluation 2010: Qualitative research report.* Pretoria: UNICEF, with the South African Department of Social Development and South African Social Security Agency.

Evans, Peter. (1995). *Embedded autonomy: States and industrial transformation.* Princeton: Princeton University Press.

Feinstein, Andrew. (2007). *After the party: A personal and political journey inside the ANC.* Cape Town: Jonathan Ball.

Fine, Ben. (2010). Can South Africa be a developmental state?. In: Omano Edigheji (Ed.), *Constructing a democratic developmental state in South Africa: Potential and challenges* (pp. 169–182). Cape Town: HSRC Press.

Fleisch, Brahm. (2002). *Managing educational change: The state and school reform in South Africa. Sandton.* Heinemann.

Fourie, Elsje. (2014). Model students: Policy emulation, modernization, and Kenya's Vision 2030. *African Affairs, 113*(453), 540–562.

—-. (2015). China's example for Meles' Ethiopia: When development "models" land. *Journal of Modern African Studies, 53*(3), 289–316.

Hirsch, Alan. (2005). *Season of hope: Economic reform under Mandela and Mbeki.* Pietermaritzburg: University of KwaZulu-Natal Press.

Heinrich, Carolyn, Hoddinott, John, Samson, Michael, MacQuene, Kenneth, van Niekerk, Ingrid and Renaud, Bryant. (2012). *The South African child support grant impact assessment: Evidence from a survey of children, adolescents and their households.* Pretoria: UNICEF, with the South African Department of Social Development and South African Social Security Agency.

Holden, Paul, and van Vuuren, Hennie. (2011). *The Devil in the detail: How the arms deal changed everything.* Johannesburg: Jonathan Ball.

Joffe, Avril, Kaplan, David, Kaplinsky, Raphael and Lewis, David. (1995). *Improving manufacturing performance in South Africa: Report of the industrial strategy project.* Cape Town: University of Cape Town Press.

Kaplan, David. (2007). The constraints and institutional challenges facing industrial policy in South Africa: A way forward. *Transformation, 64*, 91–111.

Leibbrandt, Murray, Woolard, Ingrid, Finn, Arden and Argent, Jonathan. (2010). *Trends in South African income distribution and poverty since the fall of Apartheid.* OECD Social, Employment and Migration Working Papers no.101. Paris: Organisation for Economic Co-operation and Development.

Makgetla, Neva Seidman. (2007). Local government budgets and development: A tale of two towns. In: Sakhela Buhlungu, John Daniel, Roger Southall and Jessica Lutchman (Eds.), *State of the nation 2007* (pp. 146–167). Pretoria: HSRC Press.

Matisonn, Heidi, and Seekings, Jeremy. (2003). The politics of the basic income grant in South Africa, 1996–2002. In: Guy Standing and Michael Samson (Eds), *A basic income grant for South Africa* (pp. 56–76). Cape Town: University of Cape Town Press.

Meth, Charles. (2004). Ideology and social policy: "Handouts" and the spectre of "dependency". *Transformation, 56, 1-30*.

Naidoo, Vinothan. (2008). Assessing racial redress in the public service. In: Adam Habib and Christina Bentley (Eds.), *Racial redress and citizenship in South Africa* (pp. 99–128). Cape Town: Human Sciences Research Council Press.

Nattrass, Nicoli, and Seekings, Jeremy. (2014). Job destruction in Newcastle: Minimum wage setting and low-wage employment in the South African clothing industry. *Transformation, 84*, 1–30.

—– and —–. (2015). Should and can labour-surplus, middle-income economies pursue labor-intensive growth? The South African Challenge. Working Paper 351. Cape Town: Centre for Social Science Research, University of Cape Town.

—– and —–. (2016). Trade unions, casino capitalism and the state in South Africa's clothing industry. *Review of African Political Economy,43*(167), 89–106.

Seekings, Jeremy, and Matisonn, Heidi. (2012). The continuing politics of basic income in South Africa. In: Carol Pateman and Matthew Murray (Eds.), *Horizons of reform: Basic income solutions around the world.* London: Palgrave Macmillan.

—– and Nattrass, Nicoli. (2015). *Policy, politics and poverty in South Africa.* London: Palgrave Macmillan.

South Africa. (1995). *Annual report of the department of welfare 1995.* Pretoria: Department of Welfare.

—–. (1996a). *Annual report of the department of welfare 1996.* Pretoria: Department of Welfare.

—–. (1996b). *Report of the (Lund) committee on child and family support.* Pretoria: Department of Welfare.

—–. (1997). *White paper for social welfare.* Pretoria: Department of Welfare.

—–. (1999). *Annual report of the department of welfare 1998/99.* Pretoria: Department of Welfare.

—–. (2002). *Report of the (Taylor) committee of inquiry into a comprehensive system of social security for South Africa.* Pretoria: Department of Social Development.

—–. (2006a). *Strategic Plan 2006/7–2009/10.* Pretoria: Department of Social Development, RP 22/2006.

—–.(2006b). *Accelerated and shared growth initiative - South Africa (ASGISA).* Pretoria. The Presidency.

—-. (2012). *National development plan 2030: Our future, make it work.* Pretoria: National Planning Commission.

Styan, James-Brent. (2015). *Blackout: The Eskom crisis.* Johannesburg: Jonathan Ball.

Van der Berg, Servaas. (2005). Fiscal expenditure incidence in South Africa, 1995 and 2000. Report for the National Treasury.

—-. (2009). Fiscal incidence of social spending in South Africa, 2006. *Stellenbosch Economic Working Papers* 10/09. Stellenbosch: University of Stellenbosch.

—- and Siebrits, Krige. (2010). Social assistance reform during a period of fiscal stress. Stellenbosch Economic Working Papers 17/10. Stellenbosch: University of Stellenbosch.

Von Gliszczynski, Moritz and Leisering, Lutz. (2015). Constructing new global models of social security: How international organizations defined the field of social cash transfers in the 2000s.*Journal of Social Policy*, available on CJO 2015 doi: 10.1017/S0047279415000720.

Von Holdt, Karl. (2010). The South African Post-Apartheid Bureaucracy: Inner workings, contradictory rationales and the developmental state. In: Omano Edigheji (Ed.), *Constructing a democratic developmental state in South Africa* (pp. 241–260). Pretoria: HSRC Press.

—- and Murphy, Mike. (2007). Public hospitals in South Africa: Stressed institutions, disempowered management. In: Sakhela Buhlungu, John Daniel, Roger Southall and Jessica Lutchman (Eds.), *State of the nation 2007* (pp. 312–341). Pretoria: HSRC Press.

World Bank. (2014). Fiscal policy and redistribution in an unequal society. *South Africa Economic Update*, 6 (November). pp. 59.

The Rise and Fall of Democratic Neo-developmentalism in Brazil

Einar Braathen

Introduction

The impeachment of the Brazilian president Dilma Rousseff in August 2016 brought to an end a political movement linked to the Workers' Party (*Partido dos Trabalhadores*, PT) and its leader Luis Inácio Lula da Silva. Lula, as he was commonly known, had become president in January 2003 and was succeeded in 2010 by his chief secretary Dilma. The nearly 14 years in power of what has been termed *Lulismo* government provides a compelling case study for scholars of democratic developmental states. To that end, this chapter attempts to provide analytical insight into the essence of *Lulismo*, its sociohistorical genesis, and its broad government policy objectives, which are examined according to their political, social, and economic implications, and whose combined effect we have termed democratic neo-developmentalism.

The section that follows begins with an assessment of the similarities and differences between old and new forms of developmentalism in Brazil. This is followed by a discussion on the transformation of what has been termed *Petismo* into *Lulismo* and its implications for democracy. The primary focus of the chapter, however, is on the purported success of neo-developmentalism, which will be assessed in terms of its achievements in transforming society and the economy, and in transforming the cities.

From Old to New "Desenvolvimentismo"

Economic liberalism, characterized by submission to foreign capital and to the hegemony of Northern powers (primarily the UK), was a feature of Brazil's first republic from 1889 to 1930. Following the onset of a global financial crisis in 1929, nationalistic military officers mobilized for change and their 1930 "revolution" brought to power Getulio Vargas (between 1930 and 1945) with strong support from not only the working classes but also from large sections of the land-holding and capitalist class. After

131

a period of ideological orientation to fascism and a foreign policy aligned with Mussolini's Italy, in 1942 Vargas became an ally of Roosevelt and the USA. Following this, he organized democratic multiparty elections and stepped down from office in 1945. He resumed the presidency following national elections in 1951 and this time with a genuine democratic mandate. "Democratic developmentalism" in Brazil is chiefly associated with this, Vargas' second term in office from 1951 to 1954 (Coutinho 2008).

Vargas built his rule on several strategies. First, as Singer points out, he created a "power *apparently* above classes which led to the integration of the sub-proletariat to the proletarian condition, ... integrating rural migrants into an urban working class by means of industrialization" (Singer 2012: 45). Second, he encouraged collaboration between the working class and capitalists, a process driven by the government to avoid any possibility of communist interference. The legal and institutional legacy of this form of collaboration, termed *corporativismo*, has survived all subsequent regime and government change (Coutinho 2008). Third, he built a platform for strong state intervention in the economy as a means to enhance industrialization and modernization. One component of this strategy was the nationalization of oil resources in 1939 and the establishment of a state-owned monopoly company, Petrobras, in 1953 (Ribeiro 2001).[1] It is this economic-industrial strategy, in particular, which has been called *desenvolvimentismo*, or developmentalism, in Brazilian political discourse.

When Lula campaigned for the presidency in 2002, there were few references to desenvolvimentismo in his speeches due to the then radical socialist orientation of his own PT, which opposed class collaboration as well as state control of trade unions, both of which were features of the Vargas era. However, in his campaign for reelection in 2006 and in Dilma's subsequent campaign for the presidency in 2010, the concept of *neodesenvolvimentismo* became a common refrain in their ideological and political agenda. It also underpinned a concerted effort to eradicate the rad-

---

[1]   A few months later, President Vargas committed suicide. This was apparently due to the passing of the Petrobras law, which was considered to be a "communist" measure and was met with hysterical reactions from local and international capitalist groups (Ribeiro 2001).

icalism of PT as part of an initiative to build a broader government coalition (Sampaio 2012). More will be said about neo-desenvolvimentismo later, but first it is of interest to examine the ideological and political transformation of both Lula and the PT.

From *Petismo* to *Lulismo:* The Development of Democracy

The concept of *petismo* derives from the alliance of various working-class fractions and social movements, which was forged in the 1980s to create a socialist democracy driven by the PT, or the Workers Party, itself founded in 1980. *Petismo* in this context refers to the "PT way of governing" (*o modo petista de governar*) as it was understood by the public in the 1990s. Specifically, this related to direct democracy and to ample channels for popular participation; campaigns against corruption, patrimonialism, and clientelism in municipal and state institutions; and socioeconomic redistribution through improved public infrastructure and services that benefitted the subaltern classes. This was in stark contrast to the privatization and austerity policies then on offer by neoliberal right-wing parties. *Lulismo* refers to the transformation of this alliance into an increasingly personalized government project based on the personality of Lula da Silva who was president of Brazil from 2003 to 2010.

With the end of the military dictatorship (which had ruled from 1964 to 1985), social movements of all kinds emerged advocating a new kind of politics. These social forces were radical, yet democratic; they challenged the system, but were oriented toward a sense of the public good; and they were not only militant but also civically minded. The "new trade union unionists," the urban movement, the health movement, the feminist movement, and the black and student movements were some of the expressions of what Evelina Dagnino (2004) has described as the "new citizenship" of the time. In addition to imagining new democratic practices and institutions to challenge Brazil's deeply rooted social authoritarianism, these movements played a key role in the election of Lula da Silva to the presidency in 2002. For Lula, a former metal worker and strike leader with little in the way of formal education, this was the end of a "long march through institutions" for the party, following two decades of unsuccessful national campaigns, but which also included the successful governance of municipalities run on the principles of participatory democracy. The most famous example of this *petista* way of governing was in Porto Alegre, the capital of Rio Grande do Sul, located at the southern border with Uruguay.

It is not surprising, then, that the PT's first victory in the national polls in October 2002 raised expectations of popular participation in government. The idea of participatory governance had been enshrined in the PT's "Program for a Democratic Revolution," launched at the party's congress in 1999 (PT 1999). This program sets out the foundations for an eventual PT national administration. The *Democratic Revolution* under a PT presidency, it was asserted, would mark the beginning of a long process of transformation, which would deepen economic and social democracy, extend human rights and citizenship to the country's majority, reform representative institutions, and increase democratic and direct control over the state. While the party at the time had no intention of being in perpetual opposition, it understood that "it is not enough to arrive at the government to change the society. It is necessary also to change the society to arrive at the government." The *Democratic Revolution* was thus viewed as a long but not inevitable process. It was seen to involve the reorganization of society, politics, and the economy with a new hierarchy of values based on equality, freedom, and solidarity. Education, health, literacy, welfare, and economic well-being were all seen to be central to the democratic project (Baiocchi et al. 2013).

Perhaps the best example of the participatory measures introduced by the Lula government was the national policy conferences. Seventy-two of these events were held during Lula's two terms in office, compared to the 22 held under President Cardoso's administration from 1995 to 2002 The conferences convened by the Lula's administration dealt with 40 different themes, 28 of which were discussed for the first time. According to the available data, the conferences mobilized 5.6 million participants (2.2 million of whom attended the conferences that dealt specifically with issues of children and youth), and passed some 14,000 resolutions. That said, the number of people involved in each conference varied as did the degree to which the involvement of society influenced the resulting policies. Thus, for example, the First National Conference on Sports, held in 2006, was not well supported, involving just 42,000 people who took part in 180 municipal, 140 regional, and 26 state conferences. In contrast, the First Conference on Racial Equality mobilized existing social movements and organizations and attracted twice as many participants. In some instances, guidelines on the course of national policy action were predominantly determined during the local and regional phases of participatory engagement, as was the case of the National Environment Policy, while in others decisions were taken following the deliberations of a national conference. The National Plan for Culture, for example, was debated in the first national conference in 2005 and this led to the establishment of the so-called *Pontos de Cultura*, a network of public spaces for the production and diffusion of cultural activities, 650 of which were active in 2009.

An examination of the composition of these conferences is instructive. Based on the official data of the General Secretariat for Participation (SGP 2010), approximately 70% of participants came from civil society and 30% were members of government (from national, state, and municipal levels of government). Once we disaggregate the "civil society" component, however, we see that only 34% of representatives were from social movements, 21% represented business interests, and 15% were from the unions. The high proportion of representatives from the business sector is revealing, as part of the argument for the creation of these spaces for engagement was that they provided opportunities for those who were under-represented politically. Also represented, although to a lesser extent, were religious organizations, academic institutions, professional associations, and state and municipal councils.

In a brief and critical evaluation, the national participatory policy introduced by the Lula government may be seen to have three noteworthy features (Baiocchi et al. 2013):

> First was the uncoordinated nature of these participatory spaces, with their constitution and composition often linked to particular ministries and social movements (the ministries themselves having been assigned to particular factions and political parties as part of a political pact between the PT and its coalition partners). This arrangement served to reproduce the logic of political clientelism which had become so deeply entrenched in Brazilian politics (Montero 2005).
>
> Second, the organizing logic of "dialogue and listening" characterized these spaces far more than the previous logic of empowerment and power-sharing. Although de facto influence could be exercised through the mobilization of know-how, the capacity to formulate implementable policies, and by lobbying decision makers, this was not the general rule.

Third, civil society and the progressive sectors of unions and political parties were generally dissatisfied with these spaces due to their lack of effective decision-making power over important policies. In particular, there were concerns that they exercised little influence over economic and financial policies, which were either a continuation of the policies of the previous neoliberal president, F.H. Cardosos, or they were controlled by employers' associations and financial institutions (national and international). A source of further concern was the fact that employers' associations were also well represented in conferences that dealt with matters other than those of economic nature.

Public enchantment with the government's participatory-democratic practices peaked during Dilma Rousseff presidency as almost no new national policy conferences were convened by her government. The state's response to the mass upheavals of June 2013 (which will be discussed below) cannot in any sense be construed as a return to participatory policy making. To the contrary, when the Dilma government faced an economic and fiscal crisis in 2014, the response was the imposition of harsh austerity measures without any prior consultation with the society. These austerity measures, furthermore, were in conflict with the government manifesto presented to the electorate in the run-up to the presidential elections in October 2014. What this meant, in effect, was that the concept of *petismo* was terminated by the Dilma government. Following this development, questions might validly be asked as to what its replacement, *lulismo*, brought to the Brazilian people, and to what extent it rescued the democratic-popular aspects of "new developmentalism" if at all?

Lulismo and the Apparent Success of "New Developmentalism"

Although Lula da Silva was twice elected president of Brazil, in his second term, which began in 2006, his PT lost almost 20 million votes from the better-off organized working and middle classes in the southeast and southern states. Significantly, however, in what was once the most remarkable electoral realignments in modern Brazilian history, they gained a similar number of votes from poor subproletarian classes in the less industrialized northeast of the country (Singer 2012).

Transformation of the Society: The Subproletariat

On the one hand, the PT had experienced a decline in support from its traditional constituents, as the social movements and civil society organizations, which had stood by the party since its birth in 1980, became increasingly skeptical of the party and its leader (Hochstetler 2008). Following Lula's first election in 2002 they had hoped that the new president would advance the *"petista* way of governing,"* which had become well known from cities like Porto Alegre and São Paulo and which was associated with redistribution, good governance, and public participation. However, it was evident that no real redistribution to the organized working class had occurred. Instead, pragmatism in building a broad coalition with the conservative political and financial elites became a central tenet of the Lula administration (Kingston and Ponce 2010). Rather than becoming an exemplar of good governance, the Lula administration became embroiled in one of the biggest political corruption scandals in Brazil's history, the so-called *Mensalão*, a vote-buying scheme in the Federal Congress. This scandal alienated the left-leaning liberal segments of the middle class who had earlier voted for PT (Hunter 2011). Instead of a growing influence in policy making achieved through increased popular participation, the leaders of civil society organizations found themselves all but co-opted by jobs in the government (Baiocchi et al. 2013).

On the other hand, there was a remarkable ascendance in support for Lula and his party in the Northeast Brazil and among the poorest strata of society. André Singer (2012) argues that this was due to the sociopolitical transformation that took place under the Lula government. The policies attributed to Lula ensured the material upliftment and a degree of social inclusion for the poorest 10% of the population. This was achieved through direct federal cash transfers to the bank accounts (opened specifically for this purpose) of the female heads of poor families (through, for example, the *Bolsa Família* program), and increases in the minimum wage determined by presidential decree. Labor market reforms increased the number of formal employment workers, which both reduced the number of people working in the informal sector and ensured more socioeconomic rights to the lowest paid segments of the proletariat. Singer points out that these relatively modest reforms had a significant impact on political allegiances and led to changes in the class dynamics of the Brazilian society. What had, for almost a century, constituted "the permanently su-per-impoverished working surplus population," a statistical category which Singer refers to as the "sub-proletariat," had moved toward too be-coming a class for itself, a modern "new proletariat."[2]

Lulismo and *lulista* are the labels used by Singer to describe the new political regime connected to this social transformation. "Lulismo," he as-serts, "is in my view the meeting between a [state] leadership, that of Lula, and a class fraction, the sub-proletariat, through a program with the main points delineated between 2003 and 2005" (Singer 2012: 45). In some-thing of a contradiction, however, Lula also actively supported capitalist accumulation and secured the privileges of the ruling classes. In this way, he secured their acceptance of gradual and cautious social reform, fi-nanced by improved tax collection and economic growth rather than by a zero-sum method of redistribution from the rich to the poor. In other words, *lulismo* combined "gradual reforms" for the poor and "conservative pacts" with the rich. Montero (2005) and other political scientists have described "reforms under oligarchic-conservative control" as the main characteristic of Brazilian politics after the introduction of the new dem-ocratic constitution in 1988. Although Singer recognizes that there is a considerable degree of policy continuity between the governments of Fer-nando Henrique Cardoso (1995–2002) and that of Lula (2003–2010), es-pecially in their emphasis on "conservative pacts," from a Marxist per-spective, he argues, Lula's presidency created opportunities for social *mo-bility* as well as new conditions for social and political *mobilization* among the popular classes. "The *lulismo* makes an ideological re-articulation and pulls out the centrality of the conflict between left and right and recon-structs an ideology on the basis of the conflict between the rich and poor"

---

[2] Although usually unemployed or underemployed, the subproletariat in industri-alizing Brazil is not entirely excluded from the labor market. This distinguishes them from the lumpenproletariat and "the permanently super-impoverished working surplus population." The subproletariat is typically organized in female-headed families. They often move from rural to urban areas, or from cities in the periphery in the Northeast to the faster growing parts of Brazil, in order to pro-vide better job opportunities for their offspring. Hence, in real life there is a con-tinuum, rather than a sharp difference, between the "subproletariat" and "prole-tariat."

(Singer 2012: 32). In a comment on Brazil's largest ever street demonstrations in June 2013, Singer claimed that the protests were part of "the ascension of the new proletariat." "These people have gained employment and higher income," he maintained, "but their lives are still precarious, particularly in the larger cities (Singer 2014). "The demonstrators want higher public expenditure, while the market forces demand austerity. This will place the current Dilma government at the crossroads" (Singer 2013).

Transformation of the Economy: The Petroleum Industry

Prior to Lula's ascension to the presidency in January 2003, he had promised the electorate in a "Letter to Brazil" that he would not attack the free market, the fortunes of the richest families, or the privileges of the largest capitalist groups. The implication was that any business agreement based on laws made by the previous administration would be respected by the Lula administration. Forces on the left and the trade unions despaired, among them was the social movement *O petróleo tem que ser nosso* (The petroleum has to be ours), an ally of Lula's which had been established in the 1990s to oppose the new legislation introduced by President Cardoso, which led to the partial privatization of the state oil company Petrobras and the removal of its monopoly to explore for and produce petroleum.

However, in 2007 considerable space was created for state maneuver in the economy. Lula announced the discovery of the largest oil reserves found in the world in recent decades and certainly the largest in Brazil's history. The reserves of almost 50 billion barrels are located in very deep off-shore pre-salt layers in the coastal waters of Southeast Brazil. Labeled the *pré-sal* in public debate, Lula declared that "The pre-salt is our passport to the future," , and national euphoria was unleashed. The ambition was to triple the national production of oil and gas by 2020 and to increase their share of gross domestic product from around 5% in 2007 to 15% in 2020.

By the end of 2007, Lula had begun establishing a new legal framework for the oil industry. He advanced pragmatic arguments to justify this measure which were accepted even by the right-wing opposition, namely that the pre-salt reserves had created a new set of circumstances unforeseen when the concession regime was installed in 1998 and that existing laws need to be adapted to the new realities. The redrafting process was placed in the hands of a committee consisting of representatives of various ministries and the oil industry, including the CEO of Petrobras (Sérgio Gabrielli). Although no representatives from the trade unions or from *O petróleo tem que ser nosso* were appointed to this committee, it conducted its work in the organizational and ideological spirit of Vargas's corporatism. Trade union representatives took part in the work of the committee indirectly through their links with the top management of Petrobras (Sérgio Gabrielli was a former militant of the PT and advisor to the oil worker unions) and some government ministries. However, *O petróleo tem que ser nosso* soon distanced itself from the process when, in March 2009, it criticized many of the committee's proposals and began lobbying for its own alternatives. The campaign, which drew support from federal senators and deputies, organized public hearings that presented the views of trade unions, other social movements, as well as independent critical experts. They also mobilized mass support on May Day rallies, held throughout the country in 2009 and 2010, and in demonstrations carried out in Rio de Janeiro and in the federal capital Brasilia. A particular focus of their protest was in opposition to international auctioning of concessions and the presence of multinational petroleum companies in Brazilian waters.

How much impact did this nationalist and anti-imperialist campaign have at the end of the day? It is evident that it did have a definite influence on what the government called "the package" (of oil-related bills) presented to the two chambers of the National Congress at the end of 2009. In terms of the package, the Brazilian state would once more become the majority shareholder of Petrobras. Among specifications of the package was that Petrobras alone would be the lead "operating company" in the pre-salt fields and that the oil and gas fields would be owned by the Brazilian state, which stood to gain significantly from its shares in the production and sale of petroleum. The revenues from these shares were to be administered by a new federal agency. In this way, a regime of "production sharing" was intended to replace the old "concession" system, where concessionaries expropriated the oil resources and paid only a marginal proportion of their profits back to the state in royalties.

Despite these reforms, however, the logic of global competition and capitalist relations of production were to remain. A large proportion of Petrobras shares were offered up for sale on international stock markets and particularly in New York. The exclusive right to extract the oil from specific fields was granted to consortiums selected through international tenders. In this process they retained the lion's share of the superprofits generated and paid only a small proportion of the actual value of the oil produced (around 20%) to the Brazilian state in royalties, and a small tax on their profits. The state agency established to manage the revenue generated from the public shares of *pré-sal* invested these funds in profit-maximizing portfolios inside and outside Brazil, and only the return on capital was allocated to social and public spending in Brazil.[3]

Another important stated component of the new petroleum policy, apart from ensuring direct state ownership of the oilfields and the revenue generated by them, was to promote private Brazilian companies connected to the oil and gas industry. In that respect, a particularly important policy instrument was a regulation intended to increase the national "local content" of goods and services procured. For Lula and the PT, this was also a strategy to create skilled jobs on a large scale, laying the foundation for a stronger trade union movement and a more advanced form of capitalism. This was because Brazil, like other Latin American countries, historically had had a low-skilled workforce and what has been termed a "low skills equilibrium" (Schneider 2013), while the oil and petroleum sector, in contrast, is skills based and is in need of highly skilled workers.

Over the course of the past half century, Brazil has embraced various forms of capitalism, including the corporatist (or Coordinated Market Economy) model of the Vargas era and the liberal market model (Liberal Market Economy) adopted under the period of military rule (1964–1985) and again under the presidency of Fernando Cardoso (1995–2003). Under Lula, the corporatist "coordinated" variant of capitalism was reintroduced and this stressed the importance of cooperation between the state, educational institutions, and business associations in promoting local content (Braathen and Melby 2016). Similar arrangements to strengthen local content also existed in other sectors of the economy as evidenced in the *Lava-Jato* (Car-Wash) money-laundering scheme, which has become the largest corruption case in Brazil's history, and which has fundamentally undermined local content policies. The scheme involved the directors of

---

3   This mixed economy model was largely inspired by the system set up by Norway. Interview with the project manager for the new petroleum laws, Ministry of Mining and Energy, Brasilia, April 1, 2011.

Petrobras procurement units, major civil construction companies, as well as many leading politicians, including Lula himself, all of whom face the prospect of long prison sentences. However, whether or not he serves time in prison, Lula's entire policy legacy has been widely discredited in the media.

Transformation of the Cities: The Mega Event Projects

Encouraged by the pro-poor policies implemented by the Lula and Dilma governments after 2003, some PT office-bearers sought to promote an agenda for "urban reform" as a complement to the "agrarian reform" policy enshrined in the 1988 Constitution. This led to the establishment of the country's first Ministry of Cities, which was headed by the first PT mayor of Porto Alegre. At long last, in a country where 84% of the population lives in urban areas, a policy was formulated to bridge the divide between the "informal" city (the slums or *favelas*) and the formal city. Long overdue infrastructure development, particularly not only in basic sanitation but also in comprehensive urban upgrading, was implemented. This, in fact, was one area in which the "PT way of governing" succeeded at the national level, commencing with participatory policy conferences at the city level and culminating in a conference at the national level. This led to the unprecedented federal government investment in such large-scale urban renewal programs as the "Program for Accelerated Growth" and the "My House My Life".

However, the Ministry of Cities and progressive officials in other ministries soon lost control of the urban transformation processes and in no other sector is the dramatic demise of *petismo* so evident. It was intended that urban renewal programs would be implemented through a series of public-private partnerships, with implementation and oversight assigned to a small group of politicians and private entrepreneurs. Popular participation and oversight was noticeably left out of this process and in the vacuum the civil construction lobby and investors with interests in land speculation took over, and the urban transformation policy was subjected to a classic process of elite capture. The projects implemented were typically large-scale ones, with extremely weak oversight and accountability systems and optimal conditions for graft and the maximization of profits (Braathen 2015). This trend accelerated in 2008 and 2009 after Brazil won the bids to host both the 2014 Fédération Internationale de Football Association (FIFA) World Cup and the Summer Olympics in 2016.

In the past decade all of the BRICS countries have invested enormous financial resources and political prestige in hosting mega sports events: the 2008 Summer Olympics in Beijing, the 2010 Commonwealth Games in Delhi, the 2010 FIFA World Cup in South Africa, the 2014 Winter Olympics, and 2018 FIFA World Cup in Russia (replicating Brazils "double" in hosting both events). This reflects a trend wherein the so-called emerging economies have an affinity for the hosting of mega sporting events. These countries share three crucial features: the availability of resources; an ambition to project their image as an emerging power worldwide; and the relative weakness within them of institutions dedicated to the protection of human rights and the environment. The combination of these features enables host cities to abide by the "package" of interventions that international organizing committees such as the FIFA and the International Olympic Committee require (Horne and Wannel 2012).

In June 2013 FIFA launched its "test event" in Brazil, the Confederations Cup, and during this time the country witnessed the largest spontaneous demonstrations in its history when some 10 million people took to the streets. What started as a protest against a price hike on the public transportation system in São Paulo quickly escalated to mass mobilization against the massive overspending of public funds on stadiums and sporting infrastructure at a time when the general quality of public services was poor—their anger was expressed in the slogan "We don't need more stadiums, we need more schools." While corruption was a key focus of the demonstrations the protests were also directed against the violence used by the police forces to dispersing the crowds (Maricato et al. 2013).

The June demonstrations raised major concerns in the public domain about citizens' rights, on how the "voice of the street" might be heard, how the grievances of ordinary people might be taken seriously, and how the quality of democracy might be strengthened. The surfacing of these concerns and the accompanying street protests were a manifestation of the emergence of a new generation of urban movements which had been years in formation. A network of such organizations as the *Movimento Passe Livre* ("movement for free transport"), student movements, urban resistance movements, favela residents' associations, and movements of the *sem-teto* (for those without a "roof"/house) have, through occupations and demonstrations, challenged the formally established, but hollowed-out and top-down, spaces of participation. This new generation of urban movements and civic networks is a portent for a new form of an "insurgent citizenship" (Holston 2007). As opposed to a statist conceptualization of citizenship which assumes that "the only legitimate source of citizenship rights, meanings and practices" is derived from the state (Holston 1998: 39), this alternative conceptualization of citizenship is active and engaged one which is "grounded in civil society" (Friedmann 2002: 76). It aims to move beyond formalistic citizenship to a substantive one that includes an array of civil, political, social, and economic rights and, specifically, the right to housing, shelter, education, and basic health. As such, it espouses the notion of a "right to the city" (Lefebre 1967), which recognizes all residents as "right's holders," and, in so doing, defends the needs and wants of the majority while at the same time affirming the city as a site for social conflict.

Conclusion

June 2013 demonstrations were the beginning of the end of *lulismo* and one of the few responses forthcoming from the president and the Congress, which most probably were made out of concern for the forthcoming elections 2014, was to enact stronger anticorruption legislation. These laws gave police and prosecutors more powers to combat corruption, such as in extended phone tapping, temporary imprisonment, and "plea bargaining" to deal with those suspected of shady political-economic deals. Ironically, the main culprits of the new laws were members of the very Congress that had sanctioned them. The fallout from Operation Car Wash has swamped, some would say poisoned, political and public, life in Brazil. It has also all but swept away the memory and perhaps some of the achievements of the *lulista* era. Lula's public-private partnerships, intended to promote the growth of national industries and to transform the cities, among many other ambitious policy goals, have dissolved surprisingly quickly in the aftermath of the scandal.

The impeachment of President Dilma, however, was not based on the Car Wash scandal as she was the only top politician who was not suspected of having gained from the Petrobras scheme. Instead, the judicial grounds for her impeachment stemmed from the hasty and ill-advised fiscal measures introduced by her government to address the economic crisis in 2014 and 2015. Few observers of Brazilian politics believe the formal-juridical reasons behind her impeachment and the real reasons are to be found in the political economy of the state. In the first instance, Brazil could no longer escape from the global crisis by granting huge tax breaks to its manufacturing sector and other industries, simply because these policies undermined the tax base of the state and its capacity to generate revenue. In the second instance, the hurried imposition of austerity measures in 2015 was confronted by opposition and protests from within her own political camp and particularly by the trade unions and affiliated social movements. Confronted with this backlash, the president backtracked on the austerity program, but in so doing she also lost the support of the financial markets. Seeing her weakened position, her political opponents were emboldened to form an oppositional alliance which ultimately resulted in a majority call in the Congress for her impeachment, a development which saw even her vice president, Michel Temer, abandon her.

The incoming Temer government, which represents a broad majority in the Congress, immediately pursued a set of conservative and neoliberal policies that were implemented in an authoritarian way without widespread popular consultation. A constitutional amendment was pushed through with the objective of freezing public spending at its current level for 20 years. This was accompanied by the deregulation of the labor market, a move that threatens to reverse some of the gains of the Lula era. The petroleum mining policy was also changed to permit foreign companies a higher stake in the oil reserves of the country. These new policies, however, are unlikely to be endorsed in the next democratic elections to be held in 2018; this is because a large segment of Brazilian society considers the Temer government to be *golpista*, that is, a government that came into power through a parliamentary conspiracy which amounted to a coup d'etat.

It remains to be seen, however, whether the democratic developmentalism of the Lula era becomes a bygone chapter in the history of the global South, or whether, in the face of neoliberal reversals, there is a popular resurgence of interest in *lulismo* and, indeed, in the leadership of the former president himself. A third possibility is that of the emergence of a new democratic block, based on a reappraisal of *petismo* and a critical examination of the limitations as well as the achievements of *lulismo*.

References

Baiocch, G., Braathen, E., and Teixeira, A.C. (2013). Transformation institutionalized? Making sense of participatory democracy in the Lula Era. In: K. Stokke and O. Törnquist (Eds.), *Democratization in the global South: The importance of transformative politics* (pp. 217–239). Houndmills, Basingstoke, Hampshire (UK): Palgrave Macmillan.

Braathen, E. (2015). Passive revolution? Social and political struggles surrounding Brazil's newfound oil reservoirs. In: J.-A. McNeish, A. Borchgrevink and O. Logan (Eds.) *Contested powers: The politics of energy and development in Latin America* (pp. 195–215). Zed Books: London.

Braathen, E. and Melby, M. (2016). Skill formation in the Brazilian oil & gas sector. Mimeo. Oslo: Oslo and Akershus University of Applied Science.

Braathen, E., Mascarenhas, G. and Myrann Sørbøe, C. (2015). Rio's ruinous mega-events. In: Bond, P. and Garcia, A. (Eds), *BRICS—An anti-capitalist critique* (pp. 186–199). Jacana Media Auckland Park (SA): Pluto Press.

Coutinho, C. N. (2008). *Contra a Corrente. Ensaios sobre Democracia e Socialismo.* Cortez, São Paulo.

Dagnino, E. (2004). Sociedade civil, participação e cidadania: de que estamos falando? In: D. Mato (Ed.), *Políticas de ciudadanía y sociedad civil en tiempos de globalización.* Caracas: FACES -Universidad Central de Venezuela.

Friedman, J. (2002). *The prospect of cities.* Minneapolis: University of Minnesota Press.

Hochstetler, K. (2008). Organized civil society in Lula's Brazil. In: Kingstone, P. and Power T. (Eds.), *Democratic Brazil revisited* (pp. 33–53). Pittsburgh PA: University of Pittsburgh Press.

Holston, J. (1998). Spaces of insurgent citizenship. In: Sandercock, L. (Ed.), *Making the invisible visible: A multicultural planning history.* California: University of California Press.

Holston, J. (2007). *Insurgent citizenship.* Princeton, NJ: Princeton University Press.

Horne, J. and Whannel, G. (2012). *Understanding the Olympics.* London/New York. Routledge.

Hunter, W. (2011). Brazil: The PT in power. In: Levitsky, S. and K.M. Roberts (Eds.), *The resurgence of the Latin American left.* Baltimore, MD: The John Hopkins University Press.

Kingstone, P. R. and Ponce, A. F. (2010). From Cardoso to Lula: The triumph of pragmatism in Brazil. In: K. Weyland, R.L. Madrid and W. Hunter (Eds.), *Leftist* governments in Latin America: Successes and shortcomings. New York: Cambridge University Press.

Lefebvre, H. (1967). Le Droit à la ville. Paris: Anthropos.

Maricato, E. et al. (2013). Cidades Rebeldes: Passe Livre e as Manifestações que Tomaram as Ruas do Brasil. São Paulo: Boitempo Editorial.

Montero, A. P. (2005). Brazilian politics. Cambridge: Polity Press.

Ribeiro, J. A. (2001). A Era Vargas. Rio de Janeiro: Casa Jorge.

Sampaio, Jr., P. A. (2012). Desenvolvimentismo e neodesenvolvimentismo: tragédia e farsa (Developmentalism and new developmentalism: tragedy and farce). Serviço Social & Sociedade, São Paulo, n. 112, pp. 672–688, out./dez. 2012

Schneider, B. R. (2013). Hierarchical capitalism in Latin America. Business, labor and the challenges of equitable development. Cambridge: Cambridge University Press.

SGP. (2010). Democracia Participativa: nova relação do Estado com a sociedade 2003–2010. Brasília: Secretaria-Geral da Participação -- SGP.

Singer, A. V. (2012). Os sentidos do Lulismo. Reforma Gradual e o Pacto Conservador. São Paulo: Companhia Das Letras.

Singer, A. V. (2013). The social energy cannot be turned back (A energia social não voltará atrás). Interview in the weekly magazine Epoca, June, 21 2013. http://revistaepoca.globo.com/tempo/noticia/2013/06/andre-singer-ener gia-social-nao-voltara-atras.html

Singer, A. V. (2014). Rebellion in Brazil. Social and political complexion of the June Events. New Left Review, 85, 19–37.

New Social Democracy in the South? Reflections from India, Indonesia, and Scandinavia in Comparative Perspective

Olle Törnquist[1]

Introduction

Following the UK's Brexit vote and the election of Donald Trump as president of the United States, it has become increasingly evident that large numbers of people, adversely affected by the ills of unregulated globalization, are being drawn to populist right-wing nationalism, away from mainstream liberal welfarism and social democracy. This is apparent not only in Europe and the United States but also in states in the global South. Thus, in India, Hindu fundamentalist identity politics are thriving, accompanied by neoliberal economic policies (including the growth of private social services) that nurture an Indian version of the American dream. In the period from 2004 to 2014 this undermined the efforts of the Congress Party, and various parties on the left, to augment market-driven development with social rights and public welfare. In Brazil, ambitious attempts to combine neoliberalism with welfare programs lost popular support following a collapse of commodity prices, poor governance, and the state's failure to scale up democratic participation. In the Philippines, a brutal president rose to power, promising jobs for the poor, the suppression of drugs, and the resolution of conflict with the Maoists. In Indonesia, opponents of the reformist president and his governor in Jakarta succeeded in organizing mass street protests in late 2016 based on a combination of Muslim identity politics and the resentment of the urban poor who had been evicted to make way for property developments intended for the affluent middle classes.

‘ Although states in the global North have survived similar eras of national peril (following the depression and in the 1930s and the rise of fascist welfare states), they did so in the context of an imperialist world order

---

1   The author wishes to acknowledge vital importance for the chapter of joint research and discussions with Professor John Harriss, Simon Fraser University, Vancouver.

which did little for populations in the global South. Furthermore, states in the South now confront forms of uneven development which have led to the unsustainable extraction of natural resources, land dispossession, and rent-seeking urban property development. New globalized forms of industrialization, moreover, are characterized by subcontracting, cheap and increasingly informalized labor, and the precarious employment of professionals. This has led to biased democracy, crooked governance, environmental destruction, mounting inequality, and increasing numbers of poor people living outside the circuits of accumulation. This has also made the formation of broad coalitions extremely difficult. So, given the challenges faced in both the global North and South, what, if any, are the chances to reinvent social democracy as an alternative to populist right-wing nationalism? Are there any alternative roadmaps to those now already outdated?

The prospects seem bleak. As noted, the social and political movements that emerged during the period of rapid industrialization in the North and which gave rise to social democracy are not likely to be repeated under the current pattern of globally uneven development. However, social democracy is, generally speaking, about the capacity of democratic politics to combine equity and sustainable growth and this may still be possible, albeit under different conditions and pursued in different ways. Contradictions within globalized uneven development might also give rise to new opportunities and the prospect of new alliances and, it is in this regard, that some of insights from the past may be useful. To this end, we have specified the universal processes that we understand to be drivers of social democratic development. These are (i) the formation of democratic political collectives based on broad popular interests; (ii) democratic linkages between state and society; (iii) the establishment of equal civil, political, and social rights in society and working life; and (iv) the negotiation of social growth pacts between capital and labor, and including those self-employed in the primary sectors.[2]

In this chapter, we examine the developmental trajectories of Indonesia, India, and Scandinavia, in particular, and with reference to other states in the global South such as Brazil, South Africa, and the Philippines.

---

[2]   For elaboration of these dimensions, see Törnquist with Harriss (2016).

These country cases examine different attempts to construct social democracy over a period of three generations, along with their limitations and challenges. Methodologically this is challenging in that they do not represent similar cases with different outcomes, nor different cases with similar outcomes. Nevertheless, we hope to search for fresh perspectives that can be derived from the comparative method of observing and advancing explanations of similar processes in contrasting contexts.

First-Generation Social Democracy

The intellectual origins of social democratic politics may be traced back to the late nineteenth- and early twentieth-century critiques of the syndicalist proposition that the basis for social transformation should be workers' management of industry. This proposition was derived from Kautsky's thesis that the crisis of capitalism would generate socialism, and Lenin's position that it would take a political revolution to achieve this transformation. The dissidents, inspired by Eduard Bernstein, argued instead that socialism would not occur without politics, but also that politics should be democratic, both within one's own movements and, as far as possible, even when resisting authoritarian regimes and employers. Historically, the development of the four dimensions of social democracy alluded to was most successful in the context of comprehensive capitalist industrialization that enabled the rise of broad labor movements, especially in countries with comparatively equal citizens, democratically oriented politics, and effective public administration.

Second Generation: Democratic Shortcuts to Progress

Social democracy was particularly difficult in colonial and postcolonial contexts where industrialization had been held back, where administration was poor and indirect, and where citizens' rights and democratization were shallow or negated. In was in such contexts, as a consequence, that the argument about the need for "shortcuts to progress" was advanced. It was believed that these shortcuts could be achieved through the efforts of enlightened leaders supported by cadre parties. Such vanguard groups, it was assumed, could substitute for weak labor movements by directing national independence movements, establishing strong states, pursuing land reform and industrialization, and, in this way, developing social democracy.

The shortcuts came in many versions. Some, like the Maoists, believed that revolution was inevitable. Others wished to proceed in less authoritarian ways, but ultimately had to resort to armed struggle and centralized leadership to avoid elimination, such as the movement against Batista in Cuba, the anti-Apartheid movement in South Africa, and the anti-colonial and anti- imperialist movements against the French and the United States in Vietnam. In these cases, the command structures of an armed struggle gave rise to a logic that was anything but democratic. However, in contexts with less unequal citizenship and some freedoms, there were possibilities for more social democratic governance (in forms now associated with the notion of a democratic developmental state). For prominent leaders of independence movements, such as Nehru in India, while the idea of social rights was certainly important, it was subordinate to the need for civil and political rights. As a consequence, once independence had been achieved, social rights were often neglected.

Most popular participation in the postcolonial era, moreover, remained indirect, mediated by patrons and populist leaders, rather than by organizations appointed by the people themselves.[3] In contrast, communists, who in the early 1950s had adapted to an elitist democratic framework, prioritized social and economic change. Notwithstanding this focus, attempts to establish a democracy based on equal citizenship faded in the mid-1970s when the Communist Party of India (CPI) supported the state of emergency imposed by Indira Gandhi. This prompted a group of dissident leaders, with more grassroots support, to form their own Communist Party of India-Marxist (CPI-M), which eventually rose to power in the state of West Bengal. Although this party initially advocated democratic principles and pursued a program of decentralization and land reform, over the years their own leadership succumbed to authoritarian and clientelistic practices, neglecting the interests of poor farmers and informal laborers in their quest to industrialize the state, and after three decades in power, they suffered a humiliating defeat in 2011.

---

[3]   Populism may be delineated, generally, in terms of anti-elitism and supposedly direct relations between acclaimed leaders and a notoriously unspecified "people."

The Kerala Showcase and Stagnation

The Indian state of Kerala is a good illustration of the fact that consistent social democratic development is possible even under unfavorable conditions. During the late nineteenth and early twentieth centuries, socio-religious reform movements that occurred among Kerala's different castes and religious communities were based on the recognition that assigning equal civil, political, and social rights to all would improve their bargaining power against landlords and within commercial agriculture. Supported by the progressive views of the leadership of the Congress Socialist Party (who later became communists), these reforms laid the foundations for Kerala's unique experiment in democratic human development. This was accompanied by efforts to promote the democratic integration of the population into politics through educational movements and citizen action from below. The most prominent historical cases of this struggle for citizen rights were the library and land reform movements, along with peasant and labor organizations that balanced the influence of their communist party leader. From the mid-1950s onward, however, attempts by the leftist government to broaden the agricultural and educational reforms and to pursue a program of industrialization were blocked. First, by the central government directed emphasis on heavy industries and import substitution, which ignored the comparative advantage that the state of Kerala had developed in education and commercial agriculture, and second, by conservative forces, supported by the CIA and the Congress Party, which overthrew the leftist government.

After some time, the left managed to regain power through a process of political horse-trading. As a consequence of this compromise, the strategy of a united front was no longer driven by socioeconomic interests and popular demands from below, nor was it focused on reaching some form of agreement between employers and trade unions. Between 1967 and 1981 left-led coalition governments ruled on the basis of compromises reached between various parties and leaders with special interests. Reflective of this, as indicated, while the breakaway CPI-M retained most of their popular support in their own struggles for citizens' rights, the CPI supported the Congress Party in its imposition of the all-India state of emergency. All parties, however, used perks to attract membership and the support of interest groups representing small farmers, tenants, farm workers, informal sector workers, industrial workers, as well as workers in the public sector. This drive for membership extended to women's and youth organizations, cooperative associations, and cultural and educational groups. Increasingly, independent civil society associations, too, drew closer to politicians and parties. As a consequence of the need to balance the interests of different groups, the welfare programs and policies adopted were often chosen on a partisan basis, irrespective of their impact on economic development. That said, this process took place through networks of politically affiliated organizations and their leadership, rather than on the basis of populist appeals occurred in neighboring Tamil Nadu. Kerala was also less influenced by the hegemony of a single political party as was the case in West Bengal. Thus, despite the negative effects of party divisions and clientelism, along with some corruption, the Kerala communists have had to take into consideration the interests of a wide array of social groups and, in this way, they have thus retained a substantial following.

Catering to the disparate interests of the left's supporters inevitably affected economic development. Land reforms were finally realized in the 1970s, but these, as well as the remarkable advances achieved within health and education, did not benefit the weakest sections of the population and nor did they lead to alternative forms of inclusive development to the extent that was expected. The land reforms did away with domination of landlords but they mainly benefited the tenants, who often developed special interests of their own. Moreover, there were many exceptions: peasant farmers were only granted rights to their huts and to small plots on generally infertile land, while tribal people and fishing communities were completely overlooked by the reforms. Most importantly, perhaps, the reforms were not supported with measures to foster production. Many new owners developed interests in less labor-intensive crops, and even engaged in land speculation. In addition, the reforms were implemented during a period of conflict between the CPI and CPI-M, neither of which had elected representatives at the local level. As a consequence, better educated and more privileged groups were able to secure good jobs and develop profitable ventures outside of the agricultural sector, while former tenants from lower ranked communities gained both land and an education. However, neither group developed agricultural and other productive activities of the kind that would generate new and better jobs for the underprivileged sections of society which remained marginalized, even if they now had the ability to read and write and enjoyed some access to health services. At the same time, many investors avoided Kerala, claiming it was difficult to negotiate with its strong trade unions. As a consequence, from the mid-1970s onward increasing numbers of better educated and trained Keralites and their families sustained or improved their living standards as migrant workers in the Gulf countries in particular. From this it is evident that the, perhaps unavoidable, political shortcuts to progress taken were susceptible to misdirection, the rise of vested interests, top-down leadership, and their access to privileges and resources.

Efforts were made to change these dynamics during the 1987–1991 Left Front government in which there was no participation of caste and community-based parties. However, left-oriented civil society groups, especially the People's Science Movement (Kerala Sastra Sahitya Parishad), with its tens of thousands of members (many in educational institutions in rural and semirural areas), initiated campaigns for full literacy, more democratic and socially inclusive education, and local development planning. It was not possible to scale up these civil society initiatives, however, as the government was unwilling to devolve political power and decentralize administration. Remarkably, nevertheless, the reformists did manage to initiate a transformative political agenda and we shall revert to this and to new movements in other parts of India in due course.

The Indonesian Advances with Unintended Consequences

As in India, independence movements in Indonesia argued for civil and political rights and discussed social equity but, notwithstanding this, the ethnic Chinese were excluded and often labeled colonial compradors. Many of the movements were led by intellectuals and aspiring entrepreneurs from the progressive sections of Muslim and other religious organizations. In contrast to South Asia and the Middle East, these leaders emerged from society rather than from the remnants of old regimes. Their major priorities included support for self-help businesses and welfare schemes, but they also included popularly oriented education and the promotion of *Bahasa Indonesia* as a neutral lingua franca. The concept of a modern, united, yet multicultural, nation-state was widely supported throughout the vast archipelago. Socialist and communist organizations added demands for social equality, including land reform, union rights, and the nationalization and subsequent workers' control of foreign companies. In that respect, they were opposed to usury rather than the ethnic Chinese in general.

Following a prolonged liberation struggle against the Japanese, Dutch, and British, the declaration of an independent republic in 1945 was notable in the extent to which it recognized religious and ethnic pluralism, political and civil rights, and social justice. These ideals, however, were undermined by fierce political struggles. At the time, the incoming president, Sukarno, and the parliament depended extensively on autonomous militias for their protection—the leftists among them having been defeated as part of a precondition for independence agreed to with the western powers. The Dutch, however, who had had to concede independence to Indonesia in the aftermath of the war, attempted to retain their influence in the country through the interest groups (ethnic and political) which had been responsible for its system of indirect colonial rule. Under these circumstances, debates on whether to pursue a centralized or decentralized form of governance (federalism as in India) shifted in favor of strong central leadership. Initially, however, the parliamentary democracy which came into being in 1946, promoted full citizenship rights, accommodated opposing political views, and encouraged compromise.

It was in this way that the world's largest democratic movement came into being, based on sectoral organizations representing workers, peasants, informal labor, youth, students, artists, and many others, including and significantly for the time, women campaigning for gender equality. The most dynamic movements were led by the rapidly growing Communist Party, the Partai Komunis Indonesia (PKI). Like its Indian sister party, by the early 1950s the PKI had become reformist although it did still push for some more radical measures such as the need for land reform. It benefitted from the democratic framework and the patronage of President Sukarno, who was in need of popular support. While Sukarno avoided the language of class, he opposed western imperialism and spoke up for the common people and small producers and traders. Most other organizations were based on patron-client relations and elitist networks, in addition to ethnic and religious solidarities. Although the competition was intense it was mostly nonviolent; and the importance of interests and ideas increased as did the idea of a united nation.

In the context of the cold war, however, the conflicts became more intense and positions held were uncompromising. Following the inconclusive results of the parliamentary elections in 1955 and communist advances in the polls, communist victories in local elections in Java, and the subsequent nationalization of Dutch companies in 1957,[4] those who rejected centralized government initiated rebellions and gained active support from the West. The outcome of this was that the populist President Sukarno, with the support of senior military officers and the communists, declared martial law throughout the entire country. In the process, parliamentary democracy was scrapped in favor of what was termed Guided Democracy, run by a strong presidency and central military leadership. Under this arrangement nation building had become a top-down project and public participation was possible only through the medium of political parties, including the PKI, which supported the government. This was accompanied by state corporatism, where the representatives of so-called functional groups, such as the military, peasants, workers, women, and minorities, were appointed in a top-down manner.

"Guided Democracy" derived its support from an odd combination of actors with a common interest in centralized government and politically driven development. Some had leftist ideals of transformative reform, others sought support for traditional Muslim schools and values, while yet others wanted "strong state leadership." The latter, in particular, were guilty of abusing their political connections and state resources. Military leaders, for example, became economically independent by assuming control of nationalized companies. The communists, who had begun to drift toward Beijing, opposed "bureaucratic capitalism" but failed to acknowledge the political rise of capitalism within the very alliance that they themselves supported. Moreover, as it could no longer rely on electoral victories, it was difficult for the PKI to break out of the alliance without being themselves subject to repression. Opposition and attempted rebellion came, instead, from private entrepreneurs within natural resource-based business and modern Muslim socio-religious organizations, Singaporean-oriented "social democrats," and liberal-oriented students

---

4   The nationalist ambitions were to build an independent economy, mobilize popular support, and put pressure on Holland to give up Papua New Guinea, albeit in favour of Indonesian dominance.

and intellectuals, all with active support from the West. Their civil and political rights were restricted at the same time as the regime propagated social rights; these were to be promoted by land reform and state control of national resources. The rent-seeking and primitive accumulation of capital which ensued, however, undermined all efforts at independent economic development and, in the early 1960s, precipitated a deep economic crisis, made worse by severe drought.

General Suharto's rise to power in late 1965 was made possible by a few leftist officers and communist leaders who attempted to get around the impasse by arresting the leading generals, on charges of treason, and by appointing a revolutionary council in support of the president. Their attempted coup failed, the generals were killed or escaped, and their actions were used as a justification for a militarily, politically, and religiously instigated massacre of more than 500,000 people. It also led to the elimination of the world's largest popular movement, comprised of innumerable radical nationalists and almost 20 million reform-oriented communists and mobilized sympathizers, constituting approximately a fifth of Indonesia's population at the time.

The displacement of Sukarno and the eventual transition to the Suharto regime became a blueprint for so-called middle-class coups in the global South. These were underpinned by Samuel Huntington's theory of the need for a "politics of order," which called for strong political institutions in cases where the middle classes were too weak to win elections and to withstand popular dissatisfaction in the process of capitalist modernization. Ironically, however, Suharto's new politics of order had begun gaining ground within the centrally imposed "Guided Democracy," which had politically facilitated the accumulation of resources. In their opposition to this political order, the communists and radical nationalists had also unintentionally paved the way for the rise of repressive political capitalism. Liberal-minded students and middle-class activists who supported the military against the communists and Sukarno, with their hoped-for assistance, also looked forward to new freedoms and leading positions in government and society. Instead, and in accordance with Huntington's theory, they became the technocratic assistants of the military leaders, their cronies, and big international investors.

Although all analysts agree that there were no longer any prospects for either liberal welfarism or development that was oriented to social democracy, the research informing this chapter suggests that the potential remained for broad alliances campaigning for equal citizen rights and democracy. Such alliances were oriented not only to the attainment of basic social rights, but they were also seen as essential in the fight against dictatorial and primitive accumulation and in the struggle to achieve a more inclusive form of development. In this view, the key question was whether, and how, a broad opposition movement could emerge and, if so, what interests would gain the upper hand.

From the mid-1980s onward there were signs of resistance among farmers and workers, as well as among disadvantaged business people and professionals, against the politically facilitated accumulation of capital. Yet, the New Order regime prevented any political organizing at the grassroots level, and promoted in their stead state-corporatist mass movements. Thus, while radical dissidents advocated for the democratization of state and politics, most activists simply wanted to dismantle the repressive political system and corrupt state in general. This was, in part, due to the fact that they lacked an organized following and did not trust the "uneducated masses." Their primary focus, thus, was on human rights, the eradication of corruption, "enlightened" citizen organization, and economic liberalization. As a consequence, although the demand for democracy became the unifying slogan of the 1990s, it was mainly advocated by students and dissenting intellectuals whose demands were more about freedoms and human rights than equal citizenship and popular governance. By mid-1996, however, it had become clear that the attempts by softliners to reform the regime had failed.

The New Order, however, was never decisively defeated, or even reformed, and it simply collapsed in the face of sporadic discontent and the ineffectual management of despotic leaders who had fostered so much privatization and deregulation that they lacked the financial instruments to respond to the Asian economic crisis of 1998. This financial meltdown hit ordinary people hard and finally reduced the support of even the privileged middle classes, along with that of some prominent businessmen, politicians, and even military officers. Despite this growing opposition, none in the political mainstream, or among their foreign allies, dared to tip the balance, and it was only through massive pro-democracy demon-strations in May 1998 that General Suharto was finally deposed.

Third Generation: Democratization Against Crooked Development

The misdirected policies and vested interests which were a feature of the political shortcuts to progress in Kerala were, of course, insignificant when compared to the manner in which repressive political capitalism had been enabled in Indonesia, albeit, initially, unintentionally. Differenti-ating the two was the fact that while the Kerala case represented an at-tempt to reform a mainstream party and movement, the Indonesian case illustrates how a social order attempted to start anew following the purges of 1965.

These setbacks in the attempts to progress toward a more just polit-ical order were part of a general trend in the global South in the 1960s. Although the rise of capitalism in Indonesia was pursued in much more authoritarian ways than in India, the approach is not uncommon in other developing states such as the Philippines and countries in Latin America. However, from the late 1970s economic globalization began to undermine repressive regimes that failed to adjust to the market and this was aggra-vated by Western campaigns for democratic rights in the Soviet Union which called for principled respect for human rights. In contrast to Kerala, however, established political movements had often been destroyed or, al-ternatively, they had been proven completely wrong in their assumption that liberal democratization would inevitably lead to violent revolution. In the Philippines, for example, following the "people power revolution" which ended the Marcos dictatorship in 1986, the Maoists served to delay rather than advance progress toward a more equitable social order. From Brazil and several other Latin American countries in the mid-1980s, to South Korea, South Africa, and finally Indonesia, it was mainly new, and often scattered leftist movements that fought for citizen rights and de-mocracy and thereby fostered the general idea of social democracy.

Indonesian Challenges of Elitist Democratization and Populist Openings

When Suharto stepped down in 1998, it was fashionable for political movements to label themselves "democrats." Most of the principled activists wished for a transitional government to foster citizenship, popular organization, and decentralized and participatory governance. This, it was believed, would create the capacity necessary to establish a genuine democracy and would provide them with a fair chance of winning elections. Within four months of the transition period, however, the genuine democrats lost out. This was because mainstream critics of Suharto, together with organizations which had survived the New Order, reached agreement with moderates from the old regime to introduce various social liberties and a program of decentralization, and, significantly, to hold quick elections. This last measure ensured that the poorly organized, but authentic, advocates of social democracy were bound to lose.

The position advanced[5] was that the mainstream actors, including those from the New Order, would become democrats by adapting to the new liberal democratic institutions, while the democrats would join the mainstream or advocate for change from positions in civil society. In this way, radical political leaders were marginalized as were Civil Society Organizations (CSOs) and emerging mass movements. The latter had become increasingly fragmented and subordinated by the resurgence of the liberal elitist politics that had been curbed 40 years earlier. This time around, moreover, they were far from what had been the world's largest democratically oriented popular movement.

The strategy to advance an elitist liberal democracy generated remarkable freedoms and stability, but governance and representation remained poor. As national surveys have shown, the main causes are not, as critics often argue, solely due to the accommodation of the old elites, including the oligarchs, in systems that were persistently corrupt, but they were also due to the unfairness of representative institutions and the limited capacity of change agents.

---

[5] International scholars were flown in to provide advice on the political path to be followed.

Electoral regulations were heavily biased in favor of the dominant political parties and "money politics." For example, a new party wishing to advance from below by competing for a local council had first to be able to demonstrate a visible presence in almost the entire country (about as big as the EU). This *required* huge resources. The direct election of political executives, as a means to counter the dominance of elitist parties, opened up some windows of opportunity, but fostered "moneyed bossism" and populism. There was no system for the democratic representation of organized interests as a substitute for previous state corporatism. As a consequence, interest and issue-based organizations turned to divisive pressure politics and lobbying. New commissions and advisory committees involving civil society actors and experts were appointed from above and were accountable to their peers rather than to their potential principals. Direct participation remained fragmented and elite dominated.

The limited capacity of the progressive democrats was an even more crucial limitation. Their main focus, hitherto, had been on special interests and issues, and on emphasizing the role of civil society in the struggle against state and "rotten politicians." This led to what has been termed "floating democrats," who had neither a firm organization nor a social base—this, despite the fact that Suharto's "floating mass" policy had been scrapped from the outset in 1998. Although this situation improved somewhat in the late 2000s, their capacity to develop comprehensive long-term reform policies remains weak.

Similar weaknesses applied to the capacity to mobilize and organize people. The progressives had fewer sources of power to build political legitimacy and authority, beyond their knowledge and some "good contacts." In particular, they lacked the organizational clout necessary to counter their adversaries' economic and social capital. Fragmentation remained in spite of numerous efforts to bring together various groups. On top of ideological and personal conflicts, the already existing organizations and movements often focused on the victims of the New Order politics, making it harder to develop broader solidarities and common platforms between different social classes. In addition, the ambitions of individual group's, which emphasized the importance of their "own project," further added to the fragmentation. These projects were often advanced through personal access to influential leaders rather than through any membership-based organization with a long-term agenda for public policy reforms that most could agree on. Active citizenship was also constrained by the fact that there was a shortage of supportive broad organizations that could assist ordinary people, and they had, instead, to turn to local patrons or commercial intermediaries to get access to public services such as health care. To make things worse, international democracy programs focused their support on specific projects that embodied the ideals of New Public Management thinking, rather than on the development of public institutions and long-term organizational principles that would make broad collective and strategic action more rational.

In the early 2000s, the findings of the first participatory surveys of democratization suggested that principled activists should not permit the elite to dominate and undermine organized politics. Rather, such activists should become political and build alternative "political blocks." These political blocks were conceived as coalitions or united fronts in the political space between, on the one hand, fragmented interest organizations and citizen associations and elitist politics on the other. These efforts, however, brought new challenges. Over the years, one of the activists' strategies was to intensify classical liberal lobbying such as on human rights, the environment, the gender agenda, and against corruption. Such initiatives, however, generally neglected mass organizing and the development of comprehensive political alternatives. Another strategy was to advance comprehensive political alternatives through local or central parties and party-led political fronts. These also failed to mobilize ordinary people, to reconcile avant-gardist ambitions with those of other activists, and to overcome unfavorable rules and regulations relating to the eligibility of parties to run in elections. A third strategy was to build a loose federal party, based on the political interests of different political organizations and civil society groups. But this strategy too failed to develop a unifying political theme capable of attracting sympathetic actors and organizations within issue-based donor projects. The fourth model was to "take over" the inactive local branches of national parties that had been established by monied political players in Jakarta. A variant of this was a "diaspora strategy," which entailed joining elitist parties in an attempt to change them from within. However, lacking a base and sufficient resources to avoid being subordinated to the priorities of the elitist political bosses, the strategy resulted in the election of only a handful of successful activist-turned-politicians in recent elections. A final set of strategies were to use existing interest and issue-based organizations in order to build trade union-based parties, to develop effective extra-parliamentary political pressure, or for popular organizations to sign political contracts with leaders or parties on favorable policies in the hope of gaining influence and access to resources in return for the legitimacy (and hence votes) which they provided. In the absence of a unifying program of action, this strategy, too, became subordinated to the powers and priorities of elitist political leaders and parties.

From the late 2000s elitist democracy became increasingly populist, although transactional horse-trading, rent-seeking, and informal personal contacts still remained crucial. The new system of directly electing political executives (with increased powers and decentralized public resources) meant that successful candidates had to move beyond elitist parties and personal patron-client relations. In so doing, they had to reach out to wider sections of the population and present an attractive vision through the media. These included not only ethnic, religious, and conservative interest organizations, but also key figures in reformist unions, in groups representing the urban poor, as well as among those campaigning against corruption, environmental destruction, and gender bias. The Asian economic crisis also played a role in this process in that it had led to rapid urbanization and neo-liberalization of the economy and employment conditions. This meant that politicians had to transform popular discontent into votes, which they did through the introduction of welfare measures, in both the private and public sectors. Union leaders, in turn, had to consider the establishment of alliances with subcontracted workers and informal labor in order to sustain their bargaining power.

The critical question, then, is whether and how these structural openings transformed into effective counter-movements promoting social democratic development. To find out, we have studied the character and results of the two outstanding political processes over time: first, the development of an informal social contract between new populist leaders and urban poor groups as in the rural town of Solo, Central Java. The second is the remarkably broad, albeit briefly successful, 2010-2012 alliance in Greater Jakarta between the Social Security Action Committee (Komite Aksi Jaminan Sosial, KAJS) unions and civil society activists, and progres-

sive politicians in the struggle to introduce a law on universal health insurance. The Solo social contract model, with Joko "Jokowi" Widodo at the
forefront, gave rise to a significantly wider, and successful, campaign for
new policies in the gubernatorial elections in Jakarta 2012 and the presidential elections in 2014. The KAJS campaign led to yet more attempts to
forge broad alliances from below in the quest for further reforms.

Generally, the studies point to the potential for broader counter-
movements against the negative effects of neoliberal economic development and poor public management in favor of decent jobs and work conditions, as a basis for inclusive and sustainable economic development.
However, the potential remains only a possibility as a number of challenges still need to be overcome. First, the new populism was no panacea
for progressive politics. The main drawbacks included arbitrary definitions of who constitutes "the people" and the undemocratic nature of the
direct relations between leaders and their supporters. Jokowi's opponents often define what constitutes "the people" through religious identity politics and use this to mobilize quite legitimately dissatisfied groups.
In 2014, for example, populism was so skillfully applied by the authoritarian oligarch Prabowo Subianto that this former general and son-in-law of
President Suharto almost ascended to the presidency in a process per-
fected in the United States by Donald Trump.

Second, counter-movements need to be sufficiently strong and have
sufficient bargaining power to enforce a pact. For example, it was only
when organizations representing the urban poor become sufficiently organized to reject minor reforms and threats of evictions that the then
mayor Jokowi was prepared to negotiate a social contract. Similarly, it was
only thanks to strong pressure from outside parliament through the KAJS
alliance that supportive politicians could build a political majority in support of the law on universal public health services. Conversely, when
Jokowi campaigned for the position of governor of Jakarta, the Solo model
could not really be applied as there was a shortage of sectoral and civic
groups with popular following on the ground, beyond networking and
lobbying. Hence Jokowi and his team had to turn to quick fixes. Similarly,
when President Jokowi tried to stand up against crooked politicians by
calling on the Corruption Eradication Commission (Komisi Pemberanta-
san Korupsi) to screen all candidates for his administration, this was attacked by corrupt officials and the police and could not be countered by

popular mobilization. The anti-corruption movement had focused on "big fish" without also going after the everyday corruption of public services that affect ordinary people.

Third, there was a shortage of long-term perspectives on how certain reforms might provide better conditions for further advances. For example, once the universal public health insurance system had been accepted in parliament, informal labor groups and civil society constituents of KAJS proved too weak to proceed by developing a gradual strategy toward decent employment conditions and more comprehensive welfare reforms. In addition, there was no concept for institutional reforms toward representation of interest organizations and citizen participation. This would have made broader alliances more meaningful than lobbying and pressuring for special interests. Moreover, it would thus have been possible for unions to not only discuss wages but also link up with partners in suggesting and negotiating welfare reforms and policies to foster inclusive development. Hence the unions and their leaders returned to their own priorities. For example, the urban poor and domestic labor were left on their own. Similarly, the new vision of village-level development and participation did not come with clear ideas of how to prevent elite capture and how to scale up local efforts to address the issues proliferating in a globalized world that cannot be managed solely in town hall meetings and via anarchic social media.

Fourth, even Jokowi and his team applied "popular transactionalism" in which traditional practices of calling on supposedly vital and friendly players, rather than fostering independent organization of crucial interests persisted. Some attempts have been made to alter this, but only in relation to CSOs and not popular organizations. For example, Jokowi and his team continued to negotiate informally and individually with various actors. This gave the upper hand to discretionary decisions on the part of the rulers and undermined predictability and trust. Finally, Jokowi and his aides continue to apply quick fixes to gain popular support and contain opponents. This applied to union leaders, for example. This in turn increased the temptation among many groups and organizations, even outright supporters, to act similarly by trying to "penetrate" state and politics in search of special favors and positions, and then foster measures outside government, rather than to develop policy proposals, mobilize widespread support, and try to foster progressive public reforms.

Attempts at Renewing the "Kerala Model"

In 1987, the Left Front, which formed a government without the support of community and caste-based parties, together with leftist civil society groups, launched a number of democratic participatory development programs from below. However, the government was hampered by internal conflicts and the scaling up of the civil society initiatives called for cooperation with the politicians in the process of decentralization. So, how did the reformist manage to advance and what lessons might be learned from this initiative?

When in 1991, the Left Front lost the elections, the leadership focused on establishing alliances in favor of democratic decentralization and participatory planning and, in so doing, won support from concerned scholars, some mass-based interest organizations, and the country's most widely respected communist leader, E.M.S. Namboodiripad, Kerala's first chief minister. E.M.S., as he was known, had been crucial in the paradigmatic struggles for civil, political, and social rights during the 1930s, and he remained committed to changing the fundamental ordering of society.

As the next Left Front government was assembled in 1996, the now well-known "People's Planning Campaign" (PPC) was launched through the State Planning Board. This was in spite of stiff resistance from within the Left Front itself and from various affiliated unions and others who held on to rigid conceptions of class politics and "democratic centralism."

The PPC was based on the principle that more than a third of planned investment should be distributed to local governments, on the condition that funding proposals should be developed through participatory planning processes, facilitated by well-trained resource persons and guided by a comprehensive set of rules. Considered in terms of the four prerequisites of social democracy discussed earlier, the PPC was innovative. The lack of established growth coalitions in Kerala between organized capital, labor, and farmers, combined with social provisioning, was addressed within the framework of participatory development institutions. Conventional unions and employers' organizations were expected to take part, but space was also provided for wider participation from informal workers and the self-employed, including *dalits* and women. In contrast to the Scandinavian social corporatism, which could not be applied in Kerala, due to weak industrialization, fragmented unions and employers' organizations, and the added challenge of a "soft" public administration, the organizational basis was democratic decentralization with a number of new supplementary participatory institutions.

Initially, the PPC was quite successful but after some time it faced five major problems. The first was insufficient linkage between measures in favor of social security and the promotion of production based on Kerala's comparative advantages, including its commercial agriculture and sectors drawing on the state's relatively high-quality education services. Second, there were unresolved problems in regard to the relations of liberal-representative democracy and direct democracy in the policy process. These might have been resolved through discussions with progressive administrators, politicians, and scholars, but blurred lines of responsibility and representation undermined deliberation. This led to distrust among them as well as the abuse of funds. A third problem was the lack of a viable strategy for involving the "conventional" interest and issue based organizations among farmers, laborers, and industrial workers related to the mainstream Left. Fourth, it was particularly difficult to engage the middle classes, given that welfare and production measures were not universal but targeted. As in other efforts at social democratic development, involvement of sections of the middle class is crucial for gaining majorities and generating broader interests in the welfare state. Fifth, sections within the major left party (the CPI-M) and the Left Front made attempts to take over and benefit from the PPC. They also refused to support leading local campaigners as candidates in elections and slandered and isolated major PPC leaders. As a result, the PPC was further weakened and it became possible for the new Congress-led government to radically alter the campaign when the Left Front lost local elections in 2000 and state elections in 2001.

Consequently, the campaigners did not succeed in generating a new democratic formula for the combination of equity and growth. The increasing rates of economic growth in Kerala since the 1900s have been more related to the liberalization of the Indian economy and the extensive remittances from more than two and a half million migrant laborers, out of a population of some 35 million, primarily from the Gulf countries. The common estimate is that the migrants send back about US$ 13 billion per year, equivalent to more than a third of Kerala's gross domestic product.

Moreover, in spite of this inflow of cash, the current growth rate is only on par with the other high-performing Indian states. The remittances have not been utilized to foster and sustain Kerala's own welfare system and its economic development. Rather, these remittances have mainly been used for consumption, house construction, and investment in the property and service sectors. In turn, these often generated more imports, speculation, environmental destruction, and greater inequality. Thus, although unemployment has been reduced, Keralites became well-paid migrant workers in other countries.

Hence there is little semblance of social democratic development in the actual transformation of Kerala in the recent decades. In addition to growing inequality and reduction of earlier efforts at building a welfare state, the rapidly expanding middle classes have few expectations from the state, perceiving it to be inefficient and corrupt, and have opted for individual solutions to precarity. While sections of the old middle classes may still be interested in defending the remnants of the welfare state, the most vulnerable people including the *adivasis*, *dalits*, and workers in the old informal sectors, in agriculture, and in industry are badly affected and have little bargaining power. Many *adivasis* agitate for land, some fisherfolk claim basic rights, and numerous people resist dispossession and environmental degradation of their land and neighborhoods. And even if some support is forthcoming from leftist political parties and civil society, the outcome is rarely positive.

There is certainly new activism in civil society, mobilizing against corruption, the high prices paid for medicines by ordinary people, as well as moral policing by conservative Hindu and Muslim communities. But coordination beyond what is possible through commercial and new social media is poor. The trade unions are defensive and rarely present in the new dynamic private sectors of the economy. It may now only be the Self Employed Women's Association, which does some organizing among informal labor. The growing problems with insecure employment relations and the need to arrange social security have not generated the renewed interest in public welfare systems that has come about in Latin America, Indonesia, and East Asia.

The Left Front Government newly elected in 2016 would certainly like to alter this situation, but their priorities remain unclear. While personal networks and clientelism are characteristic of the non-left parties, the Left Front parties remain affected by centralism and a culture of loyalty and obligation in return for favor. Not much has changed with regard to the persistent dominance of parties and politicians when people try to come together and take their problems to local government, even within self-help and residential groups and in town hall meetings. There is an obvious need for institutionalized channels of autonomous representation in government of significant interest and issue organizations. While local government institutions are now in place, they remain weak and little happens without the intervention of members of the legislative assembly and state-level ministers with access to pork barrel funds. There seems to be a growing opinion within the Left of the need to combine efforts to defend the least well off with the mobilization of financial resources for industrial and other development projects and to respond to the aspirations of the middle classes. But the contours are blurred. Kerala has essentially bypassed the stage of industrial development that was never really achieved in the 1950s and onward, in favor of postindustrial activities. The state has little of the Global North's broad labor movement and production-oriented class of employers that demonstrated themselves to be capable of negotiating social pacts and allowed for the combination of growth and welfare. As a result, Kerala needs to foster democratic organization and fora to negotiate the current phase of rapid uneven development, which, if left unchecked, threatens to dispossess the weakest sections of the population of their land, livelihood, and housing.

Conclusion

Until the late 1950s, it was possible to foster conditions for social democratic development in Kerala and partially in Indonesia. During this period, the focus on top-down political shortcuts and alliances at the expense of equal citizen rights and democracy led to stagnation in Kerala and political turmoil in Indonesia. Struggles for rights and democratization resumed, which generated new freedoms and, to some extent, held back the destructive effects of capitalism. However, in the context of elitist democracy and neoliberal economic development a number of challenges continue to confront the development of social democracy. In summary, these challenges are (i) representative institutions biased in favor of dominant actors, "money politics," and "good contacts"; (ii) a shortage of capacity among progressive actors to develop broad-based transformative policies and politics; and (iii) protective and targeted welfare policy proposals introduced at the expense of productive, and universal, reforms that might be capable of attracting wider support, including that from the middle classes and employers. Local attempts to establish participatory development, moreover, have been difficult to combine with representative democracy and interest-based organizations. In that respect, it has proven particularly difficult to scale up beyond villages and town halls and to avoid capture by established elites and parties.

Yet, this is not the end of social democracy. It is true that the political shortcuts to progress have undermined democratic efforts to fight the rise of authoritarian capitalism, that today's elitist democracies are shallow, and that uneven development in the South implies that it is unlikely that the social democracies of the North can be repeated. Nevertheless, it is also evident that the shallow democratization and uneven development have given rise to new contradictions and these bring to mind Karl Polanyi's (1944) arguments about the rise of broader counter-movements in the North. These, he explained, were a response to the nineteenth-century pursuit of economic liberalism, which attempted to make a reality of the capitalist claim that markets are self-regulating. This view may also apply to the current global resistance against uneven development.

Yesterday's counter-movement in northern states depended upon the establishment of an alliance of a much broader set of social groups and interests than those of workers alone, even in circumstances of labor-intensive industrialization when there were massive battalions of more or less well-organized workers in a burgeoning proletariat. As Polanyi saw it, not only workers but also peasants and landed elites and fractions of the middle classes came together in defense of society and in favor of public policies against the destructive effects of economic liberalism. While parts of Polanyi's analysis can be challenged, his emphasis on the importance of building a broad-based coalition among key actors in support of social justice is surely theoretically valid and empirically supported in the history of the South too. Are there any prospects for the development of such broad-based coalitions and public policies, with a social democratic orientation, in the present?

The Indonesian and Indian experiences point to three such tendencies. First, unions need to link up with broader sections of labor, particularly those in the informal sector, to sustain their bargaining power in response to the very uneven character of growth. This general tendency is confirmed by the broad alliances of labor, peasants, the new middle-class precariat, and others in the historical struggle for progressive policies in Brazil and South Africa. The humiliating defeat of the left front government in West Bengal is a warning of what is to be expected in South Africa if the African National Congress (ANC) and the mainstream unions do not consider the problem of unemployment in particular (Seekings and Natrass 2015).

Second, the widening interest in the legislated regulation of working conditions, social security, and other welfare schemes is promising, specifically on the part of unions as well as broader sections of labor, rural and urban poor, and the middle-class precariat. There are uphill challenges in terms of developing and negotiating labor market institutions and social security and welfare policies that protect people, including the middle classes, and in strengthening their bargaining power while simultaneously fostering effective production. Perhaps more difficult is the lack of trust in public institutions and administration and their capacity to implement impartial programs and services.

Third, there is extensive interest in widening the long-standing middle-class struggle against corruption, in regard to preferential treatment and the abuse of tax payers' money, to a broader array of citizen concerns. While the populist Aam Aadmi Party in New Delhi is embroiled in many problems, its landslide victory in 2015 is a testament to the potential of widening anticorruption campaigns from a focus on prominent offenders to combatting undemocratic governance and the abuse of welfare and other services intended for ordinary people. Similarly, the Indonesian president Jokowi's rise to power is due in large measure to consultations and agreements with the urban poor as a precondition for metropolitan development. However, improved popular organizing and representation are absolutely necessary to sustain and foster such cooperation and agreement.

Such developments suggest that the new contradictions of uneven development can open up spaces for the renewal of social democracy through an alternative sequencing of its basic pillars. The extensive welfare state in Scandinavia grew out of the struggle by strong labor movements for citizen rights and this, in turn, led to the establishment of the social compacts which provided a platform for both economic growth and the development of comprehensive welfare states. In the global South, in contrast, it would seem that the struggle to negotiate social rights, welfare policies, and the right to decent work will need to take place before the establishment of growth pacts can be considered. Concerted struggles for welfare rights and the fair implementation of policies, furthermore, could lead to stronger and more unified organizations and the broad-based coalitions necessary to negotiate a growth path which combines equity and development.

From these specific contexts, we argue, five clusters of experiences from the Scandinavian history remain instructive. First, the problems of ineffective governance in the South call to mind the successful Swedish anticorruption reforms of the nineteenth century. These were carried out by the state before the formal advent of democracy, but they were implemented with the full support of an active and locally rooted citizenship (Svensson 2016). Without the support of an active citizenry, the focus in the South today on rules, regulations, and anticorruption agencies will not make much sense even if there are more committed leaders and bureaucrats at the top. In Scandinavia, active citizenship had developed in the old parishes and among the independent farmers, in combination with increasingly efficient states. The efforts in the South at similar citizenship have often been associated with decentralization and participatory local governance. The Kerala's people's planning campaign entailed a combination of central direction and local involvement, and the Brazilian participatory budgeting process was dependent on political intervention. While similar initiatives in South Africa were politically dominated by the ANC, which, in itself, created problems, the attempts in Indonesian have tended to be depoliticized, but without the regulations and democratic space necessary to ensure that the rights and capacity necessary to control the village elites are extended to ordinary villagers.

Second, all these efforts have suffered from localism as so many crucial issues cannot be managed solely at the level of town hall meetings. Here too the Scandinavian experiences are instructive. With industrialization it was necessary to scale up poverty relief in municipalities and through civil societies to universal state welfare programs. Agricultural communities were unable to take care of all the new laborers, and associations and unions could not assist all the vulnerable people (Sandvik 2016). In the global South today, attempts at local citizenship and self-help, such as through participatory budgeting, must also be related to universal welfare systems and social rights. Otherwise, it is impossible to contain the abuse of power at the central level (e.g., Brazil), put up a fight in global labor markets, and provide alternatives to private insurance for the rich and authoritarian and religious charity for the poor.

Third, what can be done to the poor representation of ordinary people and crucial interests in the context of elitist democratization and fragmented civil societies? What about the fake direct contacts between "the people" and populist politicians in addition to the informal transactions between the same politicians and leaders in civil society and popular organizations? Much of the unique Scandinavian trust in universal state and municipality programs was based on the representation of interested organizations in public policy making and administration. In the South, this is an unresolved issue.

Fourth, the shortage of transformative policies brings to mind Scandinavian practices, especially with regard to welfare, social rights, and rights in working life. Universal instead of targeted reforms attracted the middle classes too, thus making them willing to pay higher taxes. Protective welfare reforms, such as education, health, child care, and unemployment insurance, that were also productive attracted business too. Measures toward full employment increased production and the tax base. And when subsidies were involved, they were often less costly than handouts and resulted in important but unprofitable work being done. In addition, public welfare reforms that reduced the costs of labor, such as free higher education, were another way to foster wage compression, in addition to social pacts, thus increasing competitiveness in the economy, investments, and the number of jobs.

Fifth, not even the strong Scandinavian labor movement was able to win elections and implement reforms on its own, even when women became increasingly active. There was a need for broad alliances with the farmers about welfare for all and protection against displacement, to gain a majority in the parliament and to boost reforms and foster growth pacts.

In fact, this also contained right-wing populist fascism and national social-ism. In the South, the divisive class structure and organization, in addition to the ills of right-wing populism, makes broad alliances even more im-portant.

Finally, international "Global Deals" must be accompanied by the provision of support to local actors who can come together and enforce them. In fact, these principles should also be the bottom line in interna-tional social democratic support of democracy, given that broad counter-movements and interest-based representation are fundamental precon-ditions for alternative parties and the improvement of flawed democra-cies. To make a difference, the actors of change must include broader alli-ances that grow out of the contradictions of the current globalized and unbalanced development than the more firmly working-class-based movements in the North. An immediate step ahead would be to bring dy-namic actors together in a world forum toward sustainable social demo-cratic development which would include concerned scholars as well as ac-tivists and union leaders, social movements, civil society organizations, and their corresponding political parties with possible Scandinavian seed funding.

References

Polanyi, K. (1944). The great transformation: Social and economic origins of our times. Boston, MA: The Beacon Press.

Sandvik, H. (2016). From local citizenship to the politics of universal welfare: Scandinavian Insights. In: Törnquist, O. and Harriss, J. with Chandhoke, N. and Engelstad, F. (Eds.), Reinventing social democratic development. Insights from Indian and Scandinavian comparisons. Copenhagen: NIAS Press and New Delhi: Manohar.

Seekings, J. and Nattrass, N. (2015). Policy, politics and poverty in South Africa. New York: Palgrave Macmillan.

Svensson, T. (2016). Strengthened control or fostering trust? Indian politics and Scandinavian experiences. In: O. Törnquist and J. Harriss, with, N. Chandhoke, and F. Engelstad (Eds.), Reinventing social democratic development. Insights from Indian and Scandinavian Comparisons. Copenhagen/New Delhi: NIAS Press, Manohar.

On the Sociocultural Foundations of Democratic Capitalism: Experiences from the Norwegian Case

Ole Johnny Olsen

Neoliberal globalization, of whatever kind or form, threatens political democracy in the global South as in the global North. In the South, the evolution of young democracies is constrained, and, in the North, established
forms of democratic capitalism are in crisis (Streeck 2014). While the
South struggles to escape from the remnants of old forms of domination,
the North is experiencing increasing social inequality, the return of social
insecurity, and eroding faith in the ability of political democracies to manage the problems of everyday life. Even in Scandinavia, the home of welfare capitalism's "social democratic regimes" (Esping-Andersen 1990),
where economic growth has been balanced with social equality and democracy, these problems are seen to be growing.[1] Although the core elements of a well-functioning welfare state are still intact and, compared to
other parts of Europe, the economic and social conditions of ordinary people are above average, Scandinavians have not escaped the pressure of neoliberal globalization. The outsourcing of core industries, increased labor
competition through the extension of the EU's internal labor market, pressure on institutions regulating the labor market, increasing social inequality, and deepening political divisions on issues relating to refugees and labor migration are all part of the new reality. So too are the consequences
of these changes: growing uncertainty among ever larger parts of the population, individual withdrawal from collective organization, and growing
mistrust of public institutions and political elites. Among social scientists
and in public debate the question is not whether, but to what extent, the
Scandinavian social democratic regimes are challenged, and to what degree the democratic order of capitalism has been eroded.

---

[1]   "Social democracy" here does not refer primarily to the fact that these countries
        were governed by social democratic parties for long periods of time after World
        War II, although this was the case. Rather, it relates to the existence of a broad
        social democratic hegemony that shaped the economic, social, and political order
        which evolved in these countries during this period. See Sejersted (2005/2011).

In his essay collection *Ill Fares the Land*, which examines states on both sides of the North Atlantic, Tony Judt (2010) maintains that recent generations have reflected too little on historical development to comprehend the depth and the scope of the fundamental transformations that are underway in institutions in contemporary society. This is one of the reasons why, he argues, the agents of neoliberal transformation have had such an easy path, and why change has, so to speak, crept up behind people's backs. He may well be right. We need to examine the social and cultural foundations of democracy if we are to understand the nature and value of what is under attack, and we must look at the historical formation and institutionalization of that which is being attacked, if we wish to retain it; I shall try to do so in this chapter. In thus doing I will focus on the Norwegian case and will try to describe the principal features of the sociocultural foundations of democratic capitalism in this country, and particularly, on how this developed in the post-World War II era.

I limit the discussion to Norway mainly because this is the case I know best. I will draw on a variety of contributions by Norwegian historians and social scientists as well as on my own historical-sociological research on Norwegian labor history. When comparing Norway with the other Scandinavian countries the prominent Norwegian economic and political historian Francis Sejersted (1993) argued that the label "democratic capitalism" was especially well suited to Norway. As a consequence, analysis of the Norwegian case might be considered particularly relevant for the general purposes of the chapter. Furthermore, if the mission of a Norwegian sociologist is to understand the specific conditions for Norway's democratic capitalism, it is also to understand the conditions of democracy in general.

A particular interest of this volume is to examine the possibility of a fruitful transfer of knowledge from Scandinavian experiences to the development of democratic formations in the South. Of course such formations have their own very specific conditions, created by historical and local circumstances, and, more than ever, by global relations. The transfer of knowledge in this case, consequently, could only be of a general kind, for example as a kind of inspiration or as imaginaries of possible roads to democratization. Notwithstanding this caveat, the historical trajectories of Norway and some states in the South do, after all, share some common features. Although Norway was never a colony and, in contrast to many

other European countries, its population was never subjected by aristo-
cratic class structures, it succeeded in transforming itself from a deeply
class-divided society into a more egalitarian one at the turn of the twentieth century. It did so by transforming the nation from one governed by a
small elite of civil servants and a variety of rising industrial capitalists, and
dominated by the hegemony of the traditional patrimonialism of the large
farmers, into a society characterized by a high level of social equality in
the decades after World War II. This society, furthermore, maintained a
relatively strong cultural cohesion and consensus on the values of a welfare state and on the possibilities of individual development and democratic participation which it offered.

A hundred years ago, if a working man, whether a farmhand or a paid
factory worker, lived in poverty and conditions of uncertainty, over the
course of the century he was able progressively, to leave behind those conditions and advance to a situation of seemingly ever-growing material and
social wealth in the second half of the twentieth century. Not only this, if
a working man approached his superior a hundred years ago, he was
likely to stand cap in hand, as expected by the norms of the time. Seventy
years later, he was likely to meet his superior on equal terms, supported
by values and social norms of equity and mutual respect internalized on
both sides. The working man could see himself as an equal to his employer, on a collective level through his labor organization and, on an individual level, as a human being and citizen. Over the years, the normali-
zation of social equivalence filled up the capillaries of everyday life—in
politics, in schools, in public discourse, at work, and in civil society. Social
security provided independence and social equality opened up the possibility of reciprocity and mutual recognition, both basic conditions for the
socialization of democratic citizens and their participation in democratic
institutions (Honneth 2014; Castoriadis 1997).

Equality was always relative, of course, as was mutual recognition
between social groups. Naturally, there are disagreements between people and researchers as to exactly how egalitarian Norwegian society had
become. Nevertheless, from a historical as well as from a comparative national perspective, the nation's transformation into a highly egalitarian social democratic formation cannot be denied. However, the question posed
in this volume remains, in what way can an analysis of the conditions for
transformation in a Scandinavian country be of relevance to the struggle

for democratic development in the global South? The chapter is written with this question in mind and it will be pursued more explicitly in a concluding discussion.

Capitalism and Democracy—and the Conditions for an "Ill-Suited Marriage"[2]

In an introductory essay to his major comparative study of Scandinavian states (Sejersted 2005/2011), Francis Sejersted discusses the relationship between capitalism and democracy. His point of departure is as simple as it is insightful. "As ideal types," he asserts, "capitalism means that societal power is in the hands of the capitalists" or, as he puts it more explicitly, "of those who have control over the means of production," while, on the other hand, "democracy means that power is in the hands of the people" (2003).

This definition of capitalism is easy to grasp. The control of the means of production gives the power not just to decide what to produce, but true societal power also lies in the dependence this control creates for those without the means of production. People left with no other means than their own human labor power are totally dependent on the buyers of that labor, the capitalists. In this dependency lies the roots of heteronomy for formally free laborers and it is the basis of capitalist domination.

The problem, as Marx pointed out, is that the worker is "free in a double sense." "As a free individual he can dispose of his labour-power as his own commodity," but on the other hand, as he has no other commodities, he is free of them too. "He is free of the objects needed for the realization of his labour." For the nineteenth century's liberal democrats, the principle idea of democracy was the legal/state protection of private property, hence the legal protection of capitalism. This is why Marx and the socialists and communists of the nineteenth century dismissed the idea of bourgeois democracy. Rather than bourgeois democracy, they argued, the goal should be socialism, the abolition of private property, and control over the means of production. Their argument was that only in this way could "real democracy" be founded.

---

[2] Wolfgang Streeck's expression (2016).

Since then, historians and sociologists have repeatedly discussed why the emerging labor movement in Europe and the United States deviated from its "historic mission" (Lipset 1981) of breaking with capitalism and building socialism and opted, instead, to follow the path of transforming capitalism from within, by imposing restrictions and introducing social reforms. At this conjuncture, as we now know, it was Bernstein and not Marx (with Bebel) who won the internal struggle within the labor movement, at least in northern Europe. In German, as in the Scandinavian Labour Parties, the nonrevolutionary/reformist social democratic movement assumed the leading role as the twentieth century progressed.

The social democratic labor movement, one may say, transformed into what, in this chapter, I call democratic capitalism. They laid the ground for what Wolfgang Streeck characterizes as "the marriage between democracy and capitalism, ill-suited partners brought together in the shadow of World War Two" (2016: cover text). However "ill-suited," I don't think Streeck would hold that this marriage was a mistake but, rather, as the most reasonable option at the time, or perhaps of any time. There is no question that if democracy means that power is in the hands of the people, this also restricts the power, and the freedom, of the capitalists. As a consequence, "democratic capitalism" can be seen as a contradiction in terms. As Dietrich Rueschemeyer et al. (1992) argue: "However we define democracy, it means nothing if it does not entail rule or participation by the many." Hence, "political democracy inevitably stands in tension with the system of social inequality" and with the system of capitalism as a class-divided society. "In a class-divided society, the many have less income and wealth, less education, and less honour than the few. Above all, they have individually less power" (Rueschemeyer et al. 1992: 271).

What then does it mean to say that power is in the hands of the people under capitalism? How can we specify the conditions for, and the content of, such a form of democracy? The first step must entail a reduction of the power of capitalists. As is common in most of the literature on this subject, whether in a Marxian, Polanyian, or general economic history discourse, I accept the historical process of embedding the market economy within "democratic capitalism" as the outcome of a class compromise that balances the power of the capitalist class with the mobilized power of the labor movement.[3] History has shown that this process of embedding took various forms and paths, but a general condition was the organizing of the growing working class and its capacity to unite and defend collective interests. Union building, successful struggles for collective agreements, and management of competition between workers established the power base for a class compromise that led to employment security and pay based on a relative share of increased productivity. At the national level, states became third parties in the class compromise, introducing insurance programs that covered injury, ill health, and unemployment, and, more generally, protection against the impact of the market on individual citizens. In the history of welfare capitalism such programs have been of two kinds: one offered comprehensive insurance, where the conditions for a good life formed part of one's rights as a citizen, while another provided cover for only the most basic of social needs (Marshall 1950 2000; Esping-Andersen 1992). It is only the first, universal, kind which provides real security and freedom from the domination of the market. The second is always premised on the principle that those who are not able to feed themselves through their own labor are inferior members of society; since they need help they cannot expect the same rights and standard of living as others.

Here we arrive at the distinctive hallmarks of democracy. The "institutionalization of class conflict" through collective agreements and the mutual recognition of organizations as contractual partners were, and are, certainly an important condition for social security for working people. The systems developed for collective bargaining and labor law also constitute important arenas for social exchange, the establishment of common norms, and trust building. First and foremost, however, these

---

3   As Rueschemeyer et al. point out in their study on the foundations of democracy under capitalism, "Though the working class has not proved to be the gravedigger of capitalism, it has very frequently been capable of successfully demanding its own political incorporation and accommodation of at least some of its substantive interests." The specific results may have varied but overall both sides have seen the advantages of the compromise. "Democratic capitalism rests on a class compromise between labour and capital in which the interests of both sides are to varying extents accommodated." The outcome of this has been the significant power of both sides. We can agree with Rueschemeyer et al. that "capitalist development and democracy are related primarily through these changes of the balance of class power."

systems remain a mechanism for the resolution of class conflict. Their fundamental objective is reconciliation of the "naked power" of interests, of capital versus labor. Democracy on the other hand is a form of rule *within* a group, a collectivity. For modern political democracy this group was constituted by the people within what developed as the national state, who became their citizens through this process. And as we know, democracy developed by expanding the content of citizenship and by integrating an ever larger proportion of this group as full members of society.

Using the concept introduced by T.H. Marshall (1950, 2000), from the time of the "democratic revolutions" of the eighteenth century the point of departure was a limited form embodied in the notion of "civil citizenship" (which entailed the right to justice, freedom of speech, thought and religion, and the right to own property). It was only after a century or more of political struggle that this was expanded to include political citizenship, identified with the core element of democracy, "the right to participate in the exercise of political power" (2000: 32). People without property, such as male workers, were first given such rights in Western democracies around the turn of the twentieth century. Women, in general, were accorded these rights even later. In other words, these large groups of people were not seen as full members of society, or as proper citizens. This is why, as some historians have argued, we should not characterize the young nation-states of the nineteenth century as democracies (Stråth 2016).

But there is still one element needed to flesh out the meaning of citizenship. The formal right to participate in ruling a society means nothing if its members are not also given realistic rights and capabilities enabling them to fulfill their tasks and obligations as democratic citizens. At this point we are back to the social element of the founding principal of democracy, which involves the "rule or participation of the many." In Marshall's words, this element covers a whole range of rights, "from the right to a modicum of economic welfare and security to the right to share to the full in the social heritage and to live the life of a civilized being according to the standards prevailing in the society" (p. 32). As we see here, he points not only to the need for social security and freedom from economic dependence, but he also underlines the necessity of intellectual and cultural capacity as a condition for full membership of a society. He specifies that "[t]he institutions most closely connected with" this social citizenship "are the educational system and the social services."

In similar ways philosophers and political theorists alike have asserted that it is not enough to establish (formal) democratic political rules; equally important is the development of the capacities of the people to take part in that rule through democratic processes. In fact, a basic value in modern societies is the idea of a free, independent/autonomous individual, which is both a condition for democratic participation and a manifestation of that same democracy. Autonomy implies both independence and self-development. It represents freedom from domination and freedom to act and participate in society; it provides both security—the right to be oneself—and recognition, basic conditions for the development of self-respect, self-confidence, and self-esteem (Honneth 2014).

For a democratic society it is therefore necessary to develop institutions that further the socialization of autonomous individuals. Castoriadis (1997) argues that democracy has to do with the institutions regulating the power dimensions in a group or a society; it has to do with politics. In a democratic regime "the many" have been able to establish institutions for self-governance through participation by independent, autonomous members of the group or the society. A set of key rules and institutions are therefore precisely those that secure and develop individual autonomy. A democratic regime consists of some kind of agreement or consensus about general values, the appreciation of common goods, and how to establish norms and rules for managing them. Democracy, as procedure, is the process of participation by autonomous individuals in the construction and reconstruction of that regime. We shall now proceed to look at the evolution of the regime of democratic capitalism in Norway and the sociocultural foundations of the development of autonomy and democratic life within it.

The Evolution of Norwegian Democratic Capitalism

Norway formed part of the Danish kingdom for about 400 years, until the end of the Napoleonic wars (1814) when the peace treaty of Kiel handed the country to the Swedish king. However, in the vacuum created by unsettled state power at the end of the war, Norwegian national elites mobilized for independence and succeeded in creating a separate constitution that granted Norway autonomy in domestic affairs. In the years to come, although loyal to the Swedish king, the regime of nationally oriented senior civil servants actively supported the growth of an independent Norwegian economy based on the entrepreneurship of the local petite bourgeoisie. From a relatively weak and self-sufficient agrarian economy, what has been called a state initiated capitalism (Sejersted 1993) developed during the first half of the nineteenth century.

In the second half of the century, ideas of, and interest in, national independence grew ever stronger, culminating in the demand that governments should be appointed based on the majority in parliament and not on the independent will of the king. The liberal Left party took the lead in this process, representing a broad mixture of interest groups from the petite bourgeois and big farmers to artisan leaders and the new labor organizations. Eventually, in 1884, a parliamentary system was established, but at the time there was no universal suffrage for all men and the right to vote was restricted as both the liberal Left and, even more so, the conservative Right party were opposed to the idea. In Norway, as in the rest of liberal modernity, political elites saw universal suffrage as a threat to the propertied classes. This demand became a central issue for workers' organizations and for the new Labour Party established in 1887. Despite broad skepticism, the mobilization of the workers' associations and the Labour Party bore fruit and democratic ideas also found fertile soil among liberal elites. The right to vote was granted to all adult men in 1900 and, 3 years later, following strong mobilization in the growing progressive women's movement, this right was extended to all adult women in 1913.

In the industrial expansion in Norway which began at the end of the nineteenth century, the construction of hydroelectrical power stations played a central role. A stable supply of cheap electrical power was a basic condition for the development of chemical and electrometallurgical industries in several places around the country. Given the lack of Norwegian private capital for such investments, a farsighted nationally oriented government granted international capital concessions to produce and use power on long, but not permanent, terms. Beside wood processing and mechanical industry (especially shipbuilding), this chemical and electrometallurgical industry became the backbone of Norwegian industry in the first part of the twentieth century.

Class Compromises

With industrialization came proletarization. A growing proportion of the population became wage laborers and with that, what the public discourse in nineteenth-century Europe defined as the "social problem" rapidly increased. Those without paid work had no means of a livelihood and were dependent on the support of others for their survival (see Castel 2003). This problem was aggravated by a growing population, which saw an increase from 1 million people in 1820, to 2 million in 1890, and to 3 million in 1940. One response to this was a wave of migration to the United States, especially from the 1860s onward, and in just over a century about 800,000 Norwegians migrated to the United States alone. Another state response was inspired by Bismarck's solutions to the growing social problem in Germany and the manner in which he managed the accompanying labor unrest and threat of radicalization. Based on this approach, around 1900 the Norwegian government introduced a number of progressive labor laws and social programs. The most significant contributory factor in the movement for social security, however, came through the growing strength of the nascent labor movement. As early as 1907, the metal workers' union had succeeded in ensuring the introduction of a national labor agreement and this was the first of many such collective agreements in other sectors in the years to come. In Norwegian labor history it is often called the "first-class compromise."

A "first" compromise is inevitably be followed by a "second," and so it was. The second, and in many ways most decisive, compromise was achieved in the 1930s. The preceding 20–25 years had been a period of long and bitter class conflict, but by the mid-1930s both sides had developed policies for compromise and cooperation and this story will be discussed later.

Around the end of World War I, the labor movement in Norway went through a period of radicalization. For many workers patient union struggle was no longer enough; they wanted more direct class action aimed at immediate improvement in working conditions and, thereafter, the introduction of socialist rule and a socialist economy. The Labour Party adopted a revolutionary program, elected a group of revolutionary leaders, and became a member of the Third International (Comintern) in 1919. This membership, however, did not last long; the majority of elected delegates to the Labour Party congress in 1923 voted against the Comintern program and the party was expelled by the Third International as a consequence. Following this, a breakaway group established a new Communist Party. However, this party was only ever a little brother to the Labour Party, and it shrank even further in size in succeeding years. Although radical ideology and the rhetoric of class struggle remained a common theme of the labor movement in the years after the split, following a period of protracted contestation over the path to be followed, new ideas of social reformist policy and political orientation gained ground.

The labor movement had experienced severe setbacks throughout the 1920s. A deep economic crisis in the early 1920s had given employer organizations the upper hand, and they maintained this dominance throughout the decade and into the next. The threat of unemployment was used to fight the unions and to weaken workers' labor rights (few as these might be). Union membership declined and took years to recover to the levels of the pre-crisis era. But recover they did, and despite many strike losses and employer lockouts, the unions, and the labor movement as a whole, grew ever stronger into the "hard Thirties." On the political right and within employers' organizations, strong voices argued for a more confrontational response to the labor movement. While some wanted "a finite confrontation" (Olstad 1991), others were more reluctant to use aggressive power and foresaw the possibility of a cooperative strategy. The debate within the political right on the course of action to follow, as one of the leading historians of that period has described it, oscillated between a strategy of the "open hand" and that of a "hooded fist" (Danielsen 1984).

In the end, the "open hand" approach gained ground among employers. Despite their relative strength, and the victories that they had won in various labor disputes, they saw that unions had once again grown in size and that they had repeatedly demonstrated both a willingness and the capacity to defend their interests against hostile labor policies. At the same time, they could also see that the Labour Party, itself, was gradually abandoning its once revolutionary program in favor of a policy of social reforms within a liberal democratic order. As a consequence, in the interwar years the work of parliament became ever more central with every succeeding election. Within organized labor union, leaders expressed their support for a new tactic: a willingness to cooperate with employers in their efforts to rationalize production methods and improve productivity, provided the latter gave up their hostile labor policies.

The first outcome of this political U-turn was a general agreement reached in 1934 between the national trade union federation LO and the employers' central organization, on how all future disputes between them should be handled. A basic principle in this agreement was the explicit acceptance of the legitimacy of the unions and their shop stewards by the employers, in return for the unions' acceptance of the employers' right to manage and rule production (as capitalist, private owners). The rights and duties of both sides were described in detail and common interests and obligations in respect to improving work conditions and productivity were clearly delineated. By 1933 the Labour Party had already become the biggest political party in the national assembly, but it was not yet large enough to form a government on its own. In 1935, however, following a settlement with the political representatives of the farmers on specific interests such as improved milk prices, the Labour Party was able to displace the sitting bourgeois government a year before the scheduled elections in 1936. They remained in government after this election and held power for the next 30 years, including a five-year period during the war when, due to the German occupation of Norway, the government operated in London.

With the significant class compromise between labor and capital and a lesser one between labor and farmers, the era of social democracy reached its apogee. The interruption of World War II had not weakened the compromise that had been established. On the contrary, it found a new platform in common resistance against the Nazi regime and in the extensive political dialogue between central actors on both left and right during their years of exile in Sweden. After the war the Labour Party was able to reestablish its government based on the ideas and principles of a Common Programme which had been developed through these discussions. In the years to come, the governmental program was, in all respects, shaped by the ideas and visions of the leading figures in the Labour Party. The decades that followed would become what Francis Sejersted has described as "the happy moment of social democracy" (2005/2011). However, what were the visions of a social democracy in Norway, and what justifies characterization of this period as a "happy moment"?

Social Democratic Consensus

In the aftermath of the war there were widespread expectations, in the labor movement and among the working class in general, of social change and an improvement in the living conditions of working people. Labor received around 45% of the popular vote in all elections until the 1970s. Support for the Communists surged in the 1945 elections when they received 12% of the vote—a sign both of the recognition of their prominent role in the wartime resistance and the radical hopes of parts of the working class. However, the party quickly lost support with the onset of the Cold War and the threat of a communist takeover. In this context, there was fertile ground for social democratic policies and, indeed, even for socialism itself. At this stage, however, social democracy remained an ideal and the question was, as it always had been, conceptually what did it consist of and how might it be achieved?

Although leading thinkers in the labor movement shared the broad vision of their members, they also saw the need to caution against the adoption of ideas that had failed in the past. Within their ranks strong ideas of class politics still prevailed as did a belief in traditional labor tactics and, particularly, in the power of industrial action. For the union leadership, anxious to steer a new course, it was imperative to prevent this kind of action. In the first national LO congress convened after the war in 1946, a considerable amount of emphasis was placed on the need to rebuild the economy and on the primacy of production politics before class politics. The message, as reflected in a key address to the congress, was: "The situation is different from earlier days. It is not the time for class struggle any more. Now *we* are behind the wheel" (see Olsen 1984). Much energy was spent in imparting this message to the representatives of the labor organizations present at the congress and, through them, in informing the public on the course to be followed. Where this did not succeed and the new approach was rejected, organizational sanctions were applied against those obstructing progress.

At the central level, a number of ideas were discussed on how society might govern economic growth although only a few were eventually implemented seriously. One idea was to build a corporate system to advise and coordinate the development of different sectors and branches of in-

dustry. Another was the idea of nationalizing ("socializing") core industries. Both were implemented to some extent, but the corporate system
became much more restricted and less influential than its principal archi-
tects had hoped. The main achievement of nationalization was the construction of a state-owned ironworks. Economic governance was affected
through various state regulations and illustrative of this, a law regulating
wages was introduced early on, and was more or less accepted by all social
partners. Other legislative proposals contained more radical ideas and
were vigorously opposed by employers and the political right. These suggested enabling legislation both for the regulation of prices and for rationalization, meaning that ministries would have the right (and the duty) to
instruct firms and branches on pricing, on investment and organizational
issues, and even on such questions as whether or not the closure of a business was warranted. These proposed laws, which were hotly debated in
the early 1950s, were the closest the Labour government came to introducing what could be called a socialist program of change. Under these
laws the government would have acquired the right to intervene in the
control of private property and in the means of production.

On this issue F. Sejersted makes an interesting comment: the central
argument against the introduction of these laws was made not by those
defending private property or those concerned about the dangers of socialism. Rather, they came from the leading actors of the political right
who felt that these laws represented a severe attack on the principles of a
state governed by the rule of law (*rettsstat*). Political practice based on
these laws, they argued would restrict transparency and parliamentary
oversight and would, in effect, cede all power to the state. Concerns over
a weakening of the rule of law became the main reason for the withdrawal
of all of the most radical law reform proposals. Indeed, it is reported, some
of the leading lawyers within the core of the Labour Party circles, themselves, played a leading role in the decision to moderate these laws (Sejersted 2005/2011).

From the outcome of this debate one may draw two general conclusions about the basic values, or normative consensus, of political parties
of the time. First, if the defense of conservative values and attacks on com-
munism were part of the daily rhetoric of the political right, arguments
for the interests of private capital and for free market capitalism were not
advanced, or not at least to the same extent. Recognition of the need for,

and the legitimacy of, political regulation of the economy was widely shared across social groups. Second, if Labour Party technocrats were eager proponents of regulation, their proposals were justified not in terms of socialist ideology but rather by general concerns about the need for rational central planning. When these proposals were seen to challenge the principles of a state governed by the rule of law, they were withdrawn. In so doing, the Labour Party confirmed a position it had held since the early 1930s, namely that of the fundamental recognition of liberal democracy (Sejersted 2005/2011). With this position, the advocates of social democracy also recognized actually existing capitalism. Just as the senior state officials of the early nineteenth century had recognized the need for capitalism, the social democratic regime put forward policies for organizing and preparing the conditions for the development of the same economic system.

Following the first phase, introduced in the aftermath of World War II and characterized by legal regulation, the second phase, which began in the 1960s, saw more proactive efforts to industrialize and modernize the economy by establishing special state banks in support of development and by new investment in all economic sectors. Furthermore, a corporate system to elicit the views of different interest groups in government decision making was methodically developed and formalized along with the establishment of various expert panels that provided input on policy-making processes.

At the social level, the government delivered welfare programs based on universal principles, extended compulsory education through comprehensive schools, and laid the ground for equal access to higher education—all of these reforms were fully implemented in the 1960s. In the same period, the wage agreements entered into by business and labor began to bear fruit as productivity increased and the economy grew. To that extent, the social democratic regime had fully succeeded in bringing social and economic security to working people, but what about democracy?

What Kind of Democracy?

The character of Norwegian democracy was a central theme of debate among historians in the 1960s and 1970s. An influential proposition on this subject was advanced by the leading postwar historian, Jens Arup

Seip, in a lecture to the Student Association in 1963. His pointed argument was that postwar Norway could be characterized as a "one-party state," under the leadership of the labor movement. This, Seip asserted, was not a socialist state. Rather, he maintained with rhetorical elegance, the Labour Party had had the courage to put into practice the ideas that the social liberal Left party had embraced in the early part of the century but had been unable to implement, namely the need for social security programs. Not only this, the anxieties that industrial capital had harbored about the radicalism of the labor movement had vanished. Under the Labour Party regime, he asserted, "the managers had to their surprise entered paradise." Active state support of industrial growth and confidence in the productivity which long-term cooperation would bring had created good conditions for industry. Added to this, any internal impatience or radicalism within sectors of labor was dealt with through organizational means. "The labour movement," as he puts it "had been transformed into an apparatus with which to move people."

Seip's thesis became a central reference point for discussion in the following decades, and, indeed, for the second leading postwar historian, Edvard Bull. While Seip was politically at a distance from the labor movement, Bull identified with it and could take a different critical position. When describing the political economy of postwar Norway (1979), he followed Seip's main idea, but introduced a more nuanced conceptualization. To the system of cooperative industrial growth and political regulation of the market economy that evolved in the 1950s and 1960s, he gave the label "organized capitalism"; this was a concept which was familiar to German historians and which was later picked up by economic sociologists to describe the Fordist era of capitalism (Lash/Urry 1987). Bull's characterization of the political regime, however, differed substantially from that of Seip. The central leadership of the labor movement, he agreed, did indeed exercise strong influence. However, he maintained, the concept of a one-party state did not adequately capture the peculiar character of the regime. This could best be described in terms of a "partnership of the elites." In this formulation he pointed to the close working relationship between organizational leaders in the economy and in politics and, not least, he referred to the profound consensus which these elites shared on the main societal goals, values, and success criteria.

Although there were different views on how best to describe power structures in Norwegian society, we can see that a common critical theme in analysis of the democracy was an emphasis on the distance, if not the gulf, between central authorities and the people. Throughout the bureaucratic, and oligarchic, processes of state building and organizational development, the lively democracy that had been animated by the active participation of the labor movement had ceased to exist, or at least had become weaker. The party had become, as Seip had termed it, an "apparatus with which to move the people." Many other studies took up this theme of the internal control and bureaucratization of the labor movement as an explanation for its capital-friendly politics and the peaceful integration of the working class into bourgeois society in the post-World War II era. My own analysis of this development (Olsen 1984) was substantially in line with this understanding. In addition, I underlined that the way in which class conflict had been institutionalized though collective agreement and labor law had had a powerful and expanding integrative effect, which had become the platform for labor politics and management strategy. This is because all such agreements had the effect of legitimizing their own basic premises and of tying up their participants in dealing with formal procedures rather than in political mobilization. A profound example of this effect can be seen in the agreement on how Taylorist rationalization tools would be introduced into industry in the 1950s. Time and work studies, supervised by special shop stewards, were carried out; disagreements were sent to arbitration by a special national committee; and all local resistance was effectively absorbed within the institutional order of what Michael Burawoy has called the "internal state" of labor relations (Burawoy 1979).

I still think that analysis of this type captures important features of class relations in postwar Norway and that the institutionalization of the class compromise, both at the level of labor/employment relations and in state politics, may, from a Marxist or socialist perspective, be seen, in the words of Olstad, as having placed the "giant in chains" (Olstad 1991). After a historic phase of mobilizing working-class power for socialism in the 1920s, the postwar decades became a period of social democratic politics and of winning hegemony within the capitalist framework. The road to this hegemony, however, was partially paved with means that were not as democratic as might have been expected, and bottom-up participation in political processes was not always as strong as that from the top.

Nevertheless, in a discussion of the foundations of democratic capitalism other features of the prevailing social relations are noteworthy. First, as Edvard Bull has always emphasized, there is no doubt that this regime was supported by a broad part of the population, and that it enjoyed considerable legitimacy even outside the ranks of its own supporters. In fact, a hallmark of the social democratic regime that evolved in twentieth-century Norway was its strong legitimacy on both sides of the class divide. The hegemony of social democracy became imprinted in social practices as well as in the ideology of practical political and economic thinking. This hegemony, as Sejersted has pointed out (2005/2011), was based on the socialist movement's adoption of the basic ideas of liberal democracy, and on a general acceptance of the ideals of a welfare state on the part of bourgeois/capitalist elites.

The argument is that even though the concept of class compromise remains highly relevant, the constitution of the democratic capitalism regime must be viewed at a deeper level. This is because the regime was based on the development of a broad community. In that regard, Sejersted sees the establishment of social democratic hegemony as a process of social integration. First, it was an integration of the working class into the nation, on both collective and individual levels. The extension of political and social rights made all individuals full members of a society defined by the borders of the nation-state. Through this process, they not only achieved political and economic status within the state, and they could increasingly identify with an "imagined community" of national citizenry (Anderson 1983). The British historian E.H. Carr (1945) describes this process as the "socialization of the nation," a conceptualization that I find very apt. One must remember, however, that this did not mean integration within a fully developed nation. On the contrary, the formation of the national state and the integration of its people must be understood as a dialectical process. During the twentieth century the national state was established step by step through the integration of social collectives and individuals. After the first- and second-class compromises, all subsequent social compacts were reached at the national level. In this process, all new laws and political practices were constructed nationally, along with new imaginaries, and the same applied to the extension of welfare state programs. The process of constructing a national framework for a democratic community was an ongoing one. Political democracy was institutionalized in the rules, rights, and conditions for participation in the formation of the nation.

The significance of this process of nation building can best be understood by contrasting it to the project of internationalism which occurred within the socialist movement in the nineteenth century. It had been a strong theme within the newly formed socialist movement that full freedom from capitalism could only be achieved by simultaneous socialist revolutions and/or change in several of the core capitalist countries. "The working class had no fatherland," it was stated, building socialism would have to be an international project, and class solidarity was international solidarity. This changed dramatically in the first half of the twentieth century when, to use another very accurate concept from E.H. Carr, what occurred was the "nationalization of socialism." This, as had occurred in the establishment of class compromises and the general integration of the working-class integration into nation building, was an endogenous process. But even more influential in the political turn away from internationalism and toward the nation was the outbreak of "the big catastrophe," World War I. This war had an enormous effect on the construction of national states, as such, and on the organization of capitalism at all levels and in all dimensions. In particular, it taught political and industrial elites how to use the state and state apparatus to coordinate and support economic growth (see Hall et al. 1996; Mann 2012). It also provided a distinct push to the socialist movement to reorient itself toward nationalism, not necessarily, or solely, in terms of chauvinism and excessive patriotism, but in its adoption of practical politics for social change. In this way, as discussed above, in something of an historical paradox (or historical irony), the groundwork for a democratization of capitalism was laid. The nation became the collectivity within which the social norms and institutional practices of a democratic regime could be woven. The construction of an autonomous social collectivity, the nation-state, as the basis for democratic rule, was, furthermore, also necessary for the construction of an autonomous democratic individual, the citizen (cf. Castoriadis 1997: 5, 15).

For Norway, World War I had not been so important for this process, since the country had retained its neutrality and had not entered the war.

In contrast, the collective experiences of occupation, resistance, and peace in and after World War II had a huge impact on the establishment of Norway as a sovereign nation-state and on the emergence of an imagined national community. In that respect, it laid the ground for a new level of national unity. It should not be forgotten that there had been conflicts along social and political divides both during the war (on collusion with the occupying German forces and between different resistance groups) and afterward. Within the labor movement the conflict between social democrats and communist in the 1950s was fierce, and, at the same time, there were distinct social and cultural cleavages between the left and right in the broader political arena. Nevertheless, when the sociocultural foundations for democracy are examined it is evident that the mutual recognition and understanding that developed across social and cultural divisions in the population during the war was very significant.

After the war, as indicated, this mutual recognition and trust developed further in the rebuilding of the Norwegian economy. In this process, moreover, it was not just the working class and its organizations that were subject to integration. Employers and the representatives of capital were also socialized in particular ways. Through this process the institutional regulation of collective bargaining and conflict resolution was not only accepted as necessary, but was widely valued in setting normative standards for working life. Cooperation with workers and their unions became the norm in handling all kinds of organizational change and in determining productivity measures; shop stewards, for instance, were routinely consulted on a firm's strategic concerns. Engagements of this type were institutionalized by adding specific clauses to the original agreement guiding the format of cooperation. There were, for example, rules for establishing firm-level committees for production and organizational development, which included representatives of both white- and blue-collar workers and those of management. These institutions that were established in the aftermath of World War II were revised and extended in the 1960s, and deepened in their practical application thereafter. Having begun as a platform for information sharing and general consultation, they played a progressively larger role in the actual processes of organizational development and modernization.

Of significance for our discussion is the fact that these institutions were viewed as a vehicle for democratizing the workplace. Although the committees had no formal right to decide on organizational change, employee participation was seen as extremely important both in finding practical solutions to organizational challenges and in legitimating their implementation. Furthermore, these institutions gave workers the right to be informed and to be consulted, and employers could no longer act without such consultation process. A significant body of social research has demonstrated the positive effects of the active involvement of employees in the workplace, both as individuals and as social collectives. In certain literature on human resource management and organizational study, this form of cooperation in the workplace has been identified as one of the factors that has contributed to economic development in Norway. This may well be true, but for our discussion it is more important to bear in mind the important role that this cooperation played in the development of the norms and values of democratic participation, both in the workplace and in society as a whole. It contributed to the norms of mutual recognition between different social groups and to the norms of participation they embodied in pursuit of the common good. Not least, as indicated above, all of these varied institutions of collective behavior contributed to the formation of the autonomous individual, both as worker and as citizen.

In this last development, we have arrived at a very important contributory factor in the sociocultural foundation of democracy: the growth of autonomous individuals, with well-developed self-confidence, self-respect, social dignity, and "reflexive freedom" to act as democratic citizens. The conditions for "reflexive" freedom (Honneth 2014) are not only about the freedom of expression and other freedoms of this kind, but they are also about the possibility of cultivating the individual skills and competencies necessary for a democratic life. The development of these competencies occurs in different arenas. In the Norwegian case I have discussed the importance of workplace recognition and the transformation that took place in this arena during the three to four decades after World War II. Together with growing income, welfare programs, and social security, this affirmation of individual worth laid the groundwork for what some historians have called a "silent revolution" (Olstad 1991) in self-understanding and self-esteem among working people. The possibility of moving into a modern flat, of building one's own home, and of buying better food, cloths, and "luxury" goods, such as televisions and even cars, laid the foundation for a new type of dignity. Ordinary workers were no longer an ocean apart from the upper middle class and the social elites. Furthermore, welfare programs gave people the status of full members of society even when they were not able to work. At the same time, national radio and television presented programs that encompassed a broad cultural heritage, wherein "ordinary" working people, whether at sea, within industry, or in the countryside, could easily identify themselves.

Of further importance was the fact that the educational system was systematically expanded. Each succeeding generation themselves not only received more or better education, but they could also see the possibility of their own children going one step further. For the generation born in the 1920s, the parents of the postwar baby boomers who became the first generation to take part in the educational revolution of the 1960s and 1970s, the changes in self-expression and social identity that occurred throughout the course of their lives were enormous. From a childhood typified by simple living conditions, the large gulf between rich and poor and uneducated and educated, the understanding that belonging to a lower class was a natural destiny which demanded respect and deference to those of a higher class, the working man was able to experience an adulthood of increasing social wealth, security, and sociocultural equality and reciprocity. Once again, we can argue that the experience of independence and self-respect created by a society in which one has become an inclusive member strongly legitimates a democratic regime and builds respect for its rules and leaders.

I follow Axel Honneth in his proposition that this dialectic of mutual recognition between individual and society, and between different groups of society, represents one of the foundation stones of democratic life. I also think that the establishment of democratic capitalism in Norway can be seen to have been based on a set of institutions of recognition, as Honneth terms them (2016: 61), in working life, in the welfare state, in education and in public and civil society as a whole.

The Social Democracy Meets Neoliberalism

The children of the first generation of democratic capitalism, the baby boomers (born between 1945 and 1955), became the first beneficiaries of the institutions of democracy with growing wealth, social welfare, and educational possibilities as objective realities. They could enter higher education with public support and with the prospect of good jobs and growing income. Notwithstanding these gains, with youthful impatience, and competence in social mobilization, this new generation of Norwegians, as in many other Western states at the time, rebelled against the social order and initiated a cultural revolution against what they perceived to be the remnants of authoritarian power structures. However, in adult life this same generation strongly supported the institutions and the ideas of social democratic hegemony. With growing self-confidence all social groups and classes in this generation could assume, as natural and self-evident, the right to participate in the formation of the social structures of their own daily lives, whether in school, at work, or in the local community, and they could do so with increasing technical and social competence.

A change came with the third generation. This was not just due to the fact that educational society imparts knowledge and reflexive skills, and thereby also contributes to meritocracy and individualization. The big change came about as a result of the complex reorganization of capitalism, an effective disorganization (Offe 1985), and the development of a "new spirit" (Boltanski/Chiapello 2005) of accumulation, which brought an end to managerial capitalism and ushered in an era of shareholder value and "casino" capitalism. Long-term economic growth was exchanged for short-term gain as neoliberal globalization made its entrance. The precariousness of labor relations and a new social insecurity once again became a feature of life in capitalist nations in the North. Step by step, democratic institutions have been weakened and continue to be weakened and damaged. We have witnessed a revolution by stealth, of "undoing the Demos," as Wendy Brown describes it in her latest book. Neoliberalism, she asserts, "is quietly undoing basic elements of democracy," which include "vocabularies, principles of justice, political cultures, habits of citizenships, practices of rule, and above all, democratic imaginaries" (Brown 2016: 17). Notwithstanding this onslaught, thus far there still remains much to defend in the political and economic order of Scandinavian countries. We can only hope that their citizens are able to mobilize for this task, and, in their struggle, unite with others in the North and the South.

Conclusion

At a general level two fundamental conditions seem necessary if democracy is to survive and develop: there should be social security for the individual and social equality between groups. These are minimum conditions for individual independence, mutual recognition, social cohesion, and the trust on which all kinds of democratic activity is based. Both conditions, however, stand opposed to the fundaments of capitalism and they can only be achieved through some form of political intervention. As had occurred in other states in the North during the era of organized capitalism, the evolution of social democratic capitalism in Norway was largely determined by this type of intervention. However, as we now know, the period of organized capitalism in the North has been replaced by an era of market liberalism and a form of political intervention which has broken down social security and led to widespread social inequality.

For countries in the South, this wind of neoliberalism has been devastating. At a time when many young democracies were setting out on a path of independent economic growth, following years of colonialism and imperialism, the dominant institutions of global capitalism, including the International Monetary Fund, Organization for Economic Cooperation and Development, and the World Bank, actively advocated the adoption of neoliberal policies, whether as a conditionality of donor aid or a part of a package of technical assistance. Under these circumstances, the protection of national growth was never given a chance and nor were policies aimed at promoting social security. However, after three to four decades of global neoliberalism, there now seems to be a slow but growing recognition of the damage which this has inflicted on the social, political, and economic fabric of most societies. Emerging out of this is a resurgence of interest in political systems capable of intervening in the capitalist economy—both for the sake of democracy and for the sake of sustainable economic development. Above all, there is a growing belief globally that the existing economic order is privileging political and economic elites at the expense of the majority.

An indication of this trend is the growing mistrust between the political elites and their constituencies in European countries and in the United States. The support for Trump, Le Pen, and Brexit are reflective of this mistrust. Popular frustration and anger, stemming from growing social uncertainty and inequality, provide fertile soil for political movements that present solutions to these problems that are far from democratic. History provides ample examples of the catastrophic outcomes of such populist movements. In Tony Judt's last public lecture in 2009 entitled "What is living and what is dead in social democracy?," he reminds us of how, in the first half of the twentieth century, similar movements that grew out of the depression, unemployment, and mass anger led to Fascism and war. John Maynard Keynes, he maintained, was the first leading scholar to advise us on the importance of drawing lessons from that experience. Foremost among these lessons was that "uncertainty—elevated to the level of insecurity and fear—was the corrosive force that had threatened and might again threaten the liberal world" (Judt 2010: 323). In order to counteract this, Judt asserts, "Keynes sought an increased role for the social security state, including but not confined to countercyclical economic intervention" (*ibid*).

As empirical evidence for his argument Keynes could point to the victory of Fascism in states, such as Germany and Italy, where democratic political systems were unable, or unwilling, to provide social security to their citizenry. These examples are well known, however, but he could also have pointed to countries, such as Norway, where there was an opposite outcome. When, in the early 1930s, the Norwegian social democratic movement reoriented their strategy on national elections in a bid for power, they did so by promising working people, whether or urban or rural, that their political platform was based on state-led growth, new jobs, and social security programs. An important component of their political program was to counter the growing support for the nationalistic right-wing party, inspired by Hitler's Nazis, which was then trying to mobilize unemployed urban workers and farm laborers. Norwegian historians have ascribed the strong upsurge in support for the social democrats in 1933 to this political reorientation, and its role in blocking the growth of a Fascist movement of any serious strength in Norway (Bjørgum 2017).

Tony Judt (2010) has also reminded us that while Keynes had argued for a social security state and political intervention in the national economy, Friedrich Hayek, the doyen of the neoliberal movement at time, had strongly warned against the advance of the Labour Party in Britain which he saw as similar to the rise of Fascism in Germany. Any state-led interference on the market, he believed, was a danger to liberal democracy. History, however, has unequivocally shown which of the two economists was right in their assumptions on this question. Keynes was right, not only in his assumptions on democratic growth, but his theories on economic development also made a significant contribution to economic growth policies adopted in the postwar era. History has also shown how a democratic state, with a broad popular mandate, supports economic development in ways very different from that of Fascism. Furthermore, it has also demonstrated how the democratic regulation of capitalism led to a growing and sustainable economy.

There are, of course, major differences between a country like Norway, which transformed into democratic capitalism in the post-war decades, and African states which began their efforts to build a democratic development state in the 1980s and 1990s. Norway was able to build its economy with the support of unconditional aid from the Marshall plan in a period of organized international capitalism. International markets were regulated by Bretton Woods institutions, economies in the global North were focused on industrial growth and the production of goods, and economic theory supported the understanding that small national economies needed some protection. In this context, a national economy could be led by regulation and by direct support. For weak emerging economies in the South the situation in the 1990s was the opposite. Not only did they have to overcome the many dimensions of underdevelopment inherited from their colonial past, but international funding agencies imposed severe conditionalities in the granting of financial loans, demanding that they open up their national economies to the international market and swamping them with neoliberal economic counselors. At the same time the process of financialization became steadily more dominant in the global economy. Growth was measured in terms of the movement of stocks and shares (playing in the brokers' casinos), rather than in terms of the production and sale of real goods. For developing states building a national economy under these conditions was not easy, if, indeed, it was possible at all. This reality has been acknowledged by several of the leading actors in the international economic realm at the time and they have borne testimony to the damage to emerging economies that was wreaked during this time. Among these Joseph E. Stiglitz, a leading adviser to President Clinton and vice president and chief economist of The World Bank in the late 1990s, has published several books critical of the failures of neoliberal politics and its contribution to growing inequality.[4]

Norwegian economic growth was very much based on small- and medium-sized firms, on industrial competence, and on knowledge cultures oriented to the solution of technical and economic problems and to new possibilities for growth. These cultures provided intellectual support in formulating industrial policies, and in shaping public authorities and administrations. Government ministries, in particular, were able to draw on the support of clusters of economic and technological competence which were committed to growth of the real economy. In contrast, for example, it has proven difficult for a country like South Africa to generate political support for real economic growth in the post-Apartheid era with a National Treasury dominated by neoliberal economists responding to the signals of global investment capital.

Besides a focus on "real" economic activity, growth in the Norwegian economy came about as a result of increased productivity. This was achieved through a production model based on cooperation and worker involvement, encouraged by profit-sharing agreements. This model not only increased productivity, but it also contributed to greater social equality and, thereby, to the social integration of the working class into the welfare society. It also had an effect similar to that of the classical "5 dollar a day" approach introduced on the eve of Fordism, in that it boosted the demand for goods and services in the national economy. The "happy moment of social democracy" in the decades after World War II, as explained, was built on the basis of a broadly defined class compromise which, from the 1930s onward, gained momentum through the power of working-class mobilization. With a class compromise in place, a process of mutual recognition and trust developed across the social divide and this led to the ideological hegemony of social democracy in this epoch. Furthermore, it demonstrated the importance of institutions that support the growth of autonomous individuals with the necessary self-respect and competence to participate in the processes necessary to sustain and defend the principles of a democratic state.

---

[4]   See for example one of his latest books *The Great Divide* (Stiglitz 2016).

References

Anderson, Benedict. (1983). Imagined communities: Reflections on the origin and spread of nationalism. London: Verso.

Bjørgum, Jorunn. (2017). Kampen om arbeiderklassen. Klassekampen, April 29, 2017.

Boltanski, Luc and Chiapello, Eve. (2005). The new spirit of capitalism. London: Verso.

Brown, Wendy. (2016). Undoing the Demos. Neoliberalism's stealth revolution. New York: Zone Books.

Burawoy, Michael. (1979). Manufacturing consent. Changes in the labor process under Monopoly capitalism. Chicago: University of Chicago Press.

Carr, E. H. (1945). Nationalism and after. London: Macmillan.

Castel, Robert. (2003) From manual workers to wage laborers. Transformation of the social question. New BrunswickTransaction Publishers.

Castoriadis, Cornelius. (1997). Democracy ass procedure and democratic as regime. Constellations, 4(1). 1-18

Danielsen, Rolf. (1984). Høyres historie: Borgerlig oppdemmingspolitikk (1918–1940). Oslo: Cappelen.

Esping-Andersen, Gøsta. (1990). The three worlds of welfare capitalism. Princeton University Press.Princeton.

Hall, Stuart, Held, David, Hubert, Don, and Thompson, Kenneth (Eds.). (1996). Modernity: An introduction to modern societies. London: Open University Press.

Honneth, Axel. (2014). Freedom's right. The social foundation of democratic life. New York: John Wiley & Sons.

Judt, Tony. (2010). Ill fares the land. A treatise on our presents discontent. New York: The Penguin Press.

Lipset, S. M. (1981). Whatever happened to the proletariat. A historic mission unfulfilled. Encounter. June 1981, 18–33.

Mann, Michael. (2012). The sources of social power: Volume 3, Global empires and revolution, 1890–1945. Cambridge: Cambridge University Press.

Marshall, T. H. (1950). Citizenship and social class and other essays. Cambridge: Cambridge University Press.

Marshall, T. H. (2000). Citizenship and social class. In: Christopher Pierson and Francis G. Castles (Eds.), The welfare state reader (pp. 32–41). Cambridge: Polity Press.

Offe, Claus. (1985). Disorganized capitalism. Contemporary transformations of work and politics. Cambridge: Polity Press.

Olsen, Ole Johnny. (1984). Makt og motstand. En studie av bedriftsorganisasjon og fagorganisasjon ved Eidanger Salpeterfabriker 1945–1975. Sosiologisk institutt, Universitetet i Bergen.

Olstad, Finn. (1991). Arbeiderklassens vekst og fall. Hovedlinjer i 100 års norsk historie. Oslo: Universitetsforlaget.

Polanyi, Karl. (1944). The great transformation. The political and economic origins of our time. Boston: Beacon Press.

Rueschemeyer, Dietrich, Evelyne, Huber Stephens, and John D. Stephens. (1992). Capitalist development and democracy. Chicago: Chicago University Press.

Seip, Jens Arup. (1963). Fra embetsmannsstat til ettpartistat, i Fra embetsmannsstat til ettpartistat og andre essays. Oslo: Gyldendal.

Sejersted, Francis. (1993). Demokratisk kapitalisme. Oslo: Universitetsforlaget.

Sejersted, Francis. (2005). Sosialdemokratiets tidsalder. Norge og Sverige i det 20. Århundre. Oslo: Pax forlag.

Sejersted, Francis. (2011). The age of social democracy. Norway and Sweden in the twentieth century. Princeton University Press.

Stiglitz, Joseph E. (2016). The great divide. London: Penguin Books

Streeck, Wolfgang. (2014). Buying time: The delayed crisis of democratic capitalism. London: Verso.

Streeck, Wolfgang. (2016). How will capitalism end? London: Verso.

Democratic Development State or Competition State? Toward the New Constitution of Neoliberal Hegemony

Tor Halvorsen

Introduction

The addition of the concept of democracy to that of developmentalism has profoundly altered the nature of the debate on the essence of developmental states. This is due, first, to the fact that the focus of analysis is now preponderantly on the democratic features of such states rather than on their capacity to stimulate rapid economic growth. Second, the authoritarianism inherent in the East Asian developmental model is such that it provides little insight into the formation of democratic developmental states and it is in this context that the Nordic welfare states become of interest. Third, close attention is paid to the agency of citizens and on how state and civil society relate to each other in the processes of democratizing the state. Fourth, the conceptualization of development shifts from a focus on the conditions necessary for industrialization, to a focus on the economy as the site of societal struggle over power and popular-democratic influence and on the manner in which different social forces have contributed to the establishment of welfare states.

In this context, the continued existence of the democratic development state is counterposed by the emergence of what has come to be known as the "competition state" (Münch 2012), which has become a feature of the hegemonic global regime of neoliberalism.[1] While the idea of a strong state is not antithetical to neoliberal thinking, it is critical of democratic systems that distort what are understood to be the natural "laws of the economy." How to reign in the independence of democracies, indeed, has been a concern of the proponents of neoliberalism since the advent of the concept in the aftermath of the Second World War (Plehwe et al. 2006). The questions raised in this chapter, thus, relate to whether

---

[1] The term neoliberalism was coined by Frederic Hayek in the Mont Pélèrin society, a think tank he and a number of likeminded individuals established in 1947.

democratic development states, extant and aspirant, can survive the current global neoliberal onslaught, and whether the emergence of some form of counterhegemonic, post-national solidarity is possible without undermining democracies of nation-states.

The Neoliberal Competition State

The competition state represents an evolution of the neoliberal state as it responds to the needs of the global economy. The goal of the competition state is not the advancement of democracy, but rather that of increasing the competitiveness of its national economy within the global market. In that respect, it seeks conformity with a new global regulatory framework created by a network of international experts and think tanks. In so doing, the competition state conforms to the rules of a "new constitution" which overrides and transforms the national constitutions that gave rise to the democratic development state (Kumm and Harte 2014). This neoliberal constitution establishes the parameters for the competition state and these are strongly influenced by the interests of multinational companies that bring considerable pressure to bear on civil law, social policy, knowledge and research, and on environmental policies. According to Gill the "New constitutionalism limits democratic control over central elements of economic policy and regulation by locking in future governments to liberal frameworks of accumulation premised on freedom of enterprise" (Gill 2002: 47). The global economic order is regulated by various multilateral financial agencies, including the World Trade Organization, the International Monetary Fund (IMF), World Bank, and the Organization for Economic Cooperation and Development (OECD),[2] in a system that serves to legitimize the new constitution. The new constitutionalism, Gill asserts, has in effect become "the political/juridical counterpart to 'disciplinary neoliberalism'" (Gill 2002: 47).

---

[2] The OECD, in particular, has become a central force in shaping the new constitutionalism and in overruling the constitutionalism of the nation-state. Directing its rhetoric toward developing states, it speaks of the need for "global market inclusion" and of the role of good governance, human capital development, and innovation in pursuit of this objective.

In this new economic order, the space for the democratic development state, hitherto regulated by a national constitution created by "people searching for a government," is progressively shrinking. Historically, in the Nordic context, the constitution was intended to guide the state in its role as the custodian of a common "household,"[3] and its primary objective was the creation of the good society for all. Economic development was seen as the development of the nation-state. In contrast, the new constitution assigns primacy to the interests of the global market. Where the national constitution had evolved out of a discourse that sought to protect citizens from both the power of the state and the power of the economy, the new constitution protects the interests of economic actors, often as super-citizens, exercising rights that supersede those of the democratic citizenship embedded in national constitutions. Furthermore, while the national constitution opened up prospects for a more inclusive democracy, committed to the ideal that development should contribute to the welfare of all, and especially the protection of the weak and vulnerable, the new constitution pays scant attention to citizenship and the common good, rewards individual achievement, and has little interest in the welfare of non achievers.

In the section that follows, the manner in which the precepts of the competition state increasingly impact on the autonomy, and indeed the very future, of the democratic development state will be discussed in greater detail. Here the focus is on how the influence of political parties, parliaments, and civil society in national states is increasingly subverted and sidelined by a host of international think tanks, consulting firms, international bureaucratic forums and professional associations, and the increasingly dominant sway of transnational companies (TNCs).[4] According to Kolleck, "global companies see themselves as the most competent and

---

[3] In Norway the legislature is still called the Norwegian House.

[4] According to Kolleck: "All the world's major industrialized sectors are now controlled by five multinational corporations (MNCs) at most, while 28% have one corporation that accounts for more than 40% of global sales. In 2008 the top 20 non-financial corporations' sales were worth US$4.3 trillion, equivalent to the combined national expenditure of the bottom 163 states, and greater than the gross domestic product (GDP) of the bottom 137 states.. many of the top 20 corporations are as large as middle income or emerging states such as Chile, Algeria, and the Philippines. On the basis of national expenditure, they are as large as many of the top 30 high income states..." (Kolleck 2013: 4).

indispensable players in defining societal goals" (Kolleck 2013: 135). These global companies, she maintains, "benefit from the dominance of neoliberal norms, financial benefits, free-market systems, and structural connections between mass media and politics" (*ibid*). Under this new dispensation, commercial banks, now liberated from their national roots, preside over interest rates and currency circulation and have become more influential in shaping the course of the economy than national legislatures and parliaments. However, notwithstanding the fact that the democratic development state is under threat from the growing hegemony of neoliberalism, it is evident, as both Evans (2005) and Streeck (2013) suggest, that it still holds the potential to advance an alternative form of globalization, which strengthens democratic values within nation-states, respects national sovereignty, and gives substance to this in the policies and practices of international financial institutions.

The Democratic Development State

A democratic development state may be defined as one that is sensitive to, and ultimately is controlled by, democratic decision making. Along with this, it entails a continuous deepening of democracy as popular influence on policy making expands and, in particular, in the formulation of economic policy. A central tenet of the democratic development state is that where the interests of capital and those of democracy are in conflict, the latter will always prevail. Democratic values, thus, guide and give meaning to development and secure its expansion in the economy, in civil society, and within political decision-making structures at all levels. Contrary to the neoliberal contention that the economy is driven by a set of "laws," what Buchanan (1987) describes as value "structures," the need for "moral economics" is embedded in the social relations that shape the interaction between the state and civil society.

In terms of the definition mentioned earlier, the democratic developmental state evolves out of social relations that penetrate both the economy and politics. Following from this, the emphasis is on those "communities" that express these social relations the most, labor unions, the professions, civil society organizations, and on how democracy is shaped by their collective agency and capacity to mobilize the society at large. Central to the idea of the democratic development state, thus, is that of social solidarity and a broad commitment to the ideal of the good society. In the neoliberal competition state, in contrast, solidarity is dissembled and the emphasis is on the socio-cognitive shaping of human capital, such that individual achievement is respected, and rewarded, over that of the collective. Describing this trend Honneth asserts that:

> The most important criterion for describing this new capitalism is no longer the ability to efficiently fulfil hierarchically determined parameters within a large enterprise; it is the readiness to show initiative and bring one's own abilities and emotional resources to bear in the services of individualized projects. In this way the worker becomes an "entreployee", or himself an entrepreneur; no longer induced to participate in capitalist practices by external compulsion or incentives, he is in a sense self-motivated. (Honneth 2014: 175)

An Analytical Model

Evans, in attempting to delineate the features of a democratic development state, advanced what came to be known as the "tripod" model, which saw such states as being based on the achievement of an equilibrium between three key institutions: an effective state bureaucracy, a vibrant market economy, and a democracy meaningful to its citizens. "Without a better balance among the bureaucratic capacity, democratic engagement, and market signals," Evans maintained, "state administrations, particularly in the Global South, are unlikely to be able to surmount the daunting challenge that they now face"(Evans 2005: 43).[5] Useful as this model has been, I believe that its explanatory power can be strengthened by the addition of another leg, depicting the importance of Science and Science Based Education (S&SBE) in the establishment of democratic developmental states. The historical roots of this fourth institution go back further than the origins of capitalism, but during the course of the past half century its influence in society has grown exponentially, shaping the institutions and practices of all modern societies and the course of daily life. Within the society constituted by neoliberalism, S&SBE has emerged as a particular

---

5   Evans believed that democracy was the weakness leg of the tripod, having become a component of the developmental state long after state bureaucracy and the market economy had become more or less global institutions.

source of power, not by replacing political power, but by becoming the arena where politics and knowledge overlap and mutually reproduce one another beyond the influence of national democratic institutions.

The four institutions in the revised model, each with its own history, relate to one another in ways that may promote or undermine the democratic development state. In keeping with sociological theories of modernization, it can be seen that the autonomy of these institutions within a sphere of mutual influence is a precondition for a democratic development state. Here I do not see these as "systems" that merely interact with one another, but rather as institutions that embody certain values and norms and that contribute to the way a society shapes its understanding of such social phenomena as justice, knowledge, achievement, and economic development. Although the broad socializing roles played by these institutions sometimes conflict, these tensions frequently give rise to new modes of understanding and new institutional practices, for example, in the formulation of codes of conduct on business ethics and corporate social responsibility.

Beginning with the economic component of the model, and utilizing the ever burgeoning literature on the varieties of (nation-state) capitalism, we can see how the interplay between the four institutions has created variations over time. Notwithstanding the fact that these studies have been based primarily on stereotypical Anglo-American and Germanic economies, the most common variation discernible is between what might be considered the incremental and radical innovation strategies adopted in different types of capitalism. In the incremental economy learning, to a considerable extent, takes place in the workplace. In this system there is continuous interaction between different skill levels in an organization and this forms part of capacity building and, at the same time, facilitates internal upward mobility in an organization. This is strengthened by a human resource regime which places emphasis on internal recruitment and the promotion of people to leadership positions based on their experience in a particular industry (in contrast to headhunting). Further features of the incremental model include the progressive improvement of products (including new applications of known processes), close linkages between productive and circular capital, and the maintenance of fairly close links between education and work. The economy, in this context, is constituted as a political voice within what Streeck has termed a "corporate state" (Streeck 2013).

The radical innovation economy, on the other hand, is so named due to its focus on the "new," particularly in regard to the need for new products. In contrast to the "coordinated" economy of incremental innovation described by Hall and Soskice (2001), the radical innovation economy is characterized by its fluidity and the heavy emphasis which is placed on technological innovation. Technological innovation is seen as essential in building new markets with high yielding returns on investment. Unlike the "knowledge of the workplace" generated collectively in the incremental model, innovation in the radical model is a highly individualized process which pays also close attention to issues of cost efficiency in the design process (Hayek 1978).[6] In this process, furthermore, the site of innovation becomes the focal point of interest rather the factory, which becomes merely the site for the fabrication of new products. The transformation of fixed capital into circulating capital frees up funds for investment in innovation. The capital invested in innovation itself emanates from sources which are innovative and fluid, and which are geared to the creation of new products and new markets, but which pay little attention to the dynamics of the workplace or to the need to establish social compacts as a means to ensuring long-term stability.

In the logic of this economic model, opposition to the innovation regime is irrational since new jobs will in future be generated through radical innovation. Old jobs and professions, in and of themselves, hold no value since they have little prospect of future growth. In this context, labor unions and professional associations are trapped in a conflict between old and new forms of work and the defense of an innovation system derived from organizational learning is seen as largely counterproductive. In a far cry from the "coordinated economy," the role once played by unions in establishing an equilibrium between workers and employers has largely disappeared, and they now function more as protest movements. Qualifications have also become less clearly defined and workplace learning

---

6   See "Competition as a Discovery Procedure", in Hayek (1978: 179–190). The interaction between the economic and engineering professions is an intriguing departure point for the analysis of the two contrasting models.

counts for little in career progression. Work hierarchies and educational hierarchies reproduce one another and both promote the mobility of "human capital" in a system where promotion is based solely on individual achievement, rather than on an employee's contribution to the success of a team. In a similar fashion, as social collectives, the professions are transformed from "communes of knowledge" (which assume responsibility for ethical conducted and the quality of service delivered), into "resource bases" serving individual professionals and firms in their quest for new innovations.

Turning to the S&SBE component of the model, the influence of radical innovation thinking is readily apparent, in Anglo-American liberal variant of capitalism in particular, in the manner in which "general education" has become increasingly oriented to the development of human capital for the workplace (developing skills for the market), and in the extent to which universities have become instruments for the advancement of innovation. The outcome of this has been the emergence of a form of "academic capitalism," where universities strive both to generate knowledge relevant to the innovation industry and, themselves, to become players in the innovation economy.[7]

Universities are valued for their role in establishing innovation centers and, indeed, they are now seen as central to the success of the radical innovation economy. In advancing this understanding of the utility of science and knowledge, they themselves create "innovation hubs," develop academic programs on entrepreneurship, and pay considerable attention to intellectual property rights and the registration of patents in an attempt

---

[7] The debate on academic capitalism raised by Leslie and Slaughter in their 1997 classic *Academic Capitalism: Politics, Policies and the Entrepreneurial University* was followed by the comprehensive study on *Academic Capitalism and the New Economy. Market, State and Higher Education* written by Slaughter and Rhoades in 2004. By far the most important analytical book on this topic, however, is Münch's (2011) work on *Akademischer Kapitalismus. Über die politische Ökonomie der Hchschulereform.*

to generate their own revenue.[8] In order to succeed in the competitive world of S&SBE, universities have had to specialize and concentrate their resources. This, in turn, has led to the establishment of, often large, "centers of excellence" where academics, relieved from the burden of teaching, can dedicate their careers to the pursuit of innovation.

In the incremental innovation economy, however, in addition to an emphasis on vocational training, importance is attached to education that equips people for a broader range of jobs in the economy and, at the same time, there is recognition that learning within the professions makes a significant contribution to the overall knowledge system. In this way, links between education and work are sustained over time. The manner in which education is organized helps shape communal identities and this, in turn, serves to stabilize the working environment. In maintaining this equilibrium, there is an expectation that change will be introduced incrementally and that it will take into account both practical and abstract/theoretical knowledge. Research in this context is valued for its continuous contribution to a better life, and not solely because its novelty serves the commercial interests of the innovators. In this way, the knowledge generated by universities adds not only to the store of human capital but also to public knowledge, which is manifest in communities of public value, and in widespread civic responsibility. These two educational trajectories are to be found in most constitutional states, reflecting the inherent tension that exists in attempting to balance economic ownership and public value, individual rights and collective force. However, as Evans pointed out in his "invention" of the Weberian barometer, constitutional states have very different types of bureaucracies. In liberal states the emphasis is on a rule-oriented decision-making model that overshadows what is seen as a "goal-oriented" model of decision making. The establishment of rules regulating what economic actors do in the market is seen as more important

---

8   In their discussion on how TRIPS overtook Word Intellectual Property Organization, which had been dominated by developing countries, Montes and Popov describe the pressures that emerging economies are under to adjust to western technology/knowledge, and how much they lose due to the TRIPS system in the process: "Total losses of Western companies from piracy were estimated by the IIPA (International Intellectual Property Alliance at US$ 16.4 billion in 2007 However, losses of developing countries from the implementation of TRIPS are several times higher ...60 billion a year" (Montes and Popov 2011: 130).

than supporting the growth of successful new industries. However, there is considerable variance in how such states intervene in the economy, in the ways in which the workforce is reproduced, and the way in which the socially exclude and vulnerable are supported. In the incremental innovation economy, as intimated, education and social welfare are valued for their contribution to the common good which provides the platform for economic growth. In the radical innovation economy, in contrast, sustaining these instruments of social solidarity is seen as reactive, while a singular focus on developing human capital is viewed as both proactive and essential for economic growth. Justice, in this context, is seen as fairness, in the sense that all citizens are given the same opportunity to utilize their human capital to productive ends. The primary role of the democratic state is to appeal to economic actors to treat people fairly, as evidenced in the plethora of corporate social responsibility codes to which multinational companies are encouraged to adhere. Procedure, however, is generally seen to be of more importance than actual outcomes that are seldom, if ever, monitored.

Within the incremental innovation economy, it is the role of the state to secure access to the good society. It does so on the understanding that inequality is a collective problem and the state must assume responsibility for the costs of economic transitions in society. Justice as fairness, which has come to be associated with the work of Rawls, represents a different understanding of who is to carry the burden of these changes. According to Münch:

> Rawls regards human beings as basically rational maximizers of individual benefits. Therefore, the goal shared by all people can only be offering maximum chances for freedom and development to each individual. In Emil Durkheim's ...terms, the negative solidarity of avoidance of conflicts rules among people in a liberal society, whereas in the positive solidarity of sympathy, sharing and the common definition of a good life has shrunk to a minimum that merely ensures that all continue to take part in the game and will not withdraw or mobilize for rebellion. The illusion of being able to achieve has to stay alive, if the investments in the race for achievement are to be continued ... The two basic principles introduced by Rawls do not say, however, where the limits has to be set beyond which inequalities are no longer a benefit for those who are worse off ... Rawls' theory of justice tends towards the liberal model of

society, as it places the profit-maximizing individual above the collective. (Münch 2012: 74)

In this reading of the radical innovation economy, faced with the constant transformation of the economy, the burden falls on those who do are unable to effectively use their own human capital and available societal resources to improve their lot in life. Individual risk, in this model, is underwritten, at personal cost, by private insurance companies.[9] Individual achievement is presented as an antidote to what is portrayed as the pacifying welfare state. In the incremental innovation model, the consequences of change in the economy are a collective responsibility, as, for example, occurs when jobs are lost or certain segments of the population suffer various forms of social exclusion, and labor unions continue to play an important role in sustaining social solidarity.

Democracies, of course, vary considerably in terms of their representative structures and electoral regimes, but what is of significance is how well their democratic systems work in practice. The liberal model emerged out of an ideology where democracy and capitalism were understood to be closely interrelated. In that regard, the institutionalized modernization, educational system, and middle-class values of capitalist society are believed to have created the social base for democracy. Furthermore, as capitalism has become increasingly globalized, this understanding of democracy has traveled with it.

In the incremental innovation economy, capitalism and democracy are seen as the outcomes of fairly independent historical processes, and as institutions in essential conflict with one another. Unfettered democracy is seen as a threat to capitalism, just as it is to the authoritarian developmental state, because the need to seek a popular mandate may retard or distort economic growth. In a context where voters turn out in the liberal variant of capitalism is typically less than 50% (and usually closer to 40%), and the highest proportion of those not voting is to be found among the poor and socially marginalized, it is evident that the enormous

---

[9]   The elimination of group insurance schemes was one of the first tasks of the neoliberal competition state, in that it shifted responsibility for risk from the collective to the individual.

cleavages between rich and poor to which capitalism gives rise renders democracy meaningless for the majority of citizens.

In their modern classic *"Capitalist development and democracy"* published in 1992, Rueschemeyer et al. posed the question "what happens when capitalism and democracy confront one another?" and, in so doing, opened the debate on how the growing power of global capitalism has served to suppress democracy when it is perceived to contradict the logic of the new constitution. Building on this critique, it is evident that it is the way in which social classes are structured within capitalism, and the manner in which they interact with each other, which determines how democracies function, and, we could add, what prospects exist for a welfare state and what form it might take.

In the incremental innovation economy, labor unions are socially and politically influential, they have access to and respect for knowledge, and the social mobility of workers is assisted by a flexible education system. This has led to a social order committed to democratic ideals.[10] Within and between political parties, the building of alliances between the working class and a democratically oriented middle class has led to their collective support for both incremental change in the workplace and for the welfare state. Through these alliances, forms of power sharing and democratic influence emerged and these have extended into the service economy, notwithstanding the devaluation of work associated with this sector.

In the liberal variant of capitalism, workers are supposed to aspire to a "middle-class" identity, and accept the principle that upward mobility results from sound investment in the development of human capital. Political and economic individualization strategies go hand in hand and together they shape policies supportive of radical innovation. In the increasing hegemony of global neoliberalism, the power and influence of the working class and allied segments of the middle class has been severely undermined, both within the new competitive constitution and within economic organizations where power relations changed. This is especially evident in the service sector which is characterized by individualized, unprotected work relations, low wages, and a growing number of so-called

---

[10]   Contrary to liberal ideology (embodied in radical innovation economies), it is the working class that has always been the strongest proponent of democracy, rather that the supposedly enlightened middle class.

working poor (who in some countries have become supporters of the populist right).

Building partly on the varieties of capitalism literature, the revised tripod model proposed earlier provides a basis for comparative research on how, in different nation-states, interactions between the four social institutions display similar patterns. By examining common traits and terminologies the model also allows for diachronic comparisons of the ways the domination of neoliberalism is transforming these nation-state varieties and is leading to a form of capitalist convergence. My interest is on how, at the expense of the state-driven incremental economy, neoliberalism is promoting the "radical innovation economy" of the competitive state as an ideal type. The rise of the competition state and its "new constitution" is directly opposed to the underlying values of the democratic developmental state and its welfare-oriented policies.

The Nordic Variant of Capitalism

In the ongoing debate on the essence of a democratic developmental state, the model underpinning the successes of the Nordic states has received close scrutiny for the potential which it holds for emerging economies elsewhere in the world. However, taking into consideration Hall and Soskice's proposition that there are dichotomies within the "varieties of capitalism," what is not so clearly expressed in these debates is the fact that, despite their standing as incremental innovation economies, Nordic countries have for some years invested in institutions and programs supportive of the ideas of the radical innovation economy and they have embraced the rhetoric that the development of "human capital" is their most important resource.[11] The tensions this has created within the social order can be seen in the way in which the different institutions of our model now interrelate.

In order to understand how the Nordic, and particularly Norwegian, variants of capitalism are mutating it is of interest to consider how S&SBE is currently organized. As a point of departure, it is important to note that

---

[11]   This is a contradiction pointed out by German researchers studying the Nordic model as an alternative to their own failed "solidarity pact" of the 1990s. See Simon et al. (2010), and more directly Heidenreich (2004: 125–144).

the growth of the Norwegian oil industry, which plays such a dominant role in the economy, was based on a strategy of incremental innovation. The oil industry, which grew out of the ship-building industry and a network of firms linked to the sector, also received strong support from the unions precisely because they endorsed the growth model being pursued. Paradoxically, the very success of the oil industry, albeit within the corporate economy of state ownership, laid the basis for radical innovation. The primary impetus for this change came about as a result of the reorganization of S&SBE within the country.

The main reform, in this regard, was the merger of several national research councils into one on the grounds of greater efficiency and effectiveness. Through this restructuring, the advocates of radical innovation who had pushed for the merger (with strong support from the OECD) acquired a centralizing power to direct knowledge production toward a greater focus on innovation. Universities and research centers, in this new paradigm, were to be gradually transformed into "agents" of this new "principal." In the process, the new research council's commitment to economic development has overtaken the historical ideals of research-based knowledge embedded in universities as part of their contribution to democratic society.

In line with OECD policy guidelines, this development was crowned by the establishment of a network of centers of excellence, funded by the universities, but owned and directed by the unified research council.[12] The influence of this mega council is also apparent in its role as a government adviser on research matters, and as the coordinator of all the research emanating from government ministries. The old research councils, which it replaced, had had their own research centers but the linkages between agent and principal were unclear and they exercised a considerable

---

[12]   Drori et al. have shown how the number of national science policy organizations, intergovernmental science organizations, national science ministries, and a variety of nongovernmental and international science organizations proliferated from the 1950s onward (Drori et al. 2003: 3). What is missing in this analysis, however, is any discussion of the variable ways in which different nation-states have reacted to the onslaught of the globalization movement. Lacking this discussion, the advance of globalization is presented as an inexorable force and the rise of the "innovation paradigm" is thereby naturalized, as something states must simply adapt to.

degree of autonomy, pursuing both incremental and abstract models of economic change. While the new research council has not stopped funding research aimed at improving incremental change, it is clear that its focus is now on radical innovation and it has become the proverbial tail that wags the university dog.

The role of the OECD in shaping the new constitutionalism and in reducing the constitutionalism of the nation-state is an interesting one, as is its role in promoting S&SBE in the new innovation order. Formed more than 50 years ago the OECD may be considered to have come of age, having historically been seen as a "rich man's club," serving the interests of the most economically advanced states, it has reinvented itself as a global player, which now includes developing countries in its sphere of influence. It is a strong advocate of "global market inclusion," unsurprisingly so as it serves as secretariat for the G-20 nations, but following the global financial meltdown, it is has also become a campaigner for the programmatic reorganization of global capitalism as a means to secure its future. These programs focus on various thematic strategies aimed at good governance, human capital development, and innovation. Part of this exercise has entailed support for the restructuring of higher education and research by promoting academic capitalism and human capital development geared to innovation. In this process, academic and economic rationalities are conflated, such that the postnational research strategy, so central to the progression of the new constitution, now has more legitimacy than the national one.

The OECD's influence in restructuring the research and innovation environment in Norway may be inferred from a review of innovation policy in South Africa conducted by the organization in 2007. The OECD report emphasizes the importance of marshaling all available research in order to promote economic growth. Referencing the importance of S&SBE, it also asserts that the contribution of the tertiary education is the least important source of knowledge useful to the innovation economy:

> Countless surveys of OECD firms show that their main sources of technology are internal knowledge and other firms. Public sector research in general, and higher education research in particular, account for a small share of their total knowledge inputs to innovation. (OECD 2007: 113)

In this understanding, while the generalized knowledge generated by academic disciplines is of value in enlightening the public, and it may also be of potential relevance to the state in supporting its strategic priorities should the need arise, the primary focus of a knowledge strategy should be driven by an innovation paradigm.

Commenting on the status of innovation in South Africa, the review notes that the country lacks a "focusing device" (OECD 2007: 116) capable of linking the incremental process of learning and change to the potential for radical innovation. Unlike the situation that pertains in the Nordic countries, the OECD review states that in South Africa, "There is no forum or arena at the highest level of government that can play a strong integrative role across the whole of government, not least in balancing the various policies and instruments that in practice combine to make up innovation and research policy" (OECD 2007: 141). In light of this critique, it is not surprising that Nordic research structures, and particularly the centralized Norwegian research council, should be cited by the OECD as a model worth emulating. According to the OECD, "Raising the importance and profile of innovation requires greater strength in implementation. It would be useful to set up a Nordic-style innovation agency inside or outside NRF (National Research Foundation) to achieve this" (OECD 2007; *ibid*).

Neoliberalism and Globalization

Neoliberalism and globalization, which together constitute the dominant regime of our epoch, are, as discussed, based on the radical innovation model. In contrast to the ideals of the welfare state, as we have seen, the model, among other features, embraces the concept of justice as fairness rather than the ideal that justice entails the right to access the good society. Not only has economic globalization led to a reconceptualization of the meaning of social justice, it has also created new forms of state/law relations where the competition state has, in effect, become the mediator of the new constitution, established to protect and promote global capitalism.[13] In their definition of the new constitutionalism, Gill and Cutler refer to a "combination of various sets of processes" four of which are of particular significance (Gill and Cutler 2014: 7). These processes, they maintain, relate to the governance of the global market by multilateral financial institutions (and a variety of public and private interest groups); to the neoliberal reshaping of political subjects; the restructuring of the state (through, for example, the expanded influence of market forces in social and political life); and to many new legal "informalities" such as the soft laws that contribute to the self-regulatory dimensions of national economies.

The change in political conceptions of justice forms a part of the transition from social solidarity to individualism, and this, in turn, has led to attempts to restructure the welfare system (characterized, in particular, by attacks on the universal right to social support which has been a central tenet of Nordic states). Despite the challenge which this new order presents to both social democratic and conservative values, what has been significant is the fact that there has been so little consistent, organized social or political opposition. Having so stated, it is evident that the labor unions, which still retain a strong membership base and linkages to professions that endorse the notion of national solidarity, have not embraced the principles of the radical innovation economy and, in so doing, this has given rise to a dual system of innovation (where space remains for a workplace based on incremental change). The political economy of Norway, thus, still seems to hold the potential to promote the values of a democratic developmental state, while, at the same time, the country continues to adapt to the global division of labor, in terms of specialization both in the service sector and in industry, and in the liberalization of capital and trade. In this way, the protectionist strategies that stimulated industrial development in Norway have been abandoned in favor of a so-called open economy.

---

[13]   This may be seen in the internationalization of the legal profession and in the many laws and agreements relating to the mobilization of capital, investment liberalization, the alienation of state land, safeguarding the property of international companies, and intellectual property rights. States that attempt to challenge this international legal order confront the threat of litigation by TNCs and ostracization by multinational financial institutions and by ratings agencies.

The unresolved global challenge, which now is leading Norway toward becoming a neoliberal competition state, threatens to undermine the constitutionally based nation-state community which has developed partly as a result of welfare state arrangements. The solidarity underpinning the welfare state is dissipating at the same time that the social lives of experts, senior state bureaucrats, business leaders, and increasingly of professionals are becoming defined by their international linkages. The interests of these influential social agents now veer towards the competition state, and more and more towards the reproduction of the economy beyond the limits of incremental innovation. The current Norwegian regime is advancing this development agenda in several ways. First, by undermining the influence of labor unions, academic professions, and popular democracy (local government), in order to gain sufficient power to begin dismantling the collective aspects of the welfare state. This has included the proposal to deregulate labor, in line with the Danish flexicurity system, which has been rationalized in terms of the justice as fairness principle. It is also evident in the commitment to the EU and the WTO and the fact that the anticipated growth in trade is being used to justify transformation of the entire public sector. The alliances that are being formed, between internal experts and bureaucrats in Norway, the EU, OECD, and various other multilateral agencies, are emerging as a power base which is capable of bypassing the democratic institutions "locked in" by the nation-state.

If current trends persist, it could be predicted that, given its current strong commitment to the globalization of the economy, the Norwegian democratic developmental state (of which the country has, to some extent, become the exemplar) will, ultimately, align its national constitution to fit the rules and regulations of the neoliberal economy. In that regard, it is evident that the influence of those sectors of the state which envisage Norway becoming the competitive edge of global capital is now in the ascendancy.[14] As can be seen in the case of S&SBE, this shift in state power is already providing momentum to the radical innovation strategy. In this new regime it is only through share ownership in large corporates (and, by implication, representation on their boards) that the state is able to

---

[14] A recent government White Paper on "Ownership" confirms this trend; see St. Meld 27, 2013–2014.

gaining insight into and influence the "global capital" located within own borders. At the same time, publicly funded innovative research and "human capital" are offered up in support of the globalization of the Norwegian economy.

The consequences of these developments for democracy in Norway are threefold: first, the economy is becoming increasingly insulated from political oversight in that it is governed by laws (those of the global constitution), which are beyond national regulation. Second, the individualism of the human capital strategy which is being pursued undermines the political solidarity engendered through community participation and deliberation. Third, the re-conceptualization of fairness as justice embedded in the legal framing of the new constitutional dispensation has altered understandings of the good society and its moral obligation to care for all its citizens. It is also evident that the policies and strategies that have facilitated the transition from the democratic developmental state constitution to that of the global neoliberal constitution have given rise to hybrid institutions which embody elements of both economic orders. This hybridization has led to organizational instability and conflict within state institutions. Nevertheless, the broad trend has been toward a reconfiguration of the democratic welfare state toward a society based on human capital achievement, the seemingly inescapable imperatives of the global division of labor, specialized services, and the mobility of the so-called highly skilled. Returning to our model, the shift toward neoliberalism in Norway is illustrative of how a state bureaucracy, engaged in various national and international expert networks, is responsible for importing the hegemonic multilateral economic policies (particularly those of the OECD) into the country's legal system and public administration.

Conclusion

Despite the fact that polls in Norway reflect 90% support for the welfare state and almost as much support for the level of taxes levied, democracy in the country, as elsewhere, has been weakened by globalization. Jürgen Kocka, in his book *Geschichte des Kapitalismus*, discusses the ways in which capitalism has managed to expand without democratic resistance and how, at the same time, active democracies are in decline. He refers, in particular, to the speed of financial capital, its lack of spatial attachment, lack of accountability, the complexity of its "systems," and the inaccessible of the information which drives markets, to illustrate the divide between global capitalism and the slow, space-bound, and "uniform" processes of democracy. Faced with these asymmetries, Streeck argues, democracy can only regain influence if neoliberalism is pushed back decisively. However, despite the optimism in some academic circles in Norway about the potential to renew the energies of democracy at the level of the nation-state, Streeck maintains that we are entering an era without any normative certainty as to how democracies should respond when challenged by such social phenomena as globalization, migration, and multiculturalism. It is in this context that even stable democracies, such as those in the Nordic states, are threatened by the certainties of the new constitution of neoliberalism.

Rueschemeyer et al., however, argue that it is from the contradictions within capitalism that we have come to understand the emergence of democratic action. "It was neither capitalists nor capitalism as such," they maintain, "but rather the contradictions of capitalism that advanced the cause of political equality" (Rueschemeyer et al. 1992: 302). Looking at the future, then, it is unlikely, as Olsen (2014) suggests, that the lasting tensions within democracy can be resolved discursively and that this could lead to some form of global democratic constitutionalism. Rather, it is by focusing on the many contradictions of contemporary capitalism, as is evident in the work of Scholte and colleagues (Scholte 2011), that some indication emerges as to how democracy might reform the new neoliberal constitution. They do so by analyzing how different levels of social activity, particularly within civil society, are challenging the opaque neoliberal regulatory system created by multilateral financial agencies. The question raised in their research is "how can democratic forces make the World Bank, IMF, OECD more accountable, and to what extent can the accountability to which these organizations agree to be called democratic?" Put differently, can global economic oversight and accountability be linked to nation-state democracies? Alternatively, might it be possible to forge global civil society coalitions that transcend the boundaries of nation-states and that mobilize to transform the new constitution and to ensure that its regulatory system is legal, transparent, and fair? Thus far, the center of this opposition has been fragmented but the rise of a broad range of social movements across the globe demonstrates how human agency is being mobilized across borders, both challenging the lack of accountability in global capitalism and seeking to democratize the new constitution.

References

Buchanan, J. (1987). The constitution of economic policy. *American Economic Review*, 77(3), 243–250.

Drori, Gili S. et al (2003). (Eds.), *Science in the modern world polity. Institutionalization and globalization.* Stanford, CA: Stanford University Press.

Evans, P. (2005). Harnessing the state: Rebalancing strategies for monitoring and motivation. In: D. Rueschemeyer and M. Lange (Eds.), *States and development. Historical antecedents of stagnation and advance.* New York: Palgrave McMillan. 26-47

Gill, S. (2002). "Constitutionalizing inequality and the clash of globalization". *International Studies Review, 4*(2, 1 June), 47–65.

Gill, S. and Cutler, C. (Eds.). (2014). *New constitutionalism and world order.* Cambridge: Cambridge University Press.

Hall, P. A. and Soskice, D. (Eds.). (2001). *Varieties of capitalism.* Oxford: Oxford University Press.

Hayek, F. (1978). *New studies in philosophy, politics, economics and the history of ideas.* London: Routledge and Keegan Paul.

Hayek, F. (1978). *The constitution of liberty.* Chicago, IL: University of Chicago Press.

Heidenreich, M. (2004). Innovation und Soziale Sicherung im Internationalen Vergleich. *Soziale Welt* 2/2004.

Honneth, A. (2014). *The I in we. Studies in the theory of recognition.* Cambridge and New York: Polity.

Kolleck, N. (2013). In: J. Mikler (Ed.), *The handbook of global companies.* West Sussex, UK: Wiley-Blackwell.

Kumm, M. and Harte, L. (2014). Zeiten für Rule of Law. Die Krise des globalen Konstitutionalismus. In WZB Mitteilungen. 146. Des 2014. Berlin.

Münch, R. (2011). Akademischer Kapitalismus. Über die politische Ökonomie der Hchschulereform. Berlin: Suhrkamp Verlag.

Münch, R. (2012). *Inclusion and exclusion in the liberal competition state. The cult of the individual.* Abingdon: Routledge.

OECD. (2007). *OECD reviews of innovation policy: South Africa.* Paris: OECD Publishing.

Olsen, J. (2014). *Folkestyrets varige spenninger.* Oslo: Universitetsforlaget..

Peter T, and Waterman, T.J. Jr. (1982). In search of Excellence. Lessons from Americas Best Run Companies. New York: Harper and Row.

Plehwe, D. et al. (2006). *Neoliberal hegemony: A global critique. Oxford.* Routledge.

Rueschemeyer, D., Stephens, E. H. and Stepehns, J. D. (1992). *Capitalist development and democracy. Cambridge*: Oxford. Polity Press.

Scholte, J. (Ed.). (2011). *Building global democracy? Civil society and accountable global governance.* Cambridge: Cambridge University Press.

Simon, D. et al. (2010). *Handbuch Wissenschaftspolitik.* Wiesbaden: VS Verlag für Sozialwissenschaften.

Slaughter, L. and Rhoades, G. (2004). *Academic capitalism and the new economy. Market, state and higher education.* Baltimore: John Hopkins University Press.

Slaughter, S. and Leslie, L. (1997). *Academic capitalism: Politics, policies and the entrepreneurial university.* Baltimore: John Hopkins University Press.

Streeck, W. (2013). Die Vertragte Krise des democratischen Kapitalismus. Frankfurt am Main. Suhrkamp.

Democracy, Development, and the Disciplining of Capital

Tor Halvorsen and Chris Tapscott

The primary objective of this book, as indicated in the introductory chapter, was not to attempt an authoritative definition of a democratic developmental state (if, indeed, this term is conceptually useful), but rather to contribute to the broader debate on the relationship between democracy, capitalism, and the role of the state in stimulating economic growth. In short, how can democracies mediate relations between politics and the economy and, more normatively, how can democracy be strengthened to influence this relationship such that the polity governs the economy in accordance with democratic values? There is, of course, no consensus on these issues but rather a number of interpretations of how the history of social formations might have been shaped by these relationships. The chapters in this book confirm that the idea of a democratic developmental state remains a highly contentious one, and that the ability (or willingness) of states so labeled to overcome the inherent contradiction between capitalism and democracy is at best limited or nonexistent. The concept of a democratic developmental state, nevertheless, remains of interest not least because it raises fundamental questions about how economic growth can be reconciled with individual rights and freedoms in an increasingly globalized world order. Importantly, we maintain that possibilities do exist for what might be termed a democratic developmental state formation, and this chapter will briefly explore, from a normative perspective at least, what might be some of its constituent elements.

Political Economy

It is axiomatic that the manner in which political and economic agents interact ultimately determines the developmental path of nation-states. In linking the notion of a democratic development state to this discourse we are, implicitly, advancing a normative proposition: namely that democratic principles and systems should steer both the state (in its multiple bureaucratic manifestations) and the economy. An extension of this proposition is that development that is guided by, and which reproduces and strengthens, democracy is inherently better than other kinds of develop-ment in terms of both its economic effectiveness and durability (meas-ured in terms of limited social and political dissonance and resistance).

Although it is difficult to define this mode of democratic development with any precision, it is still possible to differentiate between those re-gimes that (in different historical epochs) have embraced such a model (or continue to do so), and those that have not. Following this line of think-ing, based on their history of social democracy, Nordic states, as Olsen, Törnquist, and Halvorsen argue in this book, could be seen to approximate the ideals of a democratic developmental state. Conversely, as discussed in Chapter 2 by Cruz-Del Rosario, most Asian countries (including those labeled developmental states) would be viewed either as authoritarian states or as hybrid ones, manifesting elements of democracy with residual authoritarian tendencies. Reflective of this, in the *Oxford Handbook of Asian Business Systems* (Oxford 2014) China is labeled "authoritarian cap-italism," Indonesia "oligarchic capitalism," Japan "coordinated capital-ism," Malaysia "personal Capitalism," the Philippines "trapped capital-ism," Singapore "open state-led capitalism," South Korea "plutocratic state-led capitalism," Taiwan "SME-oriented capitalism in transition," Thailand "post-developmentalist capitalism," and, finally, Vietnam is termed "post-state capitalism." Significantly, the "democratic" prefix is not attached to any of these states, even though the original developmental states, such as Japan and South Korea, subsequently transitioned to mul-tiparty democracy. This is largely due to the fact that the authoritarian traits embedded in their social order, and reproduced by close networks and closed circles of power, have prevailed and combine to influence eco-nomic and political life.

The varied names assigned to these Asian states, including most of those known as developmental states, are suggestive of a political order where elites have sacrificed democratic principles for the sake of their own economic interests. As was the case in the era of the ascendant de-velopmental state, the justification remains that continued economic growth demands state power undisturbed and unfettered by popular in-fluence. Implicit in this standpoint is the presupposition that there are in-herent contradictions between economic growth and democracy and that the former is inhibited by the latter. Somewhat paradoxically, the recogni-tion of this latent contradiction seems to admit to what is a truism in the

Nordic regimes, albeit from a different departure point, that there is, indeed, a real conflict between democratic values and capitalism. In this Nordic understanding, democratic values refer to the pursuit of equal opportunity, participation in decision making, reduced income inequality, the distribution of ownership, and human creativity and capability. Capitalism, conversely, is understood to entail the concentration of both ownership and decision-making power, the growth of inequality, authoritarian consumerism at the cost of citizenship, and the exploitation of human capital at the cost of creativity, to mention but some of its characteristics. Expanding on this view, Wolfgang Merkel argues that:

> Capitalism and democracy follow different logics: unequally distributed property rights on the one hand, equal civil and political rights on the other; profit-oriented trade within capitalism in contrast to the search for the common good within democracy; debate, compromise and majority decision-making within democratic politics versus hierarchical decision-making by managers and capital owners. Capitalism is not democratic, democracy not capitalist. (Merkel 2014: 109)

From this perspective it might be inferred that the establishment of a democratic developmental state would be premised on the conviction that democratic values should work counter to the organizing principles of capitalism, which create social cleavages, inequality, and a concentration of ownership. However, as the experiences of Nordic countries during the ascendancy of social democratic rule (now less dominant) have demonstrated, democracy and economic growth are not inherently contradictory and can reinforce one another in the disciplining of capitalism and in the development of an economy both respecting and reproducing of democratic social relations.

The Anglo-American world, characterized by neoliberalism and by a state that is primarily oriented toward the creation of markets and, where possible, the privatization of public services (Crouch 2016; Mirowski 2013), has generally seemed unconcerned whether or not developmental states are democratic. This is because the Anglo-American social and political culture has tended, conceptually, to conflate the idea of democracy with that of the market economy. Following this logic, "democracy" naturally follows the expansion of the market economy, consumer freedom is democratic freedom, and choices, irrespective of their significance, are choices. Under this formulation, because citizens have the freedom of choice, whether in the choice of politicians or cars, capitalism should not be seen as antagonistic to a democracy but rather as its creator. After all, the question is asked, has there ever been democracy without capitalism in the modern world? Furthermore, as the middle classes are the drivers of democratic (liberal) values, the more the economy grows the stronger will "liberal democracy" become embedded in the culture of political life.

Following this reasoning further, the developmental state (as opposed to the classical liberal state) represents a logical step in the path toward democracy since this state will gradually be transformed by the demands of the market. However, the occurrence of such transformations, as Rueschemeyer et al. (1992) have pointed out, is not supported by empirical evidence. This may be ascribed to the fact that neoliberal regimes are typically concerned more with how market relations are regulated by the state, than with how democratic systems and processes guide state regulation of the economy in ways that reproduce democratic values. The focus instead, as Chapter 9 by Halvorsen points out, is on the transformation of the developmental state into what has been termed a *competition state*, which has little interest in the pursuit of democracy as an end itself. This logic also permeates the thinking of multilateral funding agencies created in the cultural image of the Anglo-American world. This is evident, for example, in the extent to which the World Bank strongly encouraged both South Africa and Brazil to accept the principle that an open capitalist economy equates to democracy and that the latter would be best served by free trade and limited regulation (see Chapter 6).

South Africa, as Chapter 4 by Penderis and Tapscott reveals, appears to have added the democratic prefix to its notion of a developmental state more as a means to justify the "ideology of conflation" of democracy and capitalism, as described earlier, rather than as a way to address the contradiction between the two—a contradiction that is probably more pronounced in this country than in any other nation-state. The situation in Brazil is broadly the same in that it has a similar regime and equally high levels of inequality. As illustrated in various chapters in this book, both countries changed course from an initially declared intent to ensure the disciplining of capitalism through democratic processes to the ultimate adoption of a neoliberal path. This, for many of their citizens, has led to a situation where democracy has become synonymous with the hegemony of capitalism (in the experience of daily life if not always in political discourse). In both countries, as Chapter 6 by Braathen and Chapter 4 by Penderis and Tapscott illustrate, there are forces in civil society, in the unions, in opposition parties, and, indeed, even within the ruling party, which are concerned about the growing levels of inequality, and are trying to advance the idea of a "democratic developmental state" as a means to mobilize public support for a reorientation of the political order (as will be discussed briefly later).

From earlier discussion in this book, it is evident that the proponents of the original model of the developmental state (characterized by its promotion of industrialization, an export-led economy, the strengthening of education, and, among other attributes, a strong strain of authoritarianism), viewed democracy as a direct threat to state power. Furthermore, even where democracy has subsequently taken root in some of these states, the process, as indicated in the *Oxford Handbook* cited earlier, has been partial and the polity remains elite driven. Of concern is the fact that attempts to replicate the model in a contemporary setting, albeit with a democratic prefix, as is the case of Ethiopia discussed in Chapter 3 by Gebremariam, has yielded much the same outcome—rapid economic growth with lip service paid to democratic values. There is, nevertheless, a tolerance of such regimes in the global North where undemocratic and authoritarian states are excused, or only mildly censured, provided they pursue a capitalist path. It is also evident from the discussion in several chapters in the book that the growth of the market economy will not cure the ills of highly dualistic countries like Brazil and South Africa. Instead, it is far more likely to undermine the democratic values enshrined in their respective constitutions. Furthermore, if democratic mobilization is unable to counter current trends, unregulated economic growth will increasingly benefit the very few and the current ownership model will lead to an even further concentration of wealth and further polarization of society.

Following this proposition, it is argued, a democratic development state deserving of the name will need to grow out of a political culture which recognizes that democracy and capitalism represent two different value systems. Linked to this, it is the extent to which the ascendancy of democracy over capitalism is embedded in power structures and institutionalized in society which will determine whether we can speak of a democratic form of economic development and, relatedly, of a democratic society.

The section that follows looks at the concerted attempts to establish a new democratic order in South Africa in the lead up to democracy in 1994, and the manner in which the social democratic ideals that surfaced during this time were ultimately subverted by neoliberal nostrums advanced by the World Bank and various Northern states. Of interest is the fact that there were thinkers in South Africa at the time who were seriously considering the merits of pursuing a Nordic social democratic model.

A South Africa—Nordic Intermezzo

In 1993 a book of some significance was published in South Africa. Entitled *Making Democracy Work: A Framework for Macroeconomic Policy in South Africa*, this book bore witness to how, in the transition from Apartheid to democracy in the early 1990s, academics and other political commentators from various Nordic states joined forces with like-minded thinkers in South Africa to advocate for a social democratic program or, what was also called, "democratic capitalism." The group of researchers called themselves MERG, short for Macroeconomic Research Group, and the book was stated to be a gift to "Members of the democratic movement of South Africa." Its significance lies in the fact that it was the first to place the idea of a democratic developmental state on the agenda as an alternative to what, in that era, was known as the "Normative Economic Model" (NEM), then in vogue with the World Bank and broadly embraced by the outgoing Apartheid regime. The NEM, which was based on neoliberal principles, focused on trickle-down effects, a supply-side economy, lower taxation for capital (though higher taxes for wage earners), swift privatization, even swifter deregulation, and, as in the Anglo-American world, the promotion of competition in all institutions of society. Explicit in this approach was the expectation that the market would serve as a coordinating mechanism in the delivery of public services, in promoting future investment, and in steering the flow of capital to new entrepreneurs. Capi-

talism, it was believed, produced growth and, in so doing, it would ultimately provide a platform for democratic participation through growing
consumer awareness.

The members of MERG (MERG 1993), who broadly embraced the
ideas of the Congress of South African Trade Unions (COSATU), contested
the idea that the NEM was the only viable alternative for a democratic
South Africa and posited a more egalitarian approach that would actively
seek to address issues of social exclusion and poverty:

> The MERG strategy contrasts sharply with the approach of the Norma-
> tive Economic Model (NEM) of the government .... The NEM favours the
> advantaged section of society and assumes that the trickle—down ef-
> fect will distribute the benefits to the disadvantaged. The MERG ap-
> proach, however, targets the disadvantaged directly (p. 4).

In an endeavor to develop a broad consensus MERG attempted, with
mixed success, to build a network, if not exactly an alliance, between civil
society organizations, progressive state officials, trade unions, representatives of big business, and the leadership of various democratic movements at both national and local levels (MERG 1993). They were also con-
vinced that the mass social mobilization, then underway country-wide,
could be transformed into genuinely democratic forms of local and regional government. Reminiscent of the Scandinavian model of corporatism from below, it was asserted that in addition to organized labor and
capital, the state should engage with all social strata in society before set-
tling on the economic strategies that it would pursue. Some of these ideas
were embodied, both in the process of its formulation and in its content,
in the African National Congress' (ANC) first policy document the Reconstruction and Development Programme (RDP), which was produced in
1994 shortly before it assumed power. However, despite the wide popular
support for this approach, particularly among trade unions and civil society organizations, MERG proposals for a social democracy ultimately
found little traction in the leadership of the incoming ANC government
and they were soon discarded.

Another book of interest to this discussion was a review of the first
10 years of South Africa's democracy and which, reflecting the uncertain-
ties of its editors, was entitled *The Development Decade?* Published in

2006, the book presented the views of a number of leading South African scholars and included their reflections on the extent to which the ideals of MERG had found expression in government policy. Most authors concluded that although some of the ideals of a social democratic state were still popular in certain circles of the ANC and its alliance partners, and a residue of this approach had found its way into the official RDP White Paper released in November 1994, this was a watered down version of the original RDP policy document and it had, in any event, been completely supplanted by the Growth, Employment, and Redistribution (GEAR) macroeconomic framework launched in 1996. Formulated by economists who appeared conditioned to view the world through the lens of a liberal market economy, GEAR afforded little space for a coordinated market economy and it simply repeated many of the prescriptions of the World Bank, International Monetary Fund (IMF), and other multilateral funding agencies,[1] including the need for "a competitive platform for a powerful expansion by the tradable goods sector; a stable environment for confidence and a profitable surge in private investment; a restructured public sector to increase the efficiency of both capital expenditure and service delivery; new sectoral and regional emphases in industrial and infrastructural development; (and) greater labour market flexibility" (Department of Finance 1996: 2).

Following the publication of GEAR neoliberalism was broadly embraced by ANC legislators and found its way into numerous state policies from this time forward. The adoption of a neoliberal framework, furthermore, was accompanied by a progressive decline in the influence of the ANC's tripartite alliance partners, the South African Communist Party and COSATU, both of which had expressed their strong dissatisfaction with GEAR. At the same time, social movements and civic organizations, which had been the bedrock of mass protest during the struggle against Apartheid, were decoupled from political mobilization at the local level. In this way (as Chapter 4 by Penderis and Tapscott has discussed), instead of becoming a vehicle for grassroots democracy, local government became simply a vehicle for the distribution of central state services, devoid of any meaningful political influence.

---

[1]   The team responsible for drafting GEAR included two representatives from the World Bank and the two from the Development Bank of Southern Africa.

A growing trend of "financialization" (Rona-Tas and Hiss 2011), in the first decade of democracy, led to a deepening divide between the so-called modern and international economy, on the one side, and the "traditional and informal" economy on the other. As a consequence of this, Newman and De Lannoy assert, democracy was seen to have brought few advantages to the poor:

> For ordinary people, the most visible changes were the disappearance of 'Whites only' signs, separate queues in shops and other humiliating forms of forced segregation and labor control that divided families. (Newman and De Lannoy 2014: 225)

Thus, it was the NEM program that informed economic strategy and real politics in the first "Developmental decade" in South Africa, and which thereby led to GEAR. With hindsight, it can be seen that far from promoting the trickle down of resources and opportunities to the poor majority, the current economic strategy has led to widening social cleavages and a growing distrust in democracy. May's chapter in the book, for example, relates how the reforms needed to address poverty (including land reform, reform of the banking sector, and reform of working conditions) are generally missing. According to May:

> These (reforms) would need to involve redistribution measures that improve the access of the poor to productive assets, such as through land reform, the delivery of infrastructure and financial market reform.

In the two books discussed earlier, the first, as indicated, made frequent reference to the social democratic experience of the Nordic states. In the second, there are no such references and the only two growth models considered are those of state capitalism (pursued in China) and the Anglo-American and neoliberal free-market economy.

The Relevance of the Scandinavian Experiences

Despite the predominance of neoliberalism in countries such as South Africa and Brazil, there is evidence of a pushback against this economic paradigm. In South Africa, in particular, there has been renewed interest (in academic circles at least) in some of the ideas first raised by MERG including that of a democratic developmental state (Edigheji 2010). Speaking of the need to alter relations between the state and the market, Mothabi asserts:

> The fundamental challenge facing South Africa is the manner in which state-market relation are structured. The neo-liberal paradigm that has shaped the post-apartheid policies has further entrenched unequal power relations and ensured that government was capture by capital, making it difficult to pursue radical reforms. To significantly move forward, state-market relations should be tilted in favour of the development project. (Mothabi 2017: 99)

The idea of a developmental approach is also to be found in the government's *National Development Plan, Vision 2030* (NDP), albeit that the essence of such a state is ill-defined. "A South African developmental state," according to the Plan, "will intervene to support and guide development so that benefits accrue across society (especially to the poor), and build consensus so that long-term national interest trumps short-term, sectional concerns" (National Planning Commission 2011: 54). Significantly, the NDP makes reference to a "capable and developmental state" rather than to a democratic one, suggesting that the democratic component of this project is of secondary importance.

Prospects for a Renewal of Social Democracy and Democratic Developmental States in the South

Despite a renewed interest in the developmental state in South Africa, there had been a marked shift from the ideas of social democracy espoused in the transitional era to the current embrace of neoliberal policy. Although the country was by no means unique in following this path, where welfare states in Europe transitioned to the so-called third way, this had taken place over the course of one or two decades (thus permitting their societies more time to adjust to a neoliberal order), in South Africa the transition was precipitous and its impact profound. Despite a strong tradition of democratic mobilization by trade unions and civil society organizations (such as the United Democratic Front) in the lead up to democracy in 1994, as indicated, following the adoption of neoliberal principles and the gradual financialization of the economy (Halvorsen 2016), ideas of a democratic developmentalism dissipated, leaving the rhetoric of such a state but without any commitment to its substance.

In discussions on the prospects of a democratic developmental state, there is typically an implicit assumption about the compatibility of democracy and capitalism, and, as in the case of social democratic states, that a form of "embedded capitalism" may be adjusted to "the will of people." Following the rise of neoliberalism, however, the inherent contradiction between capitalism and democracy has grown to the extent where democratic values have effectively been crowded out. The success of neoliberalism may be ascribed to the fact that it has been both the cause and effect of the globalization of the economy and, particularly, the financial economy. As Wolfgang Merkel has so clearly demonstrated, the expansion of globalization went hand in hand with the growth of neoliberalism and, together, they have succeeded in dismantling both state regulation and democratic influence in the economy:

> The globalization of capitalism did not and should not bring with it effective global governance structures beyond the G-7 or G-20. The balance between the market and the state shifted to the disadvantage of the regulatory state and hence to the disadvantage of democracy. Legitimate democratic political regulations were dismantled into many different economic spheres, such as labor and financial markets. (p. 116)

Although Nordic countries still retain a form of welfare state, and one capable of some regulation of the economy, it is no longer the democratic developmental state of old and by 1993 political support for its core principles had waivered considerably. As a consequence of this, the international appeal of the Nordic model had greatly diminished and in South Africa, it was set aside in favor of the principles of the "third way," then being championed by Tony Blaire's New Labour and advocated by multilateral and bilateral agencies and by a host of consultants who descended on the country in its transition to democracy. These stressed the need to link into the global economy, for financial and monetary deregulation, for privatization, and for the introduction of a tax regime favorable to the growth of capital, among other measures.

The neoliberalism that underpins this approach to the economy, as Halvorsen discusses in Chapter 9 in this book, amounts to a new global "constitution," created to protect the mobility of capital and with the capacity to overrule the democratic constitutions of nation-states when these are seen as an impediment to growth. This is because the constitution of globalized capitalism imposes on nation-states a form of deregulated financial capitalism, which has led to some of the greatest concentration of wealth that the world has ever seen. Crouch, citing Organization for Economic Cooperation and Development (OECD) data (OECD 2011), provides an indication of the extent of this concentration:

> A closer approximation is the top 0.1% which was taking 7.9% of US national income, 7.0% of Norwegian, (and) 5.0% of British...Put differently, between 1975 and 2007 the top 0.1% of the US income distribution took 46.9% of national economic growth, leaving the remaining 99.9% with little more than half (...) in France, Italy and Norway it was over 11%. (Crouch 2015: 62)

These extremes of inequality serve to undermine democracy both by limiting its capacity to address issues of redistribution and inequality and by de-legitimating the idea of active citizenship (a reality apparent in the low participation levels of the poor in national elections), since involvement in political processes is seen to yield so little. Even in Norway, traditionally known for its egalitarianism, inequality has grown as a new economic elite has linked its fortunes to global capitalism and the expense of the majority.

Those who govern the system of global capitalism, that is those who make up the rules of global financial engagement, including the IMF, OECD, ratings agencies, and central banks (now free from state influence), promote tax policies favorable to big business and financial capital. This system not only undermines the ability of states to formulate policies dictated by their own electorate, but it also holds them responsible for rectifying the misdeeds and failure of global capitalism, as was illustrated in the aftermath of 2008 financial crises, where public funds were used to bail out banks and businesses deemed "too big to fail." According to Merkel, the constitution of global capitalism confronts two fundamental principles of democracy as follows:

> The democratic core principles that authoritative political decisions can only be taken by those who are legitimized by constitutional-democratic procedures, and the principle of political equality, which is diluted by the asymmetric distribution of socioeconomic resources among citizens largely to the disadvantage of the lower societal classes. All OECD democracies are affected by these two developments, even if to different degrees. The more de-nationalization progresses, and the more capitalism loses its social ties and turns into neo-liberal financial capitalism, the more its negative effects on the quality of democracy can be observed, all other things being equal. (Merkel: 2014: 118)

Thus, it would appear, there is limited space for the emergence of a democratic developmental state in countries, such as South Africa and Brazil, which remain deeply embedded in neoliberalism. Furthermore, as Chapters 8 and 9 by Halvorsen and Olsen in this book illustrate, even social democratic states such as Norway have not escaped the influences of the constitution of global capitalism and the competition state which it has ushered it has done much to undermine democratic values and, in particular, the capacity to steer the economy toward more equitable outcomes.

As a consequence of this, there are, as Jürgen Kocka (2016) argues, very good reasons to closely analyze and discuss the relationship between democracy and capitalism in public debate. This is because unregulated capitalism, as the global financial meltdown in 2008 has amply demonstrated, is likely to become increasingly self-destructive if it is not continuously confronted, and disciplined, by strong opposition. As a consequence, if a democratic developmental state is to emerge, and this remains a political goal in South Africa as in many other developing countries, this objective will only be realized through democratic mobilization.

In recent years a number of scholars have written about both the resilience of neoliberalism and the ongoing resistance to its global hegemony. In addition to analyzing the factors that have propelled neoliberalism to become such a dominant force, some writers have examined the types of resistance that have blocked its penetration of all societal institutions (Hall and Lamont 2013; Schmidt and Thatcher 2013). The genesis of this resistance, it is maintained, may be traced back to the pre-1980 types of democratic capitalism (a theme discussed in Olsen's Chapter 8) and it is likely from the ideals of this era that the embryos of a new phase of the democratic developmental state might emerge.

Based on an analysis of historical trends, there seems to be some consensus that strong labor unions, capable of influencing relations in the workplace and in political life through centralized collective bargaining and negotiation with the state, would be an important force in the creation (or recreation) of a democratic developmental state. This is because the establishment of "democratic capitalism" would entail, as a precondition, an acceptance of the principle that all citizens in society have a right to a share of economic growth. This would include protection against the periodic impact which this growth might have on labor, such as during times of unemployment and redundancy, or in instances where reskilling and mobility are called for. Strong labor unions, thus, have the capacity to activate for wider redistribution of growth and for a more equal society. This is borne out by the fact, as OECD (2011) data confirm, that societies where neoliberalism has led to significant social cleavage and a growing inequality are typically those where unions, both at firm level and as a centralized collective force, have been weakened.

Linked to the ideal of a social contract, where all parties are committed to the sharing of economic growth, the construction of democratic capitalism would also entail a commitment to a number of other democratic values, including the right to relevant education and learning, the right to work and a living wage, and to social protection in times when capitalist transitions have deprived workers of their livelihoods. While labor unions still play an important role in protecting these rights in Nordic countries, in South Africa the influence of organized labor, once a powerful force in the latter years of the anti-Apartheid struggle, has been progressively eroded under the neoliberal order. As a consequence, as Seekings discusses in Chapter 5, despite gains in their access to basic services, large segments of the population have not benefitted from economic growth in the democratic era and the social divide has, in fact, widened.

The importance of unions is also to be found in their oversight role in the management of the economy. Where, for example, they have a strong presence, policy makers are less likely to attempt lowering company tax (a central tenet of neoliberal strategy intended to stimulate investment) while raising wage taxes. Similarly, they have the ability to expose companies attempting to circumvent taxation by moving their accounts offshore or by other forms of creative accountancy. Furthermore, labor unions that are committed to a "growth with redistribution contract" tend to insist on reinvestment in the companies they work for (rather than the investment of profits in the market). In addition, by sharing their practical knowledge of company operations they are able to contribute to technological advancements and to more rational investment. Stemming from these positive engagements in the workplace, citizens are also encouraged to engage in social and political life. The net outcome of this is that the tax base is better secured (due to minimal industrial action and improved productivity), welfare services can be adequately financed, and there is overall growth in the economy due to increased consumption. The experiences of the Nordic states reveal that, in contrast to the top-down model of the East Asian developmental state, a democratic developmental state will need to be constructed from below. That is, it is only through democratic mobilization that civil society will be sufficiently strong to engage with both the state and capital in shaping a new social and political order.

The key question, of course, is what will be the drivers of the institutional reforms needed to bring about change and where will they come from? Relatedly, how will the class alliances necessary to underpin this process come about? These are questions frequently posed by Wolfgang Streeck, perhaps the leading analyst of the inherent contradiction that exists between capitalism and democracy under neoliberalism:

> Who is to demand and force through the democratic reforms that will, for example, end and reverse the growth of precarious employment, stop privatization and restore equitable public services, tax Google and its like; increase public social investment, to make for more equal starting positions and opportunities in the marketplace, less oligarchic and less dangerous?. (2015: 55)

It remains uncertain how, and from whence, the mobilizing forces for a democratic developmental state will emerge in such states as South Africa, Brazil, Ethiopia, or Indonesia. It is also unclear how Nordic societies, themselves, will strengthen their resistance to the globalizing neoliberal forces that are threatening the future of their own variant of the democratic developmental state. It is, nevertheless, hard to accept Colin Crouch's fatalistic assertion that it is "too late to save democracy from being anything other than a façade for the operation of private economic power" (2015: 61). While the reversal of this trend will not easily be achieved, the evidence of human agency and resistance is, nevertheless, to be seen in the global rise of social movements that are pushing back against unfettered neoliberalism, whether this is trade unions opposing privatization and outsourcing, or local organizations fighting against the commercial exploitation of their land and resources.

References

Crouch, Colin. (2016). The knowledge corrupters. Hidden consequences of the financial takeover of public life. Cambridge: Polity Press.

Crouch, Colin. (2015). Comments to Wolfgang Merkel, "Is capitalism compatible with democracy?". Zeitschrift für Vergleichende Poitikwissenschaft. 2015 9: 61–71). Published online May 8, 2015. Springer VS.

Department of Finance. (1996). Growth, employment and redistribution—A macroeconomic strategy. Pretoria. Retrieved from www.treasury.gov.za/pub lications/other/gear/chapters.pdf

Edigheji, Amano. (2010). Constructing a democratic developmental state in South Africa: Potentials and challenges. Cape Town: HSRC Press.

Hall, Peter A. and Lamont, Michèle. (2013). Social resilience in the neoliberal era. Cambridge. Cambridge University Press.

Halvorsen, Tor. (2016). South Africa, the OECD and BRICS. In: Einar Braatehn et al. (Eds.), Poverty and inequality in middle income countries (pp. 48–73). London: Zed Books.

Kocka, Jürgen. (2016). Capitalism. A short history. Princeton: Princeton University Press.

MERG. (1993). Making democracy work. A framework for macroeconomic policy in South Africa. A report from the Macro-economic Research Group (MERG) to Members of the Democratic Movement in South Africa. Cape Town: Center for Development Studies. University of the Western Cape.

Merkel, Wolfgang. (2014). Is capitalism compatible with democracy? Zeitschrift für Vergleichende Politikwissenschaft. (Published online July 26, 2014).

Mirowski, Philip. (2013). Never let a serious crisis go to waste. How neoliberalism survived the financial meltdown. London: Verso.

Mothabi, Thabileng. (2017). A need for developmental interventions in South Africa. In: Godfrey Kanyenze et al. (Eds.), Towards democratic developmental states in Southern Africa (pp. 62–106). Harare: Weaver Press.

National Planning Commission. (2011). National development plan: Vision 2030. Pretoria.

Newman, Katherine S. and De Lannoy, Ariane. (2014). After freedom. The rise of the post-apartheid generation in democratic South Africa. Boston: Beacon Press.

OECD, (2011). Divided we stand: Why inequality keeps on rising . Paris: OECD.

Oxford handbook of Asian business systems. (2014). Oxford. Oxford University Press.

Schmidt, Vivien A. and Thatcher, Mark. (Eds.). (2013). Resilient liberalism in Europe's political economy. Cambridge: Cambridge University Press.

Rona-Tas, Akos and Hiss, Stefanie. (2011). Forecasting as valuation: The role of ratings and predictions in the subprime mortgage crisis in the United States. In: Jens Beckert and Patrik Aspers (Eds.), The Worth of goods: Valuing and pricing in the economy. Oxford: Oxford University Press, 223-240.

Rueschemeyer, Dietrich, Stephens, Evelyne H, and Stephens, John D. (1992). Capitalist development and democracy. Cambridge: Polity Press.

Streeck, Wolfgang. (2015). Comments to Wolfgang Merkel, "Is capitalism compatible with democracy?". Zeischrift für Vergleichende Politikwissenschaft. (2015 9: 49–60). Published online February 7, 2015. Springer VS.

***ibidem*-Verlag / *ibidem* Press**
Melchiorstr. 15
70439 Stuttgart
Germany

ibidem@ibidem.eu
ibidem.eu